D0097981

Order to View

Order to View

by

RENÉ CUTFORTH

FABER AND FABER
London

First published in 1969
by Faber and Faber Limited
24 *Russell Square London WC*1
Reprinted 1969, 1970
Printed in Great Britain by
the Bowering Press, Plymouth

ISBN 0 571 09103 2

Contents

Foreword

I should be sorry if anybody mistook this book for an autobiography: it is a report on my life and times, and reporting is an exercise in extraversion.

Great tracts in anybody's life are not susceptible to a reporter's techniques, and that is why this book is hour-glass shaped. The constriction in the middle, almost the whole of the thirties, represents a period when internal landscapes, conflicts and dialogues were often so overwhelmingly significant to me that the outside world could not be brought into any relationship with them, so that they remain outside a reporter's range.

I am grateful particularly to Francis Dillon for his sensitive production of the radio versions of some of the material in this book, and to Karl Miller for permission to reprint those which appeared in 'The Listener'.

My thanks are also due to Elizabeth Rowley, Lord Archie Gordon and Patrick Harvey of the B.B.C., and to Lane Kinsman for help with the manuscript.

For
Sheila and Sarah

I

Swad

Swadlincote is a little town in South Derbyshire. It's known locally as Swad, and it is a bit of a joke, being no beauty-spot by anybody's standards. George Brown, the Labour politician, has declared that Swadlincote helped to shape his policies. In this he is not the first: it certainly shaped mine. I was born within a mile or two of Swad and lived there until I was seventeen—the time of my life during which I became, for better or worse, irretrievably me, myself and nobody else.

I have never been back, so I don't know what Swadlincote looks like now. When I was there, it was so ugly it made you laugh. The whole district was a loose assemblage of gigantic holes in the ground, some of them half a mile across, where clay was dug out for the various works which made drain-pipes and teapots and crockery and jugs, bowls and chamber-pots, and large, hideous vases of a poisonous green to put aspidistras in. Along the edges of these great holes, dividing them one from another like threads in a spider's web, ran the dark grey spoil heaps, a tangle of derelict railway lines, and the little black streets of houses, steeply up or down hill. No proper grass grew anywhere, but a sage green vegetation like little prehistoric Christmas trees covered the older tip-heaps, and at some point on every skyline the twin wheels and black scaffolding of pit-head gear would mark the shaft of a coal-mine. Deep down below the clay holes the whole earth was worm-eaten with tunnels, many of them lost and forgotten for decades, so that streets were always falling in a foot or two, and most of the houses were cracked somewhere or held together with iron braces, and a sad smell of gas from broken mains hung over it all.

At the centre of all this mess sat, rather smugly, Swad, at the bottom of a steep hill. A town hall and a space in front of it called the Delf or the Jetty, where market stalls were lit by naptha flares on Saturday nights, one comparatively broad street of good shops, with a tram-way in the middle that went on to Newhall and Burton-on-Trent one way, and on the other soared up Swad hill through Woodville and out into the country between the barley fields like a ship, to finish up at Ashby-de-la-Zouche, which was sleepy and handsome and county and Conservative and had shops which sold outrageous foods like smoked salmon and Stilton cheese and coffee beans. And anyway, it was in Leicestershire—a nesh lot.

In Swad it was the colliers who set the tone of the place, and their tone was a mixture of independence and resentment. Independence based on pride, because as one of them carefully and slowly explained to me once, as to a foreigner, 'A collier is a man as is a bloody man.' It was a more than regimental pride, and a better one, because it was spontaneous and unorganized and knew nothing of officers. The resentment was due to the fact that this pride was constantly affronted. During the whole time that I knew Swadlincote, the owners and the miners were at war, or at best in an uneasy truce, and men squatted at street corners, unemployed, scowling, and quite often hungry. This pride and this resentment expressed themselves in a ferocious solidarity which excluded anybody who was not a collier or related to one. The typical collier was a rather small, lithe, dark, round-headed man, with lively eyes and an air of holding violent emotions in an iron grip. The same people had been fanatics for Cromwell in the Civil War. The place was full of chapels—chapels and pubs, often in livid yellows and greens. Women didn't stay young long in Swad, and after that they wore men's caps held on with hat-pins, and carried beer about in jugs. The normal greeting between man and man was a brisk 'Eeh-oop,' given with a single sideways twist of the head; but when times became very bad it was 'Are you working?' and the reply was 'No, are you?'

It was a brutal society which took pride in its harshness, and the sight, for instance, of the drunken carters, no doubt with every reason to be drunk, flogging their screaming horses over the slippery cobbles up the steep hill from the coal yard, is a childhood memory I still feel I'd sooner be without. Under the naptha flares on Saturdays nights on the Delf round the little town hall the drunks lay so thick it was like picking your way through a maze. When grimmer times came along, the unemployed starved proudly, squatting on the pavements outside the public houses. Swad was heroic and tough, but not altogether barbarous. It had its own culture of brass bands and Handel-singing choirs, but it's fair to say that there was always a bigger following for cock-fighting than there was for the colliery band, and what Swad loved more than anything was a fight in the street, hacking with steel-shod clogs. It was that sort of society, contrast in very strong colour. Fighters in any sphere were what it admired most, and you had to be pretty good even to survive in it.

This harsh, heroic, intolerant and unlovely world surged right up to our front door, which was on the Ashby-de-la-Zouche side of the tramlines from Swad, and there the door was slammed and held against it with Roman devotion by my mother who loathed and despised every manifestation of it, as if it was some contagious disease. It was the enemy. 'Class' in Swad had an odd structure in those days. There was still a veil of mysticism hanging about what were thought of as 'the real old people', the heirs and assigns of the Norman army of occupation. Fortunately, there was only one in this category. Way out on the edge of the industrial tip-heaps was Castle Gresley, fully equipped with owls and Gothic tree-trunks, and one member of the ancient family still survived; but though he had a castle it was in ruins, and though he was Sir Nigel, a sort of name very suitable for such people, he had no money and didn't appear anywhere and so he was written off as a sort of misty blessing on tradition and the social system. That left the Owners. The coal-owners, of course, were very rich indeed and much too big to live anywhere near a place like Swad. So that left the works owners and that's where I came in.

Both my grandfathers were rich Victorians, but in very different styles. In one of the larger spaces left between the clay holes, and totally enclosed behind ancient walls of red-brick and groves of trees to shut out the sight of Swadlincote, my mother's father lived in some style in a very large and inconvenient 18th-century house, with 2 or 3 acres of garden, a paddock, greenhouses, ferneries, arbours, grottoes, beehives, smooth lawns, heavy linen tablecloths, and every inch of furniture which wasn't ornate mahogany or splendid marble buttoned and stuffed with horsehair until it was on the point of bursting. The household was run with masterful ease by my Aunt Minnie, who smoked incessantly, and was an addicted card-player—if at any time, day or night, she couldn't make up a four for bridge she'd play patience until a four turned up. Maids in that house were starchily uniformed and quiet and efficient. There was a proper scarlet-faced cook in the kitchen, and a wooden-faced chauffeur in charge of a wonderful vehicle known as 'The Motor,' which was about as big as a small bus and had brass pillars like barley-sugar sticks holding up its roof. My grandfather was not an extravagant man: he was small and very neat and bright-eyed, with a little grey beard and pince-nez on a broad black ribbon. He dressed in a double-breasted jacket which buttoned right up under his chin. He had tight checked trousers and one of those hats which Winston Churchill wore in the blitz, which couldn't make up its mind whether to be a top hat or a bowler. He had a good bottle of claret every night of his life with his dinner. He could read Dickens like a pretty good actor, and he used to cry over Hardy's *Tess of the D'Urbervilles*, but that was late at night. His sons were careful to call him 'Sir'. That was my grandfather as I knew him, but there were stories of an earlier, broader tradition. His works was a pottery, and works weddings in the old days were celebrated on my grandfather's lawn with a chamber-pot full of champagne passed round among the guests, with a good deal of coarse wit. You wouldn't have believed it of my grandfather. I think his daughers had put an end to such tribal customs. I can remember my mother ticking off her brother for telling me the story. My mother was the youngest, prettiest, and most brilliant of his daughters, who had all been educated at a famous girls' public school in the Midlands, only the second generation of women to have the chance. They were very modern, rode bicycles, played tennis, read books of a chancy kind. When my grandfather discussed the works of Thomas Hardy with my father he always wound up in great excitement 'but he is wrong, Edwin, wrong; in his assumption that the Almighty doesn't care, he is wrong. We know that He counteth the sparrows.' 'Well, there, sir,' my father would say, 'I cannot go all the way with you.' He was as modern as that.

My mother made a romantic marriage. My father was nothing if not romantic. He was a quite excessively good-looking man in a heavy saturnine way, so that men didn't like the look of him much, but he was exceedingly good at all the managerial, social sports—dancing and skating and golf. He played the violin like a wizard, and he had a good voice for sentimental ballads. He feared no foe in shining armour. Besides all these attractions my father was under a cloud. He had quarrelled with his father, a thing held to be sinful in those days. This was no great feat, since the quarrel was my other grandfather's favourite art-form. He was, almost to the point of parody, a product of his times. The Cutforths had been farming in a small way for centuries around Spalding in Lincolnshire when, suddenly, towards the end of the eighteenth century, one of them got rich. My grandfather was his grandson, and by his time the advance had been well consolidated; they owned claypits and potbanks and coal-mines and breweries all over the Midlands, many of them brought as dowries by their wives. My grandfather Walter was the first of them to be born free of the muck where the money was made. He lived in an enormous house at Redhill in Surrey, where he was given over body and soul to quarrelling and foxhunting. His fetish was the horsewhip. Its liberal application had alienated all his sons, the eldest to such an extent that, returning to Europe from a seven-year exile in South America, where he had been bundled off at the age of nineteen for 'insolence and insubordination' he made a special excursion to Redhill and flogged his father all round the stables one summer afternoon. 'Not a groom raised a hand in his defence' was his only comment on the expedition. Besides his sons, my grandfather had horsewhipped at least two of his neighbours, and one of them had brought him into court for it, and been awarded damages but little sympathy. A vigorous line about affronted honour had carried the local gentry.

My grandfather's day often began with a reference to the great panacea. As a child I ate three terrified breakfasts with him. Basically the ritual was the one I was to encounter twenty years later in the Officers Mess of a rather old-fashioned Regiment of the Line. You helped yourself in silence (and liberally, if you wanted to be spared aspersions on the virility of your generation) from a great sideboard of marble and mahogany, where spirit lamps flickered blue under a dozen meals: porridge, kedgeree, kippers, bacon and eggs, scrambled eggs, devilled kidneys, sausages, mutton chops and God knows what. Before sitting down with your plateful you were obliged to address the *Times* at the head of the table with these ritual words: 'Good morning, Sir,' and if you were lucky you were vouchsafed a brief glimpse of God's face. It was a red face with a high nose, tangled black eyebrows, a bullying eye, and a great white moustache like a seagull. The ritual response came in a throaty shout—'Good morning to yer,' and then silence descended again, except for the clicking of knives and forks, until behind the *Times* a small commotion like someone having a stroke began to grow, and finally the faith was promulgated . . . 'Feller should be horsewhipped!'

They were not a cosy family, the Cutforths. My grandmother, who had been a beauty, sat apart from them all in elegant detachment, creating distance with her faint ironic smile and long, disdainful eyelids. Long ago, in some reverberation following an eruption of the volcano, she had found her formula: 'Walter is so upright.' Enunciated in bell-like tones, it had been known to silence even Walter himself, since it was precisely that quality of his which was liable to misinterpretation. During the course of his career as an industrialist he had made several major killings, none more astute, it was said, than his sale of a brewery to a man who turned out to have a country house near Redhill, and who, thereafter, whenever he saw my grandfather in the street, raised a shout of 'Stop thief.' He had been horsewhipped, of course, but the scandal remained.

The horsewhip, together with my grandmother's obsessive need of worship, had launched a drama which, by the time my grandfather first frightened me at breakfast, had been raging for a generation. It was a production in which Byron and the Brontës might have had equal shares. They were certainly a striking lot, my father and his brothers and sisters, with their crow-black hair, their long, heavy, melancholy faces, their fine eyes alight with neurosis, their lowering silences, their furious eloquence. Heathcliff had been the model for the men. The girls, my aunts, were handsome level-browed Cassandras, prophesying doom. My aunt Dorothy declared that there was a curse on the whole race of them. Hell, she said, was their natural habitat. And, in a way, it was. Family life, Cutforth version, was a saga of remembered traumas, of renunciations and betrayals, of runnings away and cryings all night, of undying hatreds and small insane revenges, slow-burns kept up for years, obstinacies maintained though the skies fell. A long diet of this strong curry had ruined them for ordinary fare. Departing one by one, never in daylight by the front door to a chorus of goodbyes, but thrown out or running away or, in one case, threatened with the police, they still went with some reluctance, as if aware that the greenest valley they might find outside would seem insipid by comparison: and they were always coming back to sniff the sulphurous air of Old Volcano Country, where the ground shook and the thunder rolled and geysers spouted underfoot.

My father held the ignominious position of youngest but one in this hierarchy. 'Edwin's a weakling' his father would assure anyone within earshot, that is, within about a quarter of a mile. 'Kiss the girls and make 'em cry. Plays the fiddle and that's his lot. Can't understand it. Bad blood somewhere.' The rumpus which finally sealed my father's marching orders was about somebody's daughter. As might have been foreseen, he 'went running to his mother,' who gave him a special dispensation in the form of a vacant assistant managership in a pottery she owned most of the shares of, far away in the murk of the Midlands, whence she had emerged.

So there my father went, a young man of striking appearance, in whom the office of 'youngest but one' had developed a formidable charm, a man with two deep pre-occupations, the violin music of Mozart, Beethoven and Schubert, and the pursuit of women, not, alas, in sensuality but in passion.

So it's 1909. My father has achieved the managership, my parents have married and gone away in a spirit of adventure to live in what used to be the doctor's house on the Ashby side of Swadlincote. They are very modern. They share a deep disdain of the nineteenth century, its horse-whips and its hypocrisy. My mother's world is that of E. M. Forster, my father's that of H. G. Wells. Everything is going to be new, scientific, and eventually, Utopian; if not by force of reason, then by evolution. The stage is set for the arrival of René Cutforth.

I was born, and sung to sleep to the tune of *The Dollar Princess*, which was the last piece my parents had been to see in London. But the first sound I really remember was both ancient and modern, and it nearly frightened me out of my wits. There was a windowless dark room in our house—really a large cupboard—known as 'The Black Hole', and used for storing junk. I dreaded it, and one wet day—I must have been about 3 then—my father, to amuse me, disappeared into the Black Hole and rootled around until he found an old phonograph, the kind with cylinders instead of discs. He put the record on, wound it up, and there issued from it in a tinny scrape of telephone quality, that highly depressing chorus of *Il Trovatore*. It went on for half a minute and then I began to scream as if I'd gone out of my mind, and continued long after I'd been whisked off to bed to be read to about the Three Bears. My fit was a five-day wonder, but there was a simple answer. I had always known there was something in The Black Hole better not thought of. I had not expected it to be so small and intricate and malign. I had not expected a horned monster. I had certainly not expected my father to be in league with it, or to let loose on me its terrible humanoid voice, a sound of such concentrated sorrow and despair that my worst fears about the human lot were confirmed.

It was a prophetic noise. On just such a note of overwrought romanticism the crack-up arrived—in the year of the great universal crack-up, 1914. My father bought the very latest toy for a tuned-in young man; an enormous motor-bike called an Indian, a thing as big as a small horse, and almost immediately he smashed himself up. When he left hospital he was always going to walk with a limp. He was not in future going to be better than anybody else at skating and tennis and golf and walking and running. Most of these he wasn't going to be able to do at all, and the rest rather badly. Well, what's a motor smash? Nowadays you almost expect them. But in those days we didn't kill a dozen a day on the roads. Life was slower and deeper. Things had time to be significant and Englishmen were more involved then in their physical manhood, as Americans still are. Anyway, my father spent most of that long glorious summer in a wheelchair in the garden, and I have a picture of him in my mind there. A completely unsentimental child's picture, mostly concerned with the fascinating intricacy of the wheelchair's mechanism, but equipped at the same time with the strange quality of sunlight, like a promise, which we can see through the memories of childhood and not again. What afflicted my father was humiliation, and what he mostly did was curse as if his life depended on the vigour and fluency of his language. And what he cursed mainly was that he had missed the war. To this day the sentimentality of the early war tunes has a special quality for me, and affects me as if it were emotionally true; as if this caterwauling was really stating the facts about the world, as if it had really come to this, romanticism, quavering on its last legs. It was quavering in the family, too. My father still couldn't walk, but he remembered that he could still play the violin. He stopped cursing and now he sat all day long Byronically hunched in a room with the curtains drawn, and all day long he ploughed a long, desolate furrow with Beethoven.

On Sunday afternoons particularly the situation in that house was well summed-up in sound. We faced two ways. One way lay the barley fields and Hartshorne village, as medieval as its name, and the bells of its splendid church of the establishment came wafting a mile across the barley fields towards us. The other way, Swad, like a pox on the face of the planet, and from that direction an urgent clamour of dissent from the bells of chapels, and an occasional back-garden practitioner on the cornet, for Swad is Brass Band country, and in the silences underneath it all the infernal weeping of the Kreutzer Sonata. My mother told me years later that often that summer she thought she had lost her reason. But just before lush sentimentality ceased to be the prevailing mode of expression it released, in 1916, one very bad tune which still excused itself and somehow seemed without offence to sum up the whole thing, and it was about the time of the Long Long Trail a-Winding, that I got the fright of my life. Literally. I have never been so frightened since, even in the war. I was padding about the house in slippers. The wailing of the violin had ceased for a moment. There was a half open door, and I could see my mother and father: my mother sitting very still and my father standing there with his heavy Valentino face full of emotion. My mother said slowly and distinctly 'I shall have to leave you, Edwin.' My father said nothing sullenly. My mother said 'I shall have to go.' and stood up. I whisked out of sight like a flash—not because I didn't want to be seen so much as that I felt that if I disappeared, disappeared altogether if possible, I might make unsaid the dreadful thing that I'd heard. I was cold and sweating and I shook. I was also in perpetual motion, walking and running aimlessly about under the poplar trees at the end of the garden, blind and deaf. I had heard my mother move across the tiled hall, click clack, click clack, click clack, and then the front door had slammed behind her, and that was that. She returned, of course, in a couple of hours, but nothing was quite the same again. And the incident must have touched a vital spot. More than twenty-five years later, at the end of my war, the 1939 one, I was having a mild psychiatric check-up along with a lot of other ex-prisoners of war. I had two troubles. The most obvious was a total inability to descend an escalator on the underground. I just couldn't go down. And the other thing was a recurring dream which I'd had for years, and from which I used to wake in terror.

In this dream, I was standing under the poplar trees at the end of the garden. It was bright moonlight, and very cold. I went through the trees, and there suddenly was a cottage, all ruined and cracked. Inside it I could see by the bright moonlight that the trees were growing up through the cottage, their great roots twined about in the downstairs room. I climbed, with rising terror, the creaking stair in the heavy silence. In the room above stretched out on a bed was a dead girl, like a marble on a tomb, and the girl and the bed and the walls were all dappled in the moonlight with the little tagged rectangular shadows of the poplar leaves. Then I woke up. It wasn't until I had this trouble with the underground escalator that I realized why poplar leaves loomed so dreadful in my life. And what I suddenly remembered in a flash, was that when my mother had got up to go, twenty-six years before, I had seen that she was wearing a veil of the kind fashionable then, with little black rectangular patches fixed on the silk mesh. Poplar leaves on their stalks.

If this were one of C. P. Snow's scenes from provincial life, and it sounds remarkably like one in parts, there'd be no trouble at all. I should have hordes of friends, who'd been in on every scene of my life, observing and reporting. But my life was not like that. My mother had that high-nosed, old-English bazaar-opening face. She was fashioned for opening church fêtes, and being intelligent on Conservative party committees. What she required of the human race was quite simple. First, they should speak the King's English, and next, they should have the right views, and then they should have easy manners and not give way to exhibitions of emotion. 'A rather hysterical person,' she would say of some poor chap who'd lost his nerve in her presence, quite an easy thing to do. Furthermore, they should be high Anglican, though she had nothing against a decent Roman—no Irishman though—and should be able to talk intelligently about politics, the new immorality, the decline of the Church, gardening and kindred topics. As I grew older I failed her in every one of these requirements, and my mother became convinced that my father was 'dragging us all down'. My contacts with other children of my age were therefore rigidly prescribed. There was an absolute class apartheid. Any Derbyshire expressions I'd picked up from the maids were wrenched out of my mouth and consigned to the flames. In the end I met only my own relations and one or two management children. But there was, thank God Florrie.

Florrie was a big, lean, high cheek-boned woman of extraordinary intelligence and heart enough for ten, the wife of a Swadlincote collier. She came in to give a hand with the housework, and to look after my brother John, who was only about five then. She ran the whole place. She was never intimidated by my mother, who she admitted was not mardy, though nesh. The two women fought fierce battles in their different idioms, but always in private. Florrie would come hot out of one of these sessions, seize me by the arm, and shout 'Yo' dunna want believe yo'r mam goin on about yo' feyther. E's noan so bad. Mony a woss.' And after some sermon on dissenters, and the wicked working classes, she'd say, shaking my arm to drive home the point, 'Yo'r mam knows nowt. Nay.' If it hadn't been for Florrie, I would have missed Swad altogether, except the depressing look of it. But under the guise of being taken out for walks in the country, I spent hours in her little black cottage, with its huge collier's fire roaring up the chimney, and fat Joe in his pit dirt, sitting in a tin bath by the fire having his back scrubbed. I picked up proper Swad speech from their two boys, the eldest about my age. South Derbyshire is not so much an accented English, as a separate language, full of old Danish words. Florrie used to take me to the Wakes at Swad and Ashby, where I saw a folk play which must have been touring a hundred and fifty years ago. It lasted eight minutes and it was called *The Death of Nelson*. You could see the shoulders of the men under the stage heaving it up and down to represent the pitching deck of a battleship. From a mast, high up in the circus tent, a man with a villainous black moustache fired off a musket with a great bang and Nelson fell on one knee. Then the dialogue went like this: 'Kiss me, Hardy, for I am wounded.' 'What, mortually, my Lord?' 'Ay, so I am afeared.'

But, until I went away to school at the age of eight, my life, as I remember it now, is no more than a flicker of episodes, like a string of beads, but the string they were threaded on I can remember: it was a sickening intuition, which solidified month by month, that life in our house was coming to an end. It's easy to see now that my father was launched on one of his love affairs, always of a highly tempestuous and romantic nature, and of a manic egocentricity. But it was my mother's death of the heart which preoccupied me and held me rapt, so that I had to detach about three quarters of my attention from life to deal with this climate of dread. It was worst when my mother made great efforts to talk to me and play with me as she had done before. All I knew was that it was a fake, and that terrified me: if that was a fake, then life had failed.

I sat about under tables and behind curtains, catching such fag ends of communication on the conflict as came my way, and all that I got out of it was that in some ways my father, whom I loved, behaved like a fiend, and that my mother always behaved in the way best calculated to rouse the fiend in him. There was no way to get at the truth, or away from it, and I was about five before a life-belt alighted on the cold water. In the garden there was a small building of two rooms, which had been, and was always called, the Surgery. Appropriately playing at doctors in there one day with a visiting girl cousin, I discovered sex. I had no sisters, and sex took my breath away; it leapt at once into an exactly sex-shaped cavity in my mind, previously hardly suspected, and settled there to grow. Its great advantage was that, unlike everything else, it didn't have to be tied in with any other consideration. It just was itself, and its own reward.

My mother caught us one day in our delicious indecencies, and one glance at her face showed me that it was a Jesus matter. 'And so you must never, never even think of anything of that kind again,' my mother finished her sermon. I wrestled with the Angel for about half a day, and then I fell. I realized that I was going to think of everything of that kind again, often and deliberately, since it was the only thing exciting enough to dismiss dread, often for twenty minutes at a time; and I would have to take my chance with Jesus who, in any case, had failed my mother in her calamity. So, from that day I began to take a long, slow, grieving, cold-stricken, guilty farewell of my mother. We met thereafter as actor and actress in a play which ignored reality. The short word for ignoring reality is madness, and my mother's production of this play afflicted me with exactly that sick chill of horror felt in the presence of the insane.

All this heavy luggage had now to be bundled out of sight because I had to go away to school.

II

Illuminations

It was the 'Lower School' of a famous public school in the Midlands, a 'preparatory school for the sons of gentlemen', as the prospectus said. The first notable thing I did was to run away. It was rather a snobbish school in the old-fashioned way: we were expected to take a deep and passionate interest in horses, and be keen about the meet of the local foxhounds. It mattered a good deal what sort of car your parents came down for half-term in. Old Kip, our headmaster, had several bees in his bonnet, about what he called 'Moral responsibility'. He would summon the whole school into hall, and make a speech. 'It has come to my ears that there are boys in the school who have not written to their parents for some weeks. As you know I never interfere. Writing home to parents is a boy's own moral responsibility. But if a further example comes to my ears, I shall name the boy and shall leave him to the disapproval of his fellows.' Old Kip forceably enrolled us all in the Boy Scouts, and after that, what had been minor crimes became all at once moral sins. Orgies of moral responsibility went on in the dorms, where patrol leaders solemnly poured cold water down the sleeves of boys who in loose moments had said 'damn' or 'bum'. But there were times when the disapproval of one's fellows was a serious business, and a howling mob trundled the victim over to the stables, where a supply of dried orange peel was kept for such occasions. This was ceremonially ignited with matches, and when properly smouldering, stuffed down the back of his shirt. This usually used to make the victim run screaming around the grounds in circles with the whole mob after him, armed with thin switches, specially cut for the job. I'd have got by, though, if it hadn't been for Mr Seaton. Mr Seaton was a new master who'd become devoted to Old Kip's ideas, and had even invented a new variety of moral responsibility. He was the mathematics master, and his new invention was that you marked your own maths papers according to a complicated system which I never understood. At the end of the week he asked you what your marks were, and you told him on your 'Scout's honour'. I never had the remotest idea what my marks were and I used to award myself a figure I hoped would be low enough not to attract attention, and high enough to keep me out of trouble. But one morning I had the misfortune to be asked first, and I said 85, glibly enough, and then realized in the silence that that was very high indeed. So I said, 'Oh—no sir, I mean 35,' and I peered at my exercise to make it appear that I'd mistaken a three for an eight. Mr Seaton came striding up and, of course, was unable to find evidence of either figure, among the muddled miseries of my calculations. So he began to shout. 'Stand up, boy. Admit, boy, you have no idea. Does your Scout's honour mean nothing to you? Are you prepared to cheat and lie your way through life?' He went on and on and finally barked out: 'I shall inform the headmaster that I've a cheat in my form.'

It was the last lesson in the afternoon of a perfect July day. Mr Seaton, I knew, would inform the headmaster at dinner that night. The school would be summoned after lunch the next day. Meanwhile there was an hour's free time before tea. The heavy sweet smell of the country drifted in through the elm avenue where the rooks were cawing away like mad, the classroom was dusty, ink-stained, and suddenly very narrow and confining like a jail. Outside you could hear the country breathing sleepily and calmly in the sunshine. I made up my mind. I'd go—now. And with that decision, all in a second, I was as happy as Larry. I went out onto the lawn, and stood on top of the north bank among the trees for a minute or two looking around. And then I slipped through the elm avenue, under the cawing rooks, over the wall, over the road, and onto the field path which led winding up and down a thick green slope, to the field of white stones which was the limit of my explorations on Sunday walks.

For the rest of that summer evening I loafed through the sweet grass, and the long ditches full of ragged-robin, where the cow parsley was up to my waist, entirely at one with the universe: I sucked grasses, climbed trees, avoided villages, paddled in streams, and finally, when it began to grow dark, I found a cow shed, in a paddled patch of sun-baked mud in a thread-bare field on a western slope, and lay down in some old-smelling hay inside, and went to sleep. That mood was still with me in the morning. A wonderful morning with the sun sparkling all new on everything, and a soft wind and a glittering green downward slope to start my journey with, and in this delightful world, there was no washing.

But now I was getting near Leicester, and the villages grew more and more frequent and soon they were continuous. I was very tired, and going very slowly. A cold wind blew up and though I tried hard to skirt Leicester and get out into the country again, I only half succeeded, and spent most of the day bitterly among the tramlines. Clouds covered the sky. At about seven o'clock that evening, clogged with fatigue, I was plodding along a black road, through rows of ugly miners' cottages in a cold rain. I'd nothing left but obstinacy. And about a mile out of Desford on the north road towards Ashby, a bicycle came suddenly up from behind me and stopped, barring my way. It was an enormous fat scarlet policeman, with a heavy old-Bill moustache. 'Where y' going lad,' he said, beaming at me through the rain. 'I'm just walkin',' I said. 'Ah, walkin' are you?' He looked me up and down. 'Well, what about a bite to eat?' 'Yes,' I said, 'I could do with that.' 'Then us'll just tek a little walk back and fix it up,' he said. We walked back to a miner's cottage of blackened red brick, and there was his wife, if possible redder and larger than he was. A huge fire, what they call a collier's fire in those parts, filled the grate and half the chimney. It was as hot as the tropics, and what small space was left in the room when these enormous figures sat down was filled with china dogs, bowls of plants, shepherdesses, and pictures of virgins locked out in the snow. There was a fat cat, and a proper black kettle singing on the hob. They stuffed me with bacon and eggs, and bread and butter and jam, and enough tea to float a battleship. They laughed all the time. 'Eat up, lad. That's right. Never let 'em get you down,' said the policeman. 'And how are you, eh? Fit as a fiddle, eh? Now I suppose your name—it couldn't be Cutforth, could it?' 'Yes, it is,' I said. 'Well, you've done a fair walk,' he said. 'How did you like it?' I said that up till today I'd never liked anything better. 'That's the stuff, lad. Well, I'll just go and do a bit of telephoning, and I'll be back.' When he came back he said, 'Now, how did you come to start this bit of a walk, like?' I thought he was a very sensible man. He appeared to have no moral responsibility of any kind. So I told him the whole story, with an imitation of Old Kip holding forth about the 'disapproval of his fellows'. The policeman and his wife rocked to and fro beating their sides in an ecstasy of laughter. 'Nay', the policeman said. 'Nay, it sounds a proper rum auction, that school. And that Kip, he's a proper comic cut.' Now this was to me an entirely new idea. It had never occurred to me that it was possible to criticize the set-up. Actually to think of the school in that lordly way as a 'rum auction' and Old Kip as a 'proper comic cut'—it was a new and welcome outlook.

'I can see,' the policeman went on, 'as you'd no other course, but to get out and keep cheerful. I never could abide a whinger. A whinging kid I cannot stomach. Your dad—I've just rung him on the 'phone, and he'll be here directly. Your dad, I suppose, being a gentleman, won't have the guts—er—to give that young master a bloody nose same as I would. But take my advice lad—you go back to that school, and face 'em out, and never let 'em get you down.' My father arrived in the car shortly afterwards, and my new friend immediately changed into a comic turn himself, touching his forelock and saying 'Here's my best respects,' and being tipped very heavily.

It was decided that I should go back, and two or three days later my father left me in Old Kip's study. He said, 'So you have decided to return. I think that is a wise decision. The boys have been prepared for your reappearance among them. I think an attitude of bravado will not go down at all well. You will receive no punishment. But I wish you to realize some part of the great anxiety of which you have been the cause. There is just one thing: your behaviour has caused grave sorrow to Mr Seaton, and he's waiting in the next room to receive your apology should you wish to give it. But I leave it to you. It is your own moral responsibility. Shall I tell him to come in?' I took a deep breath and shouldered my moral responsibility. 'No, sir,' I said. And went in to tea to face the school.

It took the school some time to find an appropriate attitude towards such a gross non-conformity as running away: its enormity exempted it from the self-righteousness which is the normal reaction in children's communities, and finally they decided it was funny, funny and slightly heroic. The tale of my adventures lost nothing in the telling, and before long I was given a limited license as an eccentric, so long as my eccentricities were held to be entertaining. During the whole of my life at school I held this unintegrated position, going through the motions of being a schoolboy but letting my mind run free to receive illuminations outside the routine, and though the irrelevance of what passed for my education makes me swear to this day when I think of it, it was at that school that I was blessed by one of the genuine illuminations of my life.

It came in the summer term of 1921, when I was eleven. By then I was a large, vague boy nicknamed Jenghis after the notable Tartar Jenghis Khan because of my slit-eyed, high-cheekboned and generally uncouth appearance. It was only the first day of term but already my mother's version of my personal appearance had worn out—one of my stockings was down to the ankle, one of my shoes was laced up with a furry piece of string, I had a hole in my shirt, a dirty face, and I stood in the school chapel, summoning up what defences I could muster against the hymn, which was imploring the Lord to behold us with His blessing, and which was falling on my spirit like a warrant read out.

I had been three years at school and would be leaving in another year if I was lucky enough to pass the Common Entrance to Public Schools examination. It never crossed my mind that I would pass, but then I spent most of my time making sure that as little as possible did cross my mind. No news was good news in my philosophy. It wasn't that I had any basic objection to any information, even the sort of information imparted at school. It was that none of it seemed to have any bearing on the urgent business of being alive, any reference to anything but itself. Knowledge was not a thing that was any help, so I didn't propose to pursue it, more than was necessary for the sake of conforming, and this was the crux of my problem; there was hardly a point at which my two worlds of home and school touched except to contradict each other. Two utterly different personalities were required to get by in these two environments, and I wrote them, produced them and acted them continually. In view of this achievement, my real self insisted that I ought to be excused further duty on compassionate grounds. So I excused myself.

It was a very good school. Looking back on it I am amazed at the liberality of its constitution. We wore shirts and shorts, or jerseys and shorts when everybody else at that time was wearing black suits, stiff collars and ties, and great black boots. We were allowed unlimited freedom on Sundays so long as we were back by 6 o'clock in the evening. This was amazing forty years ago.

It was also a very beautiful place. A long, low, battlemented house which had belonged to one medieval family whose fortunes perished in the Wars of the Roses, with a medieval chapel at one end and an eighteenth-century wing at the other, and a great two-storied block of stables with a clock at right angles to the main building. The place had its own little village inside the wall all on top of a hill. Smooth grass and balustrades: in spring the shot-silk effect of shooting corn on red earth, great trees where Capability Brown had cunningly put them 150 years before, and a Crusader in alabaster, with a great nose, lying in the chapel with bits of his armour above him: acres and acres of clipped grass, polite stone, and total peace. Here at least they had succeeded in pretending what all England was hoping to do—that the 1914–18 War had never been fought.

On the empty terrace at noonday you could see the doctor's car, its outlines waving in the heat, a thing like a dog cart with a cylindrical petrol tank perched like a bolster on its tail. We hadn't been able to get cars during the war and the doctor's was a Ford of 1912. And as it puttered away, nothing was left but sun and elegant stone and the sleepy clamour of all the rooks in the elm avenue. Time, you could say, stood still; indeed, our parents paid for it to stand still.

Fifty per cent of us were the sons of Northern and Midland manufacturers, newly come to money. The rest were professional people, members of the squirearchy, a scattering of the lower aristocracy. And the school had been modelled on the manners and views of the last category. Though nothing about horses was ever formally discussed, nevertheless, that tribal fetish was among us and above us everywhere. It was expected that we should own and love horses and live and breathe in terms of their use. Except, of course, it was well known that only about one in ten of us had even met the animal face to face. But those boys whose parents actually owned and used horses had a high prestige and stood about at ease in groups with the masters. And even among the boys, when they went boring on about withers and fetlocks, it was felt to be profane to tell them to shut up.

This cult came to its climax on Parents' Day, when two brothers, who even looked like horses, and whose mother was the Honourable Somebody or other, and lived on a horse, mounted the stage after the prizes had been given out and led us in a song called 'The Old Grey Fox'. This was quite obviously the parents' great moment. The faces of the old-fashioned ones—the gentry—softened and glowed at the realization that in this dreadful post-war world feeling was still being directed along the right lines. And the newly rich brightened at the thought that among the other properties they acquired when they paid the school fees, was this genuine old mystique instantly recognizable as 'the real thing'.

I found conformity to this cult and all its taboos extremely difficult. My natural mode of life at home was not cool or easy nor confined to any sort of code. I didn't understand codes and never for a moment while I was at that school did I understand what anything was supposed to be about. For instance I knew an extraordinary piece of verse about Latin which went like this: 'Common are to either sex, Artifex and opifex, Common are sacerdos, dux, vates parens et conjux.' There it was, in my mind, a piece of my education. Completely unrelated to anything else. Valuable, of course, but utterly mysterious. It was the same about God, who spoke to us through hymns. All that was certainly known about him, except that he had made the world, was that he was violently opposed to sex in any form. During the last term, a boy who certainly ought to have known that Old Kip was standing there listening to him, had given out in ringing tones a ditty which he felt to be entertaining. It went like this: 'There was a bonny Scotsman at the Battle of Waterloo; the wind blew up his petticoats and I leave the rest to you.' The consequences had been appalling. For days, masters went about with hangmen's faces. The Boy Scouts called a solemn session and poured cold water ceremoniously down Timms Minimus's sleeves and Old Kip had preached a sermon in chapel, not one sentence of which had had any definite meaning that you could pick out but which had been so solemn and so dire that some boys wept. Timms Minimus, it appeared, had greatly upset God and shortly afterwards, he spoke to us in a terrible hymn about the hosts of Midian prowling and prowling around.

Because I felt so foreign in this environment and could make neither head nor tail of it, and because, since I never stopped talking, I never stopped putting my foot in it, I had made up a character for myself to keep me out of trouble. I put it about that I was Irish and spoke all the time in what I believed to be the accent of that charming people. This was a brilliant stroke, since it dealt effectively with several strands of trouble at once. Irishmen, it was well known, were always at loggerheads with authority, and so was I. Irishmen got away with being witty about sacred subjects. Irishmen could be shaggy and untidy. They could get away with deep eccentricity such as liking Beethoven and hating cricket, at least I hoped they could. The part had certain dangers; for instance, when my parents came down at half term, if there were any boys within earshot of us, I had to speak in my accent, and my mother would say, 'Why are you speaking in that funny voice, René?' And there was, of course, the anomaly that neither my father nor my mother had the smallest suggestion of a brogue. Few of the boys and none of the masters really believed I was Irish but they played along with it on the grounds, I now believe, that I was dotty. The Irish character was based on that of an old sea dog called Barney, who lived in a book called *Martin Rattler*, which I cherished at that time. I had noticed that in books, books that you read, I mean, not school books, that there were roughly two kinds of characters: 'He said' characters and 'said he' characters. For instance, in *Martin Rattler*, something like the following moving passage occurs:

'The captain stirred the dead crocodile with his foot where it lay in the wreckage of our canoe. We were 700 miles from the coast. "There is nothing else for it," he said, "we go on foot." Barney looked along the jungle trail. "No more paddling, just an aisy stroll in the sun," said he.'

There was no doubt about it—the 'he said' chaps were run-of-the-mill. The chaps to be were the 'said he' chaps.

This was the most clearly formulated of the articles of my personal creed, the rest of which was concerned with disturbing presences and the obvious existence of another world all round the one we lived in, permeating it. In some strange places, the two worlds fused into one. There was an old, white, dead tree, for instance, which was obviously a product of this fusion, a place where the worlds met. Its shape, texture, colour and attitude were silently shouting about some other way of being alive, and more alive. It made the hair prickle on the back of your neck. There were other things which gave out this message, but not quite so loudly; green grass growing under clear water in the Spring term. Some stone formations. An overheard line of Shakespeare. 'Can such things be and overcome us like a summer cloud without our special wonder,' and the *Eine Kleine Nacht Musik* of Mozart, Schubert's songs, and anything by Beethoven.

Outside these moments of recognition, all was chaos and old night. Of course it was possible to learn off by heart that terrible piece about the square on the hypotenuse, but of what possible interest was it when you'd learnt it? William I, 1066, William II, 1087, were in much the same category. Mere lumps of unamenable fact. Mere anxieties rolling in the void. Cricket was another. When significance barely escaped you round every corner, glimpsed out of the tail of your eye, it was a wanton waste of time to bother with lessons or games or washing your face or not keeping your locker tidy or not being late for chapel. It was a sort of persecution.

This, at any rate, was the state of mind arrived at by R. Cutforth, aged eleven, Form Five, Nevill Holt School, Leicestershire, England, Europe, The Earth, near Mars, Solar System, whose school books, in addition to the above inscription, were covered all over with pictures of little men hanging by one hand from the tops of cliffs, or by both hands to trees whose roots were giving way from the tops of cliffs, or who were dancing on high wires on one leg over the sea or crawling like flies on the faces of skyscrapers.

At this ungainly moment of my life it would have occurred to nobody, and least of all to me, that on the very next day, I was to see a great light.

It happened on a run. The weather was so bad at the beginning of that term that cricket was impossible, so after lunch, we all sloshed off in the rain in a straggling column across country, shepherded by Mr Johnson, the music master, an unhappy intellectual to whom these chores fell as by some natural law.

After about a mile and a half, I was leaning against a gate between two sodden lengths of cow pasture, getting my breath back, when I suddenly saw in the scuffled mud patch under the gate a piece of stone washed clear by the rain, and contained in it, an intricate and perfect ribbed coil, like a coiled up snake, in a sort of dull gold. It was a beautiful object and a splendid find, and I was just wondering whether I could possibly carry it back or should I hide it somewhere to be recovered on Sunday when I didn't have to run, when Mr Johnson appeared, more than inclined to lean on the same gate and get his breath back. 'Oh, sir,' I said, 'what's this?' and showed him my find. 'That's an ammonite,' said Mr Johnson, puffing and blowing, 'an ammonite, a fossil shell, very old, used to live here in the sea when all this land was under the sea a long time ago.'

'Before the Romans and Ancient Britons?' I asked.

'Oh, long before, about a hundred and fifty million years ago, before there were any men at all,' he said. 'At least, I think that's right, they seem to change the estimate about every five years.'

'A hundred and fifty million years old?'

'About that.'

'Before or after the world was made in six days?'

'Well, metaphorically,' Mr Johnson said, 'about the Thursday of that week. An interesting period geologically—the giant lizards, the dinosaurs, the first flying beasts, the pterodactyls, they're all here still under the ground. This part of England is full of them.'

I don't know why this revelation of the huge continuity of the past should have been such a release to my imagination, but it was so. It was a genuine illumination—something to do with perspective, something to do with the mysterious quality of time itself: something to do with buried treasure, something which joined the separate worlds of poetry and finding out and learning and digging and the splendid look of the country. Something which put cricket in its pettyfogging place. During that summer term, I rarely emerged from the Jurassic Age. I found a quarry full of ammonites and bellamnites and terebratulae and rhynconellae and gryphaea and pecten and sea urchins. A whole sea bottom of creatures who'd lived and died and left themselves to be explained—this was the point—before anybody could have possibly explained them. With great difficulty I read that holy book, *The Origin of Species*. I sent for everything the South Kensington Museum had published about the Jurassic and the Lower Lias. I knew the names of all the creatures. The greatest day was when I found among the sharks' teeth in the blue clay the perfect imprint of a fish nearly two feet long.

Some of the hymns even began to sound sensible. 'Time, like an ever-rolling stream' for instance, except, of course, the hymn was wrong. Far from being forgotten as a dream dies at the opening day, they lay there in the Liassic clay making so strong an impression that they were remembered at the moment, now, a hundred and fifty million years later. Hymn writers, along with everybody else, failed to take the point. Sentimental.

I found my fish about 4 o'clock on a July afternoon. On a

Sunday, of course. At 9 o'clock by the stable clock that morning I put my name down to be absent from lunch and drew my sandwiches from the pantry, shouldered my haversack and builder's trowel and square-faced hammer, and set off down the chestnut avenue where all the bees were buzzing, and where the white dust of the roads of those days lay thick enough to mute my footsteps, and rise up in puffs of smoke when I ran.

I turned right over a stile and illegally along the edge of a hayfield, waist-deep in the hot, scented, multi-coloured mixture of grasses and weeds, and over the railway embankment, climbing down the long morraine of rocks which drained it and reinforced it, up the other side, down the side of the big barley field, waving like a sand-coloured sea and on down hill to a meadow badly farmed and full of ragwort under whose harsh, yellow flowers you could find millions of the black and yellow caterpillars which turned into Cinnabar moths, and over another stile into a sort of wilderness of long grass through which wound the brook in its own canyon about ten feet deep and twenty feet wide. The water was low and the biggest pool not ten feet wide or three deep. Long, bone-coloured grasses grew on the tops of little cliffs, and rushes and yellow flags at the water's edge. I heard the birds signal my arrival and then stop and fall very silent. There was the swishing noise of a cow eating grass on the cliff top. Bright blue and bright yellow, the little dragonflies flicked about like neon signs over the water and a waert rat, not quite silently, slid under and was off. I took off my shirt. The summer's geology had burnt me toast colour. I took off my shoes and put my feet in the water and just sat for ten minutes, possessing my estate—this fifty yards of brook. In the glare of the sun, eyes slightly unfocused, the yellows and tans and off-whites of the dried grasses and the coins of sunlight on the water splintered and disintegrated into zigzags of light as in a picture by Van Gogh. Everything went a little darker and the insect hum became more important. Some small degree of self-hypnosis and sun-drunkenness was an integral part in this act of worship.

I sat very still and the birds began to regain their confidence. The cow came over to look at me, and three rabbits lolloped into view. You had to sit there until you were satisfied that you were part of all this. And then participation could move on to its next stage, the uncovering of the other world. From the edge of the stream to the foot of the taller cliff—the 12 foot one, of cigar-coloured silt, on the floor of the canyon a strip of dark blue clay was laid bare. The Lower Lias in all its glory. When the spirit moved me, I walked across with my haversack, lay on my stomach on the grass and began to peel off with the trowel the first layer of clay. Fossils were to be found scattered all through the clay, perfectly preserved, but every so often a layer of hard cemented stone occurred, a flat pavement three to six inches thick, and in and under this, the life of the ancient ocean floor had become compacted and was as thick as gravel in concrete. I found one of these layers at about midday, knocked off for my sandwiches and to take a trip down to the next bay of the stream to see the kingfisher, who was streaking about as usual like blue lightning. Then I just lay in the sun and roasted and then, at about two, I got down to work. It was the richest lode I had ever struck. Every layer brought up something new, rich, strange. The heat of the afternoon was over the hill when I decided to yank out a two foot block of it which seemed separate, before I knocked off for the day. It took me an hour to haul it out—a long, oval stone covered with the hieroglyphs of shells in section and on edge and at one end something I couldn't place—a sort of wavy pattern in black and white which disappeared into the stone matrix. I took out my knife, a huge affair of many implements and tried the biggest blade in a crack at the top of the stone. Quite suddenly it fell apart like a hinged box and there was my fish from its head to the end of its tail which was the bit I had noticed, perfect in every scale: eyeplates, spines, teeth and the great, square, bony back plates of a shark.

I sat there in the sun for half an hour or more filled with the sense of a life made, for an instant, perfect, and then I emptied out my haversack, covered the contents with clay and marked the spot with a clod of earth and a stick, washed my fish gently in the stream, wrapped him in dock leaves, stowed him in the haversack and toiled up the hill. And it was the last Sunday of term.

Life at home in the holidays had a richer, thicker, hotter texture than school life and was based on the loud, prolonged discord, what could nowadays be called a 'dialogue', between my parents' two totally incompatible ideologies. This dialogue had been going on for twelve years and showed no signs of ever being resolved. Sometimes it erupted into great storms when the lightning flashed to and fro and the thunders rolled, but usually it was confined within intellectual banks as a spate of arguments and attitudes. Briefly, my father pinned all his faith in the future. For him, everything now established was due, and quite rightly, for a quick fade-out into something very different. The most subversive thought was the best one. For my mother, on the other hand, the canons of taste, belief and permissibility had been laid down, once and for all, by the Anglican upper classes in about 1905. Both of them were passionate, opinionated and immensely articulate people. It was a noisy household. But at any rate, hunting played no part in it and being quietly superior and self-contained was not an admired attitude.

My mother was rather pleased to find that my new religion was concerned with anything as clean as stones—an earlier faith had involved the stocking of a smelly aquarium in my bedroom with newts and waterbeetles which always escaped and were found with much screaming by the maids months later, sometimes in airing cupboards or folded away amongst the shirts in drawers. Now the aquarium was bundled away to make room for shelves full of rocks all labelled with their jaw-breaking names, for already I had become very learned. Nor did I wear my learning lightly. Everybody suffered from it.

But the fact was that, like any other religion, this one needed a monastic discipline to reach its highest flights. At school this was provided by the utterly boring routine and a constant state of high anxiety. Home life was secular and distracting. There was the gramophone, the bicycle, the house in the tree, my brother, John, my friend, Peter, the vicar's son. I made some attempts on the local fossils which were vegetable and carboniferous but had to realize in the end that they wouldn't do. The deity concerned was a local god presiding over just that particular stretch of stream where the fish had lain so long.

I lapsed, and gave myself up to secular pleasures, some of which I recognized as vices. For instance, whole sunny afternoons spent flat on my stomach on the dining room floor with a bag of sweets and a volume of the *Boy's Own Paper* and the gramophone. I used to choose a record with a slow rhythm and an absolutely meaningless content—nothing that said anything would do. Its function was purely hypnotic. Then pop in a sweet and begin to read. 'Captain Hunter was the first to enter the tomb of the Pharaoh, but we were close behind him. Our footsteps echoed on the stone flags of the passage floor, the first echo there for perhaps five thousand years. "If my reading of the hieroglyphs is correct," the Captain said, "the first danger spot is in the three steps that are right ahead of us there." He picked up a fragment of rock which had fallen from the roof and threw it against the lower step. There was a click as the step moved down like a piano key, and simultaneously a sound like distant thunder began far ahead of us in the gloom, and to our horror we saw rolling towards us along the passage at a rapidly increasing pace an immense stone ball ten feet in diameter. "Throw yourselves flat at the foot of the steps," the Captain roared and hardly had we done so than the ball was upon us, skimming over us by an inch or less. It rushed on down the passage and crashed into the entrance hole, cutting off the sunlight and blocking the way completely.

"Hazard No. One," Captain Hunter said grimly, "the Priests of Ammon Ra have done their work well." '

But in spite of backsliding in the holidays, the rigours of school life soon renewed the faith. In the end, it perished of its own success. The headmaster took it up. A geological society was formed. I was its secretary. I gave lectures. At one time a learned man from the South Kensington Museum came down to consult me and to take for his own glass cases a very curious shell of mine of a kind which I had never seen before. Nor, he said, had anyone else. It's somewhere in the Science Museum to this day. When, by the time of my last summer term, I had found the giant ammonites under Hallaton bridge, there were sixteen little boys digging them up and a master taking measurements. I had felt sad all day and now I suddenly knew what was wrong. I flung down my trowel in disgust. The faith had become institutionalized and I was through with it.

Against that, I had passed the Common Entrance.

It reappeared, of course, the faith, as it's reappeared all through my life in one form or another. For me, it seems, something else, something other, has to permeate the universe. I can't do without it. In its next manifestation, it had sunk to the level of physics—it was the radio wave.

I had heard somebody say, 'Of course the wave doesn't come to an end, it's not in the air, it's in the ether, it goes out into space for ever. The waves from every transmitter on earth are going on out to the moon and the planets and on past the solar system; in fact they fill the Universe.'

'What waves?' I said.

'Wireless.'

'What's that?'

It didn't take me long to learn. The fossils were all carted off to the cellar, for it was feared that attic floor would break under their weight, and now my room was filled with ebonite panels and copper wire laboriously wound in coils. It was like living in a giant cat's cradle. A copper kettle of my mother's which she had not yet missed was buried in a flowerbed underneath my window to act as an earth. My father's spare car battery which he had not yet missed was expending itself very fast on three of the great, hot bright valves of the time. The new circuit—ST 100, Scott-Taggart's greatest—was ready to be tested. I adjusted the crystal and turned the dial: a trickle of Morse piped against the thundering static. Feverishly I looked it up in the book—1750 metres; Stockholm.

'If it's not a ship,' I said, 'it's Sweden.'

My brother John dashed out of the room to the head of the stairs.

'He's got a message from Sweden,' he bawled.

My father came bounding up the stairs to listen. He was visibly impressed. 'Well, I'll be damned,' he kept saying.

I adjusted the moving coils again and turned the dial six notches down and—glory: a voice, a genuine human voice slowly intoning. 'Fastnet and Rockall: low cloud at 200 feet, nine tenths, visibility 2 miles.'

'Well, I'll be damned,' my father said.

'The wave goes right on past the moon and the planets,' I told him, 'and fills the Universe.'

'Well, I'll be damned,' he said.

Nevertheless, a few days later, I was delivered at my new school. Dressed in black like a waiter, I prowled nervously about the high arching cloisters as the evening drew in. Suddenly an awful being in a mortarboard cap accosted me.

'Hey, you.'

'Yes, sir.'

'Don't call me sir, you twit, my name's Forbes.'

'Yes, Forbes.'

'Are you a new squit?'

'Yes,' I said humbly.

'Well, you new squits are supposed to be in chapel five minutes before the bell.' He looked me over—'And have your buttons done up, and your shoes cleaned and your hair tidy. What's your name?'

'Cutforth, Forbes.'

'Right, I'll remember you. Now get along.'

'Five years to go,' I thought, as I went into chapel, and two minutes later, they were at it again. 'Lord, behold us with thy blessing, once again assembled here.'

III

No Man's Land

Being an alien is the burden of adolescence, an alien without a passport or even an identity card, and surrounded by meaningless or hostile foreigners, all claiming respect and allegiance.

I was nearly seventeen before I began to feel the full weight of this burden. It came over me in flood as I sat in the school chapel one Sunday morning, wondering, not for the first time, whether the grotesque irrelevance of my daily life would ever come to an end, whether it would ever begin to mean anything. A visiting clergyman was preaching the sermon in an Anglican dialect so etiolated as to be difficult to follow. He was making impassioned play with a monosyllable which he pronounced 'Gudd', and all along the rows of boys I could see eyes brightening and mouths moving as they rehearsed the imitations which would explode in the cloisters the moment the service was over. Normally the sight would have livened me up somewhat, but that morning it depressed me, and as I stood up for the after-sermon hymn, I noticed with anger the mental effort I still had to make, after all these years to counter the emotional blackmail of the tune.

Outside, the sun's message, no longer scrambled by stained glass, sang out loud and clear. It signalled an interval during which the motions I went through might be my own, if I could think of any. So, I decided to walk out to the village pub I'd found a few weeks before, where they were undeterred by my Sunday black coat and striped trousers, and drink an illegal pint of bitter in the back bar: anything to get away from being what had to pass as myself while I was at school. Perhaps I might meet somebody in the pub bar for whom, for a little while, it would be possible to deploy another self, which certainly need be no more fictional than the one I had to make up to satisfy the school. I might be headed for a short holiday. From reality? Who's to know?

The swooning scent of meadowsweet saturated me as I walked along the old canal towpath, meadow sweet and 'Those long purples which our cold maids do dead men's fingers call them, but liberal shepherds give a grosser name'. A few liberal shepherds among the masters might do something for the standard of education, I felt: they might have their sights on something relevant for a change. Meadowsweet, again: nature was such a fraud: promise without fulfilment. As it happened, I knew about meadowsweet: no honey-bags, just a big smell: the winged creatures crawling all over it, fertilizing it, would get nothing for their labour. There was nothing to get: a hoax. Perhaps because nature was a meadowsweet hoax people turned to God. Gudd. No, not him, fat with devotion and saccharine hymns. In this mood I turned into the twilight of the Hare and Trumpet's back bar, a private bar, normally empty. 'I suppose it's all right,' the landlord said, and passed my pint across the counter. I didn't really like bitter, but it was cool, and after a pint, and on one occasion two, circumstance nagged less knowingly: an escape clause loomed up. I kept my back scrupulously turned to the outside door, because I was illegal, and it was a revelation to me when another door, right in front of me, which led to the saloon bar, suddenly opened and disclosed my Housemaster, known to all as Crumpers. The situation was beyond me, so I froze. Crumpers, a fat man with a bishopy face, advanced upon me, holding in his hand a full pint. As he came on, I had the opportunity to observe that all the time I'd been having to endure the sermon in the school chapel, Crumpers had been doing himself very well in the saloon.

'Ah, Cutforth,' he said as he came up, 'I might have known it.' He drew in a huge breath and I stood by. There was a pause, and he then exhaled it. 'Hello,' he said at length. This threw me. My Housemaster and I were not on 'hello' terms. The reverse, in fact. When he came in I had noticed at once that he was wearing a variant of the less sinister of his two expressions—that of a man-eating rabbit—and I had consequently adopted in the two seconds at my disposal, the look of a boy who, though he would never be a house prefect, still had some good in him. Now, with an abrupt change into the minor key, Crumpers put on his more sinister expression, that of the good man unjustly denied your confidence. This I had learned to dread, and in conjunction with his astonishing 'Hello', it deprived me of the gambit. I waited, back-pedalling, holding my look of the good boy, and hoping that no trace of the 'bloody arrogance' complained of by my house captain showed through.

'Boys are the devil,' said Crumpers. 'You blame me because I know nothing about you.'

'Oh no, sir,' I said, for my simple creed had been that the less he knew about me, the better.

'Oh no, sir,' mimicked my Housemaster, to my great discomfort. 'That's as far as I've ever got with you. I tell you what, Cutforth,' Crumpers roared, 'we'll get drunk together. A pint for Mr Cutforth,' he shouted across the bar.

And so began a memorable afternoon. Soon after the second pint I was saying, 'The point is: I can't see that anything I'll ever want to do is being prepared by what I'm doing now.'

'What do you want to do?'

'I don't know.'

'Then let me be your guide . . .'

'No,' I said, 'I don't think you can be.'

'The point is, there are only a limited number of things you can do.'

'In your bloody world,' I said.

'That's right. That's where you have to live.'

'Not necessarily,' I said. 'You can opt out.'

'Into what?'

'Just living about.'

'You must go up to the University.'

'More penal servitude.'

'Oh no,' said Crumpers, shocked, 'that isn't so, you're quite wrong there. That isn't so at all.'

I said it was a memorable afternoon, full of revelation and

shouting. Unfortunately, only the early part of it lies in my memory. Crumpers, who had a deep admiration for Belloc, bought pint after pint. 'If you must drink, boy,' he bawled, old Bellocky Bill, 'drink deep.' I can remember him saying that it was boys like me who made him feel that his life was a failure, he who had fought in the war so that the ideals of a Christian gentleman should not perish from the earth: and how could I fail to realize that I was one of a tiny handful of the most privileged people on the planet. He went on from there to patriotism and 'the greatest Empire the world has ever known'. He felt it his duty to let my parents know that his methods had failed in my case, failed. He washed his hands of me. No. On second thoughts, he would persevere. I was unfortunate, a victim of the decadence of the times, of writers such as Bernard Shaw and D. H. Lawrence. And finally, did I call myself an Englishman? I shouted back as best I could, but long before I got into the taxi he presently called, he had beaten me by sheer weight of alcohol. We returned to the school deviously by the music school entrance, and I got into bed as it came round for the second time.

In times when society is changing gears it's the adolescent who has to bear the brunt of the conflict. That encounter with Crumpers, a head-on collision in 1926 between mutually incomprehensible generations, returned me to square one, the realization that I was shortly going to have to launch myself into a world run almost entirely by people like Crumpers for people like Crumpers; and that, in that world, I was utterly alien: I didn't even have a passport to it. I couldn't make out what it meant when it spoke. On its great days it was frighteningly foreign. Armistice Day, for instance, when in a cowed silence, we watched with shock some of the masters in tears. Armistice Day meant nothing whatever to us. And then, as now, there was the sound barrier.

Jazz, 'a depraved and barbaric noise' according to Crumpers, had arrived, and gramophones were pounding out in every study and class-room in the school, and this jazz opened up a window on another, more glamourous world, the one reported with so much venom and disgust by the popular newspapers. In London, it appeared, the young danced all night at parties which in the later stages became orgies. The Bright Young People, as they were called, had few sexual inhibitions and nothing whatever to do. They were all, it seemed, independent of the necessities which beset most of us, such as making a living, or being tolerated in a neighbourhood. But jazz was their music, and conversely they were the spirit of jazz, the new age. They informed our attitudes even at school, in spite of the fact that all our knowledge of them was derived obscurely from paragraphs in the *Daily Mail*, whenever one of them committed suicide or was had up on a drugs charge. We felt on these occasions that a blow had been struck against Crumpers and Hymns Ancient and Modern. A boy in my house called Tolland, hitherto nameless, became a hero overnight when a picture of his sister being hauled along by a policeman appeared in the *Mail* over the caption 'Deb drunk and incapable'. We prevailed upon Tolland to invite his sister over next time his parents came down for the weekend, and the very next weekend she appeared, with a boy's haircut, long slinky legs in shiny silk, her skirt at mid-thigh, a great scarlet mouth painted across her face, with the regulation yard of green jade cigarette holder stuck in it, and the high, loud, clipped, gabbling upper-class voice which was as much a badge of fashion in 1926 as the Liverpudlian whine is now. Everybody was having a go at it.

Tolland's sister was a great happening. It made the summer term of 1926. The fashion for Oxford bags had reached its preposterous height that summer. Oxford bags were trousers in very pale shades of colour with fancy names, silver-grey, silver sand, strawberry and cream, and moonlight, and many others, and the point about them was their enormous width of leg. Some of them were a yard wide at shoe level. They were worn with double-breasted waistcoats, little round pork-pie hats, bow ties and long cigarette holders. Permission to wear them at school at weekends had only been granted the term before, and then only to the upper school, and minus the pork-pie hats, the bow ties and, of course, the cigarette holders.

I can't give a better idea of the tremendous impact of

Tolland's sister than to report that I too felt constrained to borrow a pair of Oxford bags for that occasion, and I was a tousled boy with unbrushed hair and unblacked shoes, crumpled trousers and missing buttons, who in my first year had been frequently hauled up and caned by the prefects for being what they called 'a bloody disgrace'. I now approached a friend of mine called Allen, whose life consisted almost solely of his elegant appearance and the specialized skills and learning which that entailed, and borrowed his third pair of silver sand Oxfords, the ones with the small cigarette burn which didn't really show.

I suppose that every member of upper school must have made an occasion to show Tolland's sister his Oxford bags during that weekend, and one boy, Maryland, who was very dark, grew a small moustache for the occasion. We didn't exactly parade for Miss Tolland, but as she stood there in the quad with Tolland and their father and mother and their 'rather excessively smart car,' to quote a snobbish prefect, it was surprising how many Oxford bags found they had business in the quad, and so great an affection for Tolland, a surprised mousy boy unused to glory, that they had to shake him by the hand. We did not go unrewarded. There was, for instance, the sight of Crumpers. When Crumpers had first had his attention drawn to the newspaper photograph and caption he had crumpled up the paper and hurled it into a corner with a loud 'tchah'. Now he was caught unawares in cricket flannels and his old faded Cambridge blazer, with the corners of his mouth turned down, shaking Tolland's sister's hand as if someone had given him a firework to hold. Some of us were rewarded directly. I was there when a group of Tolland's new-found friends found enough nerve to commiserate with his sister on her adventure with the police.

'My dears, too, too kind,' she said through her cigarette. 'I was, actually, the tiniest bit squiffy—one of Jo-Jo's divine parties—but, my dears, one simply faces the dim fact that policemen simply do not care for one. So shame-making. And, I mean, where's the justice?'

I treasured these fatuous words, my only direct contact so far with the glamour of my time and period. I found myself savagely envying Tolland his father who lived in London and had made a large fortune out of boots and shoes, so unlike my father who lived in Swadlincote, South Derbyshire, and was so much better at spending money than making it that by now there was very little left. Tolland's father knew some very rich people in the neighbourhood of the school who were giving a dance that night, hiring a famous band from London. Five of us were invited and had permission to go. I was one, and before I left I had (a) kissed Miss Tolland, and called her Penelope. In fact, I'd had quite a session with Miss Tolland, who told me her brother hadn't wanted to invite me, but that she had insisted, because I had looked so sweet in those Oxford bags six sizes to small for me 'with, my dear, a simply enormous cigarette hole in the trouser seat. Oh, you looked so sweet. No, no, you must behave.' I wasn't even put off when she said, 'Don't you agree, simply the only writer is Michael Arlen?' although I knew perfectly well that apart from Shakespeare and P. G. Wodehouse, T. S. Eliot was the only writer. And (b), I had called the world-famous bandleader by his first name, and he me by mine: we'd had half a bottle of champagne together, he'd let me have a go on the jazz drummer's outfit in the interval, and when I'd finished, he'd rolled his eyes and said, 'You sure handled that great, René.' His was a name to pulverize the middle-class male opposition in Swandlincote. I bore it away with me like a piece of loot, along with the cigar Mr Tolland gave me, and the last words on the steps of Penelope Tolland, 'And do please come to my party, 26th of next month, and we'll get locked up in Vine Street together.'

Vine Street police station, the scene of Miss Tolland's late adventure, became a symbol to me of the free life as lived by happy sophisticates who had broken free. There was Vine Street and there was Swadlincote and never the twain would meet. That was the trouble. None of the worlds with which I was familiar met at any point. Impossible ever to tell my mother about, for instance, Tolland's sister, or Crumpers in the pub, impossible that any of my relations could realize the glory imparted to me by the great bandleader. Well, my father would have enjoyed all these stories at one time, but we rarely saw him nowadays, and when we did he was so sunk in gloom as to be unapproachable. He was nothing to do with us, his manner suggested.

I saw no future in Swandlincote, and there I was wrong. Of all the worlds I was in touch with then, it was the only one, as it turned out, which had a future.

It frightened me. It seemed to me then a mere squalid hangover from the nineteenth century, and I was glad that I didn't have to try to survive its rigours. I lived out on the edge of it all, isolated first by middle-classness, and then from the rest of that lot—a small, rather cowed, rather fusty 'who's for tennis' group—by the fact that our house was always loud with music and arguments about books and theories, and over and under and through all this crackled the thunder and lightning of the war which my father and my mother had been waging all through my lifetime as long as I could remember. The din tended to put people off, and the sensation of living under a volcano which might go off at any moment. 'An odd lot,' they said, and didn't come again. The day the volcano finally erupted, and my father left one morning in his car, never to return, was about a term and a half away.

One of the worlds which I knew in my youth seems now totally to have disappeared: part of the D. H. Lawrence landscape, which after all was only twenty miles away and twenty years back in time. Out in the country which surrounds the black industrial mess of Swadlincote, and it's a harsh dark country of millstone grit, with a few bright soft valleys where the limestone breaks through, a friend of mine, called Harry Blood, used to live on a starvecrow farm over by Carvers Rock, where the colliers used to stage their mains of cock-fighting. Harry was an Englishman of an ancient kind. He was tall and thin and very blond, and had the sort of roman nose you used to see on officers of the regular army. This nose was entirely countermanded by a pair of enormous dark blue eyes, with a disconcerting sort of laugh in them. He wore a long, ragged yellow moustache like a Celtic chieftain, and his cloth cap sat with the peak one way and the cap the other, and a cowslip or a rose stuck between them. Harry could make and play a wooden penny whistle better than anyone I've ever heard. He could and did make catapults which in his hands were real hunting weapons. He was the best poacher for miles around, a great one with ferrets and traps. Given five minutes any time he could tickle a trout out of the river, and he had a lurcher dog called Bowler, an only just junior partner, who worked with him apparently by telepathy. This Harry Blood was full of folk songs.

But he had his weaknesses: whisky was one, and cock-fighting was another. He'd been in the hands of the police once or twice. He took me to see a main of cock-fighting once, in the middle of the night, down under Carvers Rock which is the quarry where in the old days they hacked out the great millstones which ground their bread. In a natural arena, a small circle like a dry pond, in the light of a ring of carbide bicycle lamps they fought three mains before the lookout signalled that the police were on the way and we broke up and ran for it. I detested the cock-fighting, and I couldn't understand how Harry, the least bloodthirsty of men, could bear to act as impresario to such a savage performance. 'Those men were bloody savages,' I said. 'Ay, they wor,' said Harry, 'and they are. It's wokkin' down t'pit as brutalizes 'em so all their worrit is blood and murder. A man should have his feet on grass if he's to know 'is nature. Yes, they come for t'blood, but cock-fightin's way beyond and above such clods.' And he went on to sketch out his own feelings on the subject, in which cock-fighting figured as a sort of art-form, in which rage and cruelty, facts of all our natures, were so purged of sentimentality, so perfectly expressed in the bodies and the movements and rhythms of the fighting cocks that they became beautiful, as everything could be.

Of all the worlds available to my intuitions in the Derbyshire of the '20's, Harry Blood's world, which stretched from Hartshorne to the Trent at Swarkestone Bridge, was the one I'd have soonest been rooted in, but there were to be no roots for me. The managerial-industrial class which I was born into was the first generation of the rootless, the racing rats, the beginning of Organisation Man. Harry's shiftless, sensual world embarrassed or shocked such people; for he was altogether without the puritanism which sent them chasing after money and status. What Harry was after was delight; and he could abstract it from a huge range of natural phenomena, headed by women, on whose behalf his life was one long scandal, but adequately recompensed for living by the sight of a nest of blue hedge-sparrow's eggs, or of sunshine on yellow straw; or the taste of a particularly fine apple, or the presence of a happy child. A lazy, long-gazing life of the sort that nobody lives now. He knew where to lay his hand on anything he wanted, from the first morels of early spring, which he made into a soup I've never tasted the like of since, through the whole long succession of fruits and fungi, trout and bream, rabbits and hares, partridge and wood-cock; gastronomically, he lived a life of fabulous luxury; in love he always had his way, but his greatest conquest was Time, having always had time; and it was the sight of him, lounging gracefully about bearing his sins so lightly, that was the most bitter affront to the scurrying lives committed to the pursuit of status and money.

None of my other worlds would accept Harry; at school the whole stance was modelled on his opposite; the sensuous was not appreciated, the sensual was positively sinful; if you were full of deeply committed feelings, it was to be hoped that it was for your school or your country, and it was even more to be hoped that you would never mention it, but perhaps reveal it at the last by some sacrificial death in action. My mother, who deeply detested Harry on class grounds, seemed in those days to have dwindled into a mere embodiment of veto. 'Let me hear no more about you and this Harry Blood,' she said, 'a man with a criminal record, and two affiliation orders out against him. And that woman who house-keeps for him, no more than an immoral slut. Most undesirable.' My mother was always accurately informed.

Walking back from Harry Blood's country, up the long hill to the tollgate at Woodville, it was like sleep-walking through a no-man's-land. At the top of the hill, the road ran steeply down into the blackened saucer, where Swadlincote lay, under its eiderdown of smoke. It wasn't, except rarely, and from special angles, a vision of Blake's dark satanic mills, it was too mean and squalid, with its narrow canals full of bright yellow industrial effluent; its fences made up of old wire rope, broken into rusted paint-brush ends every yard or two; its rough cobbles, the long, blank, black, greasy walls, leaning at decrepit angles; the ubiquitous smell of gas. In this environment, the Anglican God was fearfully rejected by a stern population which still christened its sons Aaron, and Jedediah, and Habbakuk. Swadlincote's God hated sex even more bitterly than the Anglican one did; but his speciality was to make a positive little hell of Sunday, when blinds were drawn, children shushed, voices lowered, games forbidden, music and books—except the Bible—banished, and long faces compulsory. Hymns, which seemed to be advocating the suicide of all believers, were bawled out with a dreadful vitality. Sermons, mainly about drink, ran on for hours.

This society had produced another world into which I timidly stepped from time to time, the world of the children, now grown up, whose teeth had been set on edge by this prodigal feast of sour grapes. The headquarters of those in whom puritanism had gone bad was in the back bar of the big pub on the Delf; here, nearly every night of the week, the Devil's Disciples were on view, led by a gigantic fishmonger called Jed, crimson with drink, with his fair hair waist long, and long yellow moustaches like a Viking's flung back across his shoulders. When he was not in the bar, urging the disciples to new depths of violence and lechery, Jed drove his fish-float furiously through the streets, his hair and moustaches flying behind him in the wind, cursing and screaming as he plied the whip; a theatrically desperate character, with his gang of full-blooded Victorian villains, dedicated to the Devil, or whatever the chief opponent of the God of Swadlincote called himself. I felt they were on the right side in that quarrel, but the full practice of their faith, the taking off into the country on Sundays, on a hare-coursing, whippet-racing expedition, with half a bus-load of shrieking girls and several crates of Bass and bottles of whisky, was too humourless, too dedicated for me. I only tried it once, and I didn't like it; you had to belong and I didn't.

There was only one person in my life to whom I could take tales from all these various worlds and get a judgement on them: my great-uncle Charles, an ancient and eccentric clergyman, who'd spent nearly all his life in India. He didn't belong anywhere, either, and now froze in the heat of the English summer in my grandfather's well-ordered house out beyond the clay holes. Old Charles always wore a heavy black cassock with two deep pockets in the front like a butcher's apron. In one of these he carried a Greek Testament and in the other a flask of Martell brandy, and throughout the day he would dip for refreshment now into the one, now the other. His judgements were found eccentric by many, but not by me. For instance, 'Your housemaster, what d'you call him, Crumpers, is a fool,' he announced. 'His friend, Belloc, is not so much a writer as a vulgar comedian, and, what's worse, a moral bully. Harry Blood, I knew his father, a fine man, a sort of poet, but only with his hands, he couldn't read or write. A fine, sensitive man who knew a great deal. You stick with Harry Blood, my boy, you won't go far wrong. As for your, what is it, jazz band feller, they're a good lot. I played the bones in a nigger minstrel outfit years ago in Brighton, when I was reading Theology. A very fine lot they were. I gather they've come up in the world since then. Quite right, too.'

But of course there was absolutely no future in great-uncle Charles.

Meanwhile, there was a matter of pressing urgency—girls. And there were plenty of girls, not all that different from Tolland's sister, at least in intention. There was the bank manager's ravishing daughter, and the Rector of Hartshorne's delectable one. One and all, they had read *The Green Hat*, by Michael Arlen—in Swadlincote, it was quite often the only thing they ever had read, except 'Hymns Ancient and Modern,' but in their redoubtable female way they had grasped the gist of that great work, which was, that a reputation for unchastity is a great advantage to a woman, if young; so they set about acquiring one—bogusly, more often than not—and that was the basis of my complaint against them. Also they were a year or two older than I was, and were looking for experience rather than experiment.

In middle-class Swadlincote, as far as I was concerned, the male opposition was formidable. There was Teddy, for instance, three years older than me, very tall and slim, who had an aquiline nose and, much worse, green eyes which turned up, showing white all around the southern aspect of his eyeballs. As a gesture, it came off.

'Oh, do you know him?' asked an ecstatic girl partner in the kick Charleston, which, by and large, was more exhausting than a brisk ten minutes of Rugby League. 'Oh, do you know him? I adore him. He looks as if he did such very wicked things—or at any rate, thought of them.' There were five good returns to this volley, I now see. I used none of them.

'Such as what?' I asked.

'Oh, probably you wouldn't know; you're rather young, aren't you?'

As we left the dance floor, she suddenly dragged me round in a half circle, so that we bumped into Teddy. I had to introduce them, and Teddy's eyes turned up beneath my very gaze about another half inch.

And there was Bill Bantlin. Bill was a type which hasn't been seen around much since, but in the twenties women's magazines were much concerned with him. He was very large and hairy and lazy, and cultivated an air of extreme, though amiable, stupidity, and all his clothes were even larger and hairier than he was, and he was never seen without his large, hairy, lazy dog, which he had trained to assume his own expression exactly: sad, but willing to please. 'I say, what ho, jolly good' was the staple of his conversation, but it was nicely calculated, for there was a psychiatric truth beneath these fashions for short hair and cylindrical figures, and many a female eye brightened as the scent of the docile animal made its impact.

And there was a whole contingent of 'Nuts from Barcelona', small neat men, with patent leather shoes, patent leather hair, hair-line moustaches in varying positions of extreme significance on the expanses of their upper lips, and sideboards, not of the luxurious kind we know now, but small rectangles as of tar neatly dabbed on. Some of these Nuts had been to London.

My own slit-eyed, tousled and uncouth appearance, wildly gabbling about Mozart and T. S. Eliot reassured no one, enhanced no status. I didn't even have a car. All the same, aware of all this, I danced on.

In the end, it wasn't in Swadlincote, or at school, or in the country, or anywhere near Vine Street, that I found an answer. It was in France. I went to stay with the usual horribly respectable family in Dijon to improve my French. On a walk by myself one midday in the soothing heat, I came suddenly upon a group of wild-haired adolescents lying down under a tree drinking wine, three girls and two youths. One of the girls was lovely. They all had long hair, and guitars, and haversacks slung on their shoulders, and they looked so attractive I smiled across at them. One of the boys waved the wine bottle across at me, and a minute or two later we were all launched on one of those heady, seventeen-year-old conversations about the state of the world.

'We are from Germany,' said the leader of the group, whose name was Pieter. 'And in Germany everything is now very bad. We must make a new world of a new kind. Germany is full of bloody-minded old men, and so is France, and England too, I daresay, we won't have anything to do with. So we wander about, and live rough, and sing, and our friends all over Europe make room for us in barns and outhouses. We are called the Wandervogel.' I stayed for an hour and then got guiltily to my feet. Madame Perron's lunch, my God, the lunch of Madame Perron. I stood there looking at them, and Pieter said, 'Why not come with us. You will be good for Gisela; her boy left us yesterday to go to his university. You will be kind to her. She is sad.' And he pointed to this beautiful girl.

I returned from a three weeks' trip with the Wandervogel to my last term at school much refreshed, but now confirmed in every doubt and fear about the relevance of my education to any sort of real life. Every minute of it was a minute wasted: I could hardly bear to wait to leave at the end of the term. But home when I got there was worse, just as unreal and narrower, and everything seemed to have run down almost to a standstill. I'd had this fancy or intuition, if that's what it was, that everything was running down since the General Strike the year before, when, against a crimson sunset on Gresley Common, I watched thousands and thousands of miners and their wives as they listened to A. J. Cook, the miners' leader. I went with Florrie, because A. J. Cook was to her what St. Paul was to my mother. 'Yo mun understand as he's reet,' she kept on saying to me. The men were totally silent, concentrated, listening, not weighing it up; it was all weighed up. They were there to see justice done. 'Something is now going to happen,' I thought. I looked forward with some pleasure to the Revolution. But nothing happened. Everything just went on. Just went on running down.

My father had long since ceased to have any connection with any works. He was away most of the time, and what he did was a mystery. When he was at home my brother John and I used to listen at night to the swelling counterpoint of the dialogue going on downstairs between our parents into the small hours of the morning; but no longer with the dread which it used to inspire. The fire had gone out of it.

Then all the ends came quite suddenly. My mother's father died, and we were all startled by the sudden emergence like a butterfly from a grub of Aunt Minnie. She appeared suddenly in the height of the absurd fashion of the time, dressed as a tube, though a pretty substantial one, pillarbox shaped, all covered in fringes like a Red Indian outfit, and ending in a mini-skirt four or five inches up the thigh, shining silk stockings and a huge scarlet mouth with a yard of cigarette holder stuck in it. Her hair was cut short at the back like a man's, and her masterful nose jutted out below a long fringe. She wore about half a hundredweight of clashing beads and bangles. If you had to sum up her appearance in a word, it would have to be—indomitable. Nobody would have dreamt to look at my Aunt that only three months before she'd presented the appearance, and apparently enjoyed the role, of a meek Victorian lady keeping house for her father in a fossilized environment, charmingly old world, if you liked that sort of thing, with Madeira and seed cake at eleven in the morning, and the motor, all glittering with polished brass, at three, for visiting. Afterwards, in the light of hind-sight, I sometimes seem to be able to catch out my Aunt Minnie slightly overplaying this part of a dutiful daughter: half-visible through the vegetation of her herbaceous borders, for instance, in long gloves, messing about with beehives in a veil, or carrying a sentimentally-shaped basket filled with the long stems of old-fashioned roses, the flat kind with the powerful smell. But most especially in her exquisite drawing-room, a work of art, or at any rate of fiction, with thousands of fabulously wrought meaningless little objects displayed on tables or in glass-fronted cases against the palest pastel shades of blue and primrose. It was Pre-Raphaelite in intention, and certainly quite unearthly in effect. And here my Aunt Minnie used to play Mendelssohn with rather affected movements of her fat little hands, but with a glitter in her eye which might have meant that some of the obvious pleasure she had in presenting herself in these surroundings had a touch of malice in it. All this came suddenly to a stop as if it had never existed. My grandfather died, and after the briefest pause for changing gears in the South of France, Aunt Minnie returned unrecognizable. She now whizzed about in a little red sports-car, danced all night and had champagne for breakfast.

In our house the trend was in the opposite direction; and one morning my father came heavily into the kitchen, a room he never set foot in, looking meek, a thing he never looked. He was white and sweating a bit, and held a paper in his hand. My mother looked at him for a long minute, and then said, 'Edwin, what have you done now?'

My father sat down heavily in the chair and mumbled, 'Got to go. Better get away now. Can't be helped. Sorry. Put my foot in it.' Half an hour later he drove off in his car and we never saw him again.

IV

Could Do Better

I discovered once and for all that commerce was not my line in a tall dusty office in Birmingham called J. Seddaby Import/Export. I was eighteen, and I'd been there a couple of months and I was sitting as usual on a tall stool in front of a sloping desk made of wood about three inches thick to demonstrate the solidity of the firm's standing. I was writing down in a book the melancholy fact that an institution called incredibly Aktiebolaget Svenska had sent J. Seddaby a cheque for 40,000 Kroner, doubtless the proceeds of some nameless crime against the widow and orphan. In about five minutes, unless I could spin it out longer, I should make another entry of the same sort, to the same accompaniment of the round, yellow-faced clock, pompously ticking away small grey chunks of time, and a bluebottle on the window buzzing its urgent need to get out of J. Seddaby's office before it died of it.

Behind me, Mr Ransom was simpering at Miss Gold, the Secretary. I could tell that because of the cooing note in his voice. 'I do, I do indeed,' he fluted. And now he would be thumbing and fingering that spoilt child, his small moustache. Simpering was as far as he would get, I reflected, because George Seddaby, the junior partner—Mr George, as his father insisted that we called him—would be in in a minute, and there was nothing Mr George liked better than to savour the servitude in which he held Mr Ransom. And there were nearly a million and a half unemployed, so Mr Ransom minced around like a head waiter in Mr George's presence. He could, though, take it out on me. Mr Ransom detested me, because I'd been to a public school and didn't think much of it, and he had not, and thought of little else.

He wore an old school tie, and an air of off-hand insolence, which he thought of as easy and confident, thought of it so hard sometimes that it was painful to look him in the face. In my early days I'd tried to talk to Mr Ransom, treating him to the usual adolescent discourse on the iniquities of the social system, but this had been a mistake, and I was now 'the Bolshie'. And every time the word was used, Miss Gold gave a dutiful titter. 'Better not let Mr Seddaby know your views,' Mr Ransom told me; 'he's a true blue Englishman, and we could do with a few more like him.' This caution had been uttered in ringing tones, because Mr George had been striding through the office at that time, giving his well-known, his exhaustively-known, imitation of the brilliant, but over-driven, young executive, with no time to spare, constrained by filial piety to waste his talents in a Brum backstreet.

Old Mr Seddaby's performance from eleven to one daily, as an elder statesman in ripe decline, an illusion which involved a lot of business with a monocle and cigar-cutter, was pure *son et lumière*. The firm was half-way down the drain—a circumstance referred to by both partners in the phrase 'in these times'. 'In these times, Cutforth, we cannot, of course, pay the old rates, much as we would like to. In these times, we cannot afford to leave before half past six.'

Most of their energies seemed to be devoted to old, tired theatre, and Miss Gold for her part, impersonated various film actresses, as they appeared at the Gaumont, but with so strong a proviso that there was to be no funny business, that provocation was still-born. Even Mr Ransom knew that she wanted him to start something so that she could make a fuss.

Suppose everything and everybody suddenly decided to do as they liked, I thought, scribing out the second entry, about peanuts in Nigeria. Suppose the clock, instead of tick-tocking away, suddenly started to scream like a dying pig, which was what it must have been wanting to do for years. Suppose Mr Ransom suddenly seized Miss Gold and flung her down on the office table with a snarl of 'Quit stalling,' like one of her favourite film actors. Suppose Mr George suddenly hit his father over the head with a chair, stuck his agate cigar-cutter down his throat and went off with the money in the safe. As I conjured up the vision of what gratified desire would mean at J. Seddaby's Import/Export, I saw it in a flash as a diabolical machine, designed to keep desire and action held apart, year after year, while the dust settled and the flies buzzed and the spiders spun their webs, and the clock ticked on. Nothing, nothing that anybody really wanted could ever happen at Seddaby's. That was the situation, so what was I doing in it?

I turned right round on my stool as if in a dream, and said slowly and carefully to Mr Ransom:

'Why don't you seize hold of Miss Gold and fling her down on the office table, and tell her to quit stalling?' And then I heard the clock bite off three square chunks of time, and then the bomb went off. Miss Gold said:

'Well!' and then she said, 'I suppose I'm to sit here and be insulted.' And at that, Mr Ransom went through the motions of going berserk.

'Before you leave the room,' he yelled, 'you'll apologize to Miss Gold and to me.' But he didn't really go berserk until I said:

'No, seriously, why don't you? Have you an interesting reason?' After that, there was a period of thumping and yelling and kicking and fighting, and then there was the spectacle of Mr Ransom sitting bemusedly in a chair, and Miss Gold telephoning for a doctor. It appeared I'd hit him on the head with one of those round office rulers. And while this was going on, old Mr Seddaby appeared mopping and mowing at the doorway of the inner office, and Mr George suddenly rushed in from the street, pulled up a chair, so as to glare at me eyeball to eyeball, and said:

'Move an inch and I bring the police.'

During the next quarter of an hour, it was established (1) that Miss Gold would not spend another hour in the same office with me, and (2) that Mr Ransom had a blue bruise on his forehead, a very little one, which J. Seddaby spent some time searching for with his monocle, and (3) that I was not apologizing. J. Seddaby then sacked me, handing over a month's salary—£18 10s. 0d.—while Mr George addressed himself to the task of holding Mr Ransom back from making an assault on me, than which nothing was further from his thoughts.

At eleven o'clock with the yellow-faced clock chiming primly at my rear, I stood on the pavement a free and solvent man. I felt about twenty pounds lighter, and it was a May day with sunshine, but I knew all the same that my situation was serious. More than a million men were looking for jobs in vain, and I'd just thrown one away. In his sacking speech, J. Seddaby, besides mentioning 'these times' and 'hooligans' and 'no respect' and 'going to the dogs,' had made it clear that I should ask him in vain for a reference or a testimonial.

I drank a pint of Mitchell and Butler's Export, one of the few cheerful products of Birmingham in 1927, and then moved on to keep a permanent lunch date with my friend, Neil Monroe, another displaced person incarcerated in a similar concentration camp to the one I'd just got out of, called Applegates Auditors. Neil did less repining than I did. He was an optimist, a Christian and a Scot, a resilient compound. When I announced that we were going to bypass the 1s. 3d. lunch, and have the two bob one, on me, he said:

'I knew you'd left when you came in. I can always tell when you've done something damn silly. You look as if you own the place—paranoid, anti-father figure, primeval jealousy pattern, a simple case.' Neil explained everything in terms of Freud. 'Were you thrown out, or did you go quietly?'

I told my tale with much mimicking and exaggeration. It was the climax of a long soap opera that Neil and I had been producing week after week over lunch every day, based on the personalities of our business colleagues. It was the best yet. He had the grace to laugh, then the Scot took over:

'Man, you're in a terrible jam, though. What on earth will you do? How much do you owe at your digs?'

'Four pounds ten,' I said.

'That leaves fourteen pounds,' said Neil, 'and how long will that last you?' We began to talk about jobs, and we knew very well that there weren't any.

The next day, with a hangover and a thin drizzle darkening Birmingham's surly frontages, I felt the first stirrings of fear. Fear, principally, of the city of Birmingham itself, designed apparently to intimidate by sheer weight of gloom. Even if I had to go home I must get out of this. But at lunch that day, Neil had a message of hope.

'I went to see the Rev. last night,' he said. The Rev. was a Birmingham vicar, a rare man in those days, inasmuch as he thought well of the young.

'The Rev. says that unless,' and here Neil began to mimic his friend, 'unless he would care to become a curate in the Church of England, a process involving the acceptance of the 39 Articles, and which takes some time, there is no career known to me open to a young man of Bolshevik tendencies, and without qualification of any sort. Such a young man, however, can often command a hand-out to tide him over, by entering the profession of preparatory schoolmaster, purely as a temporary measure.' And the Rev. had written on a piece of paper 'Messrs Antrobus and Spong—scholastic agents,' and an address in London.

I wrote the letter on a corner of the lunch table, and Neil recast it in a prissier form.

'It's psychology you lack,' he said. 'You, of all people, should try to strike a note of plain formality.' Two days later, I had a reply from Messrs Antrobus and Spong, thanking me for my enquiry, and enclosing an odd little slip of paper, like a piece of poor quality lavatory paper, on which was a blurred copy in purple ink of this message: 'The Reverend Harold Mears of Fremlet Park School, Fremlet-on-Sea, Kent, requires a junior master to teach general subjects up to Common Entrance level, commencing at half-term, June the 12th. Salary offered—£120 per annum all found. Fremlet Park is a preparatory school for the sons of gentlemen. There are 80 boys. Write promptly, yet carefully, to Mr Mears, stating age, qualifications, and experience, if any. Two testimonials should accompany the application. If the application is successful, the agent's fee is payable on accepting the post, or it may be deducted from the first term's salary.'

'That's no good,' I said to Neil. 'June the 12th—I can't live till then on five pounds.'

'I could lend you a bit,' Neil said, 'and the Rev. has half a dozen spare rooms in the vicarage. We might manage.' But these stern measures proved unnecessary. The next morning I had another letter from Antrobus and Spong and it said, 'Since we wrote to inform you of the vacancy at Fremlet Park School, Mr Mears has let us know that he requires a junior master at once. If you were considering applying for the post, will you instead meet Mr Mears at this office at eleven-thirty a.m., Monday, the 21st of this month?' That was three days ahead, and I had to borrow a pound from Neil, to make up my train and taxi fares.

Antrobus and Spong had an office strong in atmosphere, exactly right for the job—all heavy mahogany and sudden corners and high stools and brass. I noticed that they didn't use quill pens.

In the waiting room, a young man of my own age with red hair was walking about.

'Are you after this job?' he asked me at once. 'So am I. Got to get it. In a bit of trouble as a matter of fact. Disappear quietly into the country for a bit. Matter of life and death.'

'What have you done?' I asked.

'Too complicated to explain now, but got to get out of London. Look out of the window, will you, and see if there's a chap outside.' After an inspection, I told him I couldn't see anyone waiting, and then a very impressive bald man opened the door and said to the jittery youth:

'Mr Mears will see you now.' And they disappeared.

A few minutes later a cab rolled up and the red-haired young man came bolting out through the waiting-room, and buried himself inside it. He must have summoned it on one of Antrobus and Spong's antique telephones, all hooks and plaited wires and carved with dolphins—and who would have thought that possible?

'Mr Mears will see you now,' the bald man said to me. And I stepped into a private room full of great sofas, to meet my prospective employer. The Reverend Harold had fine white hair, and an expression I was to get to know very well in the Prep. School round—that of a man who is owed a great deal, but has ceased to count on it being paid up. At some point in his childhood, his face had formed around some sweet sentiment. The rest was disappointment and petulance.

'Did you see that red-haired young man?' he asked me. 'Mad, completely mad. He actually asked me to peer through the window and try to spot a bailiff. We can't have that, you know. I don't know what things are coming to these days in education, young man. Your predecessor was scandalous, scandalous: don't let us speak of such things, though I'm sure you'll know what I mean. I had to sack him on the spot, and pay him the other half of the term's salary. Now, Mr Cutforth, to business. I have all your particulars. Are you a member of the Church of England?'

'Technically,' I said.

'Do you play cricket?'

'I know the rules.'

'Testimonials?'

'None, I'm afraid.'

'Oh well, we'll arrange that later. No doubt we can see to that. Now, how soon can you be there?'

'The day after tomorrow, rather late in the evening, but I shall have to have an advance.'

'£20?'

'Could you make it £25?'

'Very well, of course in these times ....' He suddenly turned on me a smile of piercing love, held it for five seconds and wiped it off again.

The Prep. School of forty years ago needs some explanation. It was all based on the marketing of a class image. In practice most Prep. Schools came into being because somebody like the Reverend Harold felt that the only life for him was that of a country landowner in a grand house and could only afford the grand house if he shared it for two-thirds of the year with a mob of boys. It was the last, and even then an extremely futile, gesture of the world of privilege which had been whittled down and undermined until the last residual bonus automatically payable to anybody solely on account of his expensive education was a job in a Prep. School. All the expensively educated duds in England who had no private income sooner or later found themselves in Prep. Schools, where all they had to do was, in the Reverend Harold's phrase, 'Hand on the tradition'.

So I'd arrived at the end of the line already, the proclaimed remittance man of an obsolete social system. I went back to Birmingham that night with the £25 and paid my landlady. I felt a slight pang about leaving my digs. I'd had to take a lot of trouble to persuade my landlady to take me in, because I wasn't what she called 'a theatrical' and she came of that tradition. Birmingham had a music hall in those days called, I think, the Varieties, and my fellow lodgers were all transients, who stayed a week and trod the boards of The Varieties and then moved on.

Neil and I were addicts of that theatre. And now that I was going I remembered the roaring late night suppers of mutton chops and Guinness eaten with vainglorious people who loved to show off, whose lives were a question of the right words perfectly timed. They made ordinary people seem half dead. The great Billy Merson had once looked in to see a friend and stayed for supper and paid for it, not only with his own clowning, but by the life he put into some of the rather tired old pros that night, so that we had an after theatre show on our hands.

One of the old pros, Billy Brunt, a pudding-shaped Lancashire comedian, came to the door with my landlady to see me off.

'Well, I'm sorry you're going,' my landlady said, 'and to the South an' all. Brum's bad enough, but the *South*. I cannot abide it. Folks down there, they're so fornicating, talking behind your back and kissing your behind to your face.'

'Eee, that would make a right sketch for acrobats,' said Billy Brunt, and on that note we parted. I had a glorious plan. I hardly dared to think of it.

England still existed in those days, not merely as a geographical entity, but as a dense atmosphere, an emotional climate. Englishness came off the face of the land as solid as something to eat. In these days hardly anybody is twenty years out of date. In 1927, most people were still living in 1850. In the country they even looked as if they were. Horses did the ploughing, and men with scythes did the mowing, and the rich face of the countryside, much more beautiful, in fact, than it is now since the chemists and the concrete mixers got at it, still seemed to give out the powerful Victorian blessing of security. The countryside was still local. Most people had never travelled more than ten miles from their village. It was secret and sensual. It looked as if it had been there solidly rich for forty generations. That's what Victorians admired most, and most people in England were Victorians until the Second World War.

It was still possible to feel, but not to think, that farming England was the real England, and industry a mere brutal interloper to be fought or ignored. The motor car was still an instrument of pleasure. The roads of England were emptier then than Ireland's roads are now, but the car manufacturers' competition has recently become deadly keen, so that off all the main roads, between the great cities, whole fields full of second-hand cars priced from £5 upwards, and all runners, lay spread out like a supermarket. You didn't need a test. You drove straight out on the road and took pot luck, and this, between Birmingham and the Kent coast, I now proposed to do.

I took a bus, parking my suitcases on the conductor's platform, after an altercation with him, a pure formality like the responses in church, and drove along the Stratford-on-Avon road until just before Shirley I pulled the bell. There on the side of the road was a 20-acre field full of cars over which a red and white banner blew in the soft sunshine announcing 'Ockley's Okay Cars'.

It took me a long time to select my Rover 8 and I paid £7 10s. 0d. for it. The salesman must have been a fairground man at one time. He was a cockney, tattooed on every visible inch, with a broken nose, and the fairground voice and manner, impersonal as a gramophone. 'If you want your money's worth, don't go for the paint,' he said. 'Go for something ugly and dirty. See them tyres, last you a year, they will. There's four months tax left on this and its engine is first class. Wood's gone, paint's gone, but it's a real traveller.' My Rover 8 was milk chocolate colour, a colour they haven't tried since, and it was squarish and it had two enormous air-cooled cylinders which stuck out of vents on each side of the bonnet. After a long day I was to find that they glowed cherry red in the evening twilight. Another thing I was to find was that when you started it in the morning—with the handle, of course, it had no self starter—it was powerful enough to throw you a full five yards. Its top speed was 40 miles an hour, and at that speed you took your life in your hands. This time the salesman started it and I was off. I'd only driven a car twice before, but I was well in charge before we got off the main road where I crossed through the cornland to Warwick, and then on through the wide grass country to Daventry.

For the rest of that day I was completely surrendered to the little car's sewing machine chatter and the country. The thing about England's surface is the abundance of shyly revealed secrets, small perfect arrangements a thousand years old. Smaller, even more perfect arrangements of hedge and green, dating from the eighteenth century. At every turn something new, but redolent of centuries of sleepy and possessive love. In pubs in those days you got real bread which tasted of bread, and real cheese. Stilton isn't so good now, Blue Wensleydale had disappeared, Blue Vinney no longer exists, Derbyshire Sage is a curiosity. Where have all the morels gone to and the blue-legged mushrooms which used to be sold in the Bullring market in Birmingham? The Boletus mushroom has quite disappeared and that last end product of the pig, 'scratchins,' a sort of crisp flake like a breakfast cereal, but more work for the teeth and bright with lard. I've not seen them for years. Beer was better then, or do I imagine it? Quite a lot of pubs brewed their own, and in the country nobody ever dreamed of observing the licensing regulations, which had been forced on us in the guise of a defence measure during the war.

Slowly, my monstrous little car chugged its way past the great elms and the churchyard yews and the slow broad rivers where the cattle sat, through Chaucer and Shakespeare and Tennyson and Samuel Palmer, an orgy of self indulgence for a man who knew perfectly well where all that pride had already finished up—in Fremlet Park School, Fremlet-on-Sea, Kent, and other places like it. England's ancient house still stood, though creaking. The useless furniture was all in place, but the residuary legatee was a phoney. I spent the night in Aylesbury where the bread was bread, the food was good, the ducklings, a local speciality, were local and special, and the beds had linen sheets, but there was no electric light. An old radio like a baroque commode in the residents' drawing room—'lounge' was not a word yet—was the only concession to the twentieth century.

The sun was low when I arrived at Fremlet Park School, a huge house built in the reign of Queen Anne. The staff were at dinner, a special dinner, in the Reverend Harold's private dining room to mark half term and my arrival. It was even worse than I was tuned up for: silver, and finger bowls and dinner jackets (except me). There were five of us, Mears at the head of the table, sweet and melancholy on the subject of the revival of the local folk dance which was one of the things which he hoped, as he said, to encourage.

'We must encourage the tradition. Fremlet hasn't a cinema, of course, that's one good thing. They've got one at Goshorn three miles down the road, and the maids are already insisting on two very long evenings out to get there and back.' The others were Mr Graves, an old and distinguished-looking man with a little silver beard, and a fund of anecdotes about the Czar of all the Russias whom he had met in a moment of ecstasy when he was private secretary to one of the Grand Dukes.

'We live in a terrible age,' he said. 'The vandals are massing for the kill. I've seen too much—too much.'

There was an elegant young man, a bit older than me, with beautiful manners and exquisite clothes who confined himself to giving out an air of grave attention, and remarks like 'Really' and 'Do you think so?' as an accompaniment to Mears' discourse, and there was one formidable figure: a man in his early thirties with half a left arm, a canvas glove on a bent right hand and a crutch by his side. His face was related to the Reverend Harold's, built around a sentiment of sweetness, but had gone on from there not into disappointment but into savagery. He said little during dinner but 'Pass the brandy' in a voice of command, and the brandy, which had had the stopper put back, was passed. He was obviously slightly drunk when we left Mears and moved into the staff room for a final drink.

He came over to me and stretched out his hand in his glove.

'Newland Greene is my name,' he said, 'and this paraphernalia,' and he indicated his crutch at his crippled arm, 'all this paraphernalia, since you will want to know, is because I was shot up in the War. You'll recollect the event. Began in 1914. You'd better get the hang of the situation here,' he went on, 'and I can probably give it to you better than anybody. We are, as you sarcastically told Harold at dinner, the residual legatees of civilization. The boys are here either because their fathers are in India or Africa, or wherever the Empire has called its sons to serve, or because local parents think it will give them a social leg up. Mears is here because he had ten thousand quid to invest in comfort and silly dreams. Warren is here because his uncle has a title. Graves is here,' and he pointed his chin at Graves who was rolling his eyes and raising his brows in deprecation, 'Graves is here because he will settle for comfort and he has a degree; and I am here,' Greene went on, 'because I find my chief pleasure in setting my teeth on edge, and there is nothing quite like Fremlet Park for that. Why are you here?' he enquired belligerently.

'Oh I'm a dud like you,' I said, 'without the advantage of a war to explain it.'

'Fair enough,' said Newland Greene grinning, 'another brandy.' Shortly after that we all went to bed.

Whatever the shortcomings of the establishment, the boys were in good form. I sat at the head of a table next to a bright-eyed eleven-year-old.

'What's your name?' I asked him on the first morning.

'Appleyard,' he said. 'Have a kipper, sir, I would if I were you. It's eatable, sir, it really is. The tea is called squeezer. It's squeezed out of the floor rags. Were you in the war, sir? Mr Greene was in the war, sir, didn't half make him sweat. He's been sweating ever since. What do you think of Kipling, sir? Is he a fascist beast? My father says he's a fascist beast. Sir, Mr Greene got very boggy one day and cried, and said to Marlow, "mocking at me, me, a man who fought in the war when other men skulked." Oh sir, it was terrible. There was silence, sir. That's not a thing that happens very often. Then Mr Greene went out very slowly. That's an awful car you've got, sir. I suppose Mr Mears doesn't pay you very much, sir. Have you got a degree, sir?

Only Mr Mears and Mr Greene and Mr Graves have degrees. Isn't that awful? And Mr Graves's gown is very peculiar. Mr Greene said he bought it at a rummage sale. Did you want to be a school master, sir, or did it just happen? I don't think I should want to be.'

In the classes I did very well. I found I couldn't remember about mathematics, but there was an intense boy in spectacles who could do it without thinking, so I wrote the problem on the board, and after an interval I said, 'Well, Simon?' and Simon supplied the answer. My version of history was a riot.

In the evening, except on special occasions when we dined with Mears in state with brandy and finger bowls, we all went off to the pub. Mock Tudor, phoney like the rest of us.

'I see the first act,' Newland Greene would announce after his third or fourth brandy, 'with the stage completely dominated by a grand piano. I hear a theme of Beethoven. That's the first act.' He'd been writing the play for eight years, though pen and paper had not been involved as yet. Even the landlord was a piece of theatre.

'It's lovely to hear you gentlemen talk,' he would butt in. A likely story. 'It's a privilege,' he would pronounce judicially.

'I fail to follow your drift, Greene,' Mr Graves would say. 'Surely Beethoven is a long way back. It's up to us to battle with our own time. Four bitters and a brandy.'

'When my Uncle dies,' Warren predicted, 'and I suppose he will some time . . . I'll get the house almost certainly, but what's the good of that? It will cost two thousand to put the roof in order. I could run it as a prep. school, but I haven't a degree. That wouldn't do for a headmaster, you know. Of course, there's always silver fox and dog-breeding.'

Appleyard's father lived in Stonebridge and owned a very large garage farther up the coast.

'I want the boy to have the sort of chance I never got,' he said, 'but I should like him to be able to do something. I admire Mr Mears, of course, but you know, between you and me, I'd hate the boy to turn out like him.' He rubbed his chin. 'There's something eerie about Mr Mears, if you get what I mean. As if he didn't live here like you and me. Somewhere else like. Somewhere that never existed except in his head. Now that car of yours, it doesn't look much, but that was a snip at seven pounds ten. You couldn't have done better. I'm thinking of opening . . . well, I'll tell you about it some other time. Come up for a bite to eat tonight.'

It was a week before the end of term and it had been a heavy night at the pub. I'd missed breakfast. Prayers, I could hear, were not half over. I walked out on the gravel to cool my head. Had it come to this already—alcoholic hallucinations? A posse of men was pounding up the drive, led by a massive official in one of those cast-iron bowler hats, who looked impervious to the human lot. The rest wore green baize aprons and had the bright, furtive expressions of men who were enjoying themselves in repressive conditions.

'Name of Mears?' asked the man in the bowler.

'No, no,' I said, 'Mr Mears is in London. He's been at a conference for the last three days.'

'Little matter of a debt,' said the bowler-hatted man. 'Distraint. That's what we are here for. Here's the order.' And he produced a document. Without another word, they all moved on into the house and as prayers broke up the first of the furniture began to appear on the lawn, and a pantechnicon rolled into sight up the drive. 'You can't take the dormitory beds,' I shouted, inspired. 'They're the tools of his trade.' The boys were fascinated.

'Oh, sir, Mr Mears won't half be mad when he comes back. Oh, sir, they're taking the furniture away. Is that right? We can't possibly do any work, sir, while the desks are being moved.'

'I think I shall go home,' said Appleyard, 'it's coming on to rain.'

'You will all be paid,' the Reverend Harold assured us. 'Sometime, but not now. I shall pay each of you half of what he is owed and send the rest after. My life work is over. I shall shut down the school. There will be no more lessons as from today. You are at liberty to go as you want to. I shall give each of you first-class testimonials.'

'Fifteen quid and a testimonial and what I stand up

in, that's about what I'm worth,' I told Mr Appleyard over drinks in his house. 'I can't invest anything in your project.'

'I didn't mean that,' he said. 'Couldn't me and you get together on ideas and selling like? I've never been any good at selling. I'm no good with the words. Here, you know the thing is bound to go. They've got them all round London and Brum already. Open-air car sales and they're selling like hot cakes. But mine is going to be a bit different. It's going to be sports-cars and racing cars. Something with a bit of life in them for the young, you know. And for that I need a salesman. Eight pound a week and commission, and, of course, expenses and the use of a car. What about it?'

'That suits me,' I said, and we shook hands. Later, he said, 'And what are we going to call it?'

'Appleyard's OK Cars,' I said with finality.

'You don't think something a bit more refined?'

'Certainly not,' I said. 'Less, if anything.'

I suppose the nearest I ever came to a comfortable season ticket on life's bus was Appleyard's OK Cars. The sports-car project flourished like a fungus, and Appleyard was in the real money in no time. He was a generous man, and I could see a directorship looming up for me in, say ten years time. Nevertheless, I was back in Swad inside six months.

The trouble, diagnosed by my mother time and again as 'exactly like your father', was a temperamental one. As an adolescent I was fundamentally of the graceless, scowling kind, but most of that kind have the virtue of being more or less dumb, whereas I was hideously articulate. Moreover, I had managed to detach from my total entity another character, a descendant of the Irishman I had created to get me through the school world. This fellow's chief characteristic was an absolute refusal to suffer; an actor, producing himself in a new play every minute, his life was a dance of ideas, a juggling of attitudes, rather like a woman trying on hats. I talked the whole time, and always against everything, and though the incessant spate of words undoubtedly saved me from active delinquency, in the way nosebleeding can save you from a stroke, safe, sound members of society knew

I was the enemy and tended to lock up their daughters. 'Mummy says I oughtn't to see you again' was a refrain I grew very tired of.

It wasn't a good age for the indigent young; the newspapers of the time were full of pathetic advertisements: 'Young man, public school, own car, go anywhere, do anything.' I hadn't even got 'own car'. But the biggest disaster of all had been love. In practice, among the 'Mummy says I oughtn't to see you again' girls, my sexual affairs had resolved themselves into a series of agonizing farewells, nearly always in a fog and on the banks of the River Trent and in November, and I had longed to break out of this formula. When eventually I did so, the whole thing took a turn for the worse.

One of my father's friends, greatly disapproved of by my mother, had been a very entertaining and rather drunk colliery manager. Over the years he switched the adjectives, and became rather entertaining and very drunk. Then he was just very drunk, and then he disappeared, leaving a wife and daughter to the tender mercies of that smug little management society. The daughter, who was beautiful, had gone off to London at the age of seventeen to sink or swim, and at the age of twenty-one she returned to visit her mother, and I met her at the hospital dance.

She was something altogether outside my experience, and not only in the matter of looks. My dance of ideas, regarded as a sort of lunacy in Swad, was bread-and-butter stuff to her, and, what I chiefly admired, she made no concessions to Swad's dreary third-rateness. Back now, equipped with power, she had put them through their hoops like a circus master. She cut a swathe that week which was remembered for years. In due course I followed her back to London, borrowing the money, though I would have stolen it if necessary, and I'd lived with her in her flat in Chelsea for about a week—a week of disaster, because I'd been totally unable to find any way of staying in London. She'd said, 'I can't imagine why you choose to live in that frightful place,' but it was no use, I had to go home, and incidentally to walk the last five miles, and since then the whole subject has thickened up and become an intolerable witches' brew simmering in the back of my mind at all hours of the day and particularly the night.

Briefly, what happened at Appleyards was that I telephoned this girl, went straight up to London, lived with her for three weeks, and then the painter she normally lived with came back, and I failed to dislodge him.

Back in Swad I spent what was left of Appleyards money getting drunk night after night in the pub on the Delf. I used to sit there with my head well down, focussed on the pattern of the grain in the floorboards, with a poem running through my head:

While I was fishing in the dull canal
On a winter evening round behind the gashouse
Musing upon the king my brother's wreck
And on the king my father's death before him.
White bones naked on the low damp ground,
And bones cast in a little low dry garret,
Rattled by the rat's foot only, year to year.

One evening, the Kreutzer sonata had taken over from Eliot.

'That's the tune the old king died of,' I heard myself saying, and then thought 'My God, I'm pretty drunk.' I heard a sudden commotion followed by an astonished silence, and there stood my Aunt Minnie, garbed in an extraordinary tube of sackcloth with heavy lumps of amber clattering around it, over two very solid silk legs. All her features were extinguished by a cloche hat except a bright red mouth with the usual yard of cigarette holder in it.

'Oh, there you are,' she said in her new, high, clear twenties voice. 'Been looking for you everywhere. Do you know the latest? I'm off to India. Would you like to come? Needn't stay with me, of course. Yes, a large gin, please, with French *and* Italian and a cherry. My dear, your *face*! For God's sake, cheer up!'

V

Aunt Minnie's Passage to India

When I went off to India with my Aunt Minnie in the very early thirties, I was nearly twenty-one and she, I suppose, was about forty-six. We were an odd pair.

The fact is, Aunt Minnie has been reprieved in the nick of time. One of the rather frequent English social revolutions was in full blast in the twenties—a new age had crept up while I was wasting my precious time at school and Minnie had made a snatch at it as it went by and held on. The new age in the twenties resembled the latest new age of the sixties in two ways at least; its chief effect was that nobody under twenty could hear ten consecutive words from a member of the older generation without wanting to scream and run up the wall, and the other similarity was that it was all arranged around a certain sort of sound. The sound which inaugurated the new age of the twenties was the Charleston. It was a genuine revolutionary trumpet call. In the generation before mine, it had seemed perfectly natural that the young should have to plough a hell of a long furrow of filial obedience and general servitude. In the provinces, particularly. In Swadlincote, I knew dozens of people who were listlessly going through the motions of being dutiful sons and daughters well into their dessicated middle age. The manifesto of my generation declared total war on those who ate their young. It had a few other modest demands, too, such as complete sexual freedom and racial equality, and it made a start on the demolition of the class structure, but its main feature was an immense consumption of gin: it was the cocktail age. Of these cocktails the best, one of the few still with us, was the Dry Martini, but any decent barman in the twenties could be expected to make anything up to a hundred different types of cocktail, most of them with very high-flown names like 'Pink Sensation,' 'White Lady,' 'Blue Devil' or 'Green Sin,' and it was this last which was the temporary favourite of my Aunt Minnie, and to see her in the throes of the old kick Charleston with a 'Green Sin' in one hand and her cigarette holder in the other, being given lots and lots of room by everybody else on the floor at the Bretby Park Hospital dance was to know that the new age, though it had taken some time about it, had blossomed at last in Swadlincote.

My Aunt's devotion to the new ideas was perfectly genuine, since she herself was a splendid example of the victims we were determined to snatch from servitude, and since she was not like me, born to take the new climate in its stride, but was a convert, her devotion was wholesale. She had, in her view, been liberated, and it was only right and proper that she should now devote her energies to liberating someone else, and her eye fell on me. I suppose it was bound to, really, simply because I was in so many ways the most unsatisfactory member of the family.

I went to India in a quite simple mood, the mood of the beatnik. Since there seemed no way at all in which my life could go forward, I was ripe for an escape in any direction. And India was obviously the right place, foreign enough possibly even to provide some absolutely new sort of life—somewhere to escape from the wheel of circumstance, and yet not entirely strange, for mine was one of those British families which had got itself mixed up with India.

There was Great-Uncle Charles, for example, about the only member of the family of whom I completely approved. He'd been in India for sixty years, completely immersed in Sanskrit roots and the translation of bits of the New Testament into Marathi. He was also wildly eccentric to the point, some people said, of insanity. For instance, on one of his rare spells of leave, he'd once spotted me, as a boy, walking along with a jam-jar and a net on a newting expedition to a pond.

'You going fishing boy?' he roared through the window. 'You going fishing for what? What are they called, those things?'

'Newts,' I said.

'Newts, that's what they are,' my Great-Uncle shouted in triumph. 'Newts. Hold on, boy, hold on, I can show you a pond which is full of the most tremendous newts.' I had to hold on for nearly ten minutes while my Great-Uncle struggled into the huge overcoat he wore over his cassock in the English summer air. His room was as hot as a Turkish bath.

'What think ye of Christ, pussy?' he asked the cat as we set out. We crossed the paddock and a couple of fields until we came to a circle of enormous trees. It had a small hollow filled with leaves in the middle of it and my Great-Uncle began to wander about in it like a lost old retriever dog, humming in a gnat-like voice the only tune he'd ever mastered, 'Champagne Charlie is me name'.

It finally occurred to me, while he was still poking about in the hollow, that in some prehistoric age this must actually have been a pond surrounded by bushes which were now the enormous trees . . . and I gazed in awe at my Uncle Charles who'd been a newt hunter when these were saplings, and all he said was: 'Most extraordinary—the whole thing has disappeared.' But to my mind the best thing about my Great-Uncle Charles was the manner of his departure from India. He left under a cloud. I don't believe a word of this story now, but among us children it was an article of faith: it was the great thing about Uncle Charles. He'd been in charge of a little church at Miri on the Bombay side, and what with the Sanskrit and the Marathi and the heat and living all by himself miles away from any other English people, he'd begun to fashion the Anglican service more to his own way of thinking, and when some ecclesiastic called in there when Charles was in his seventies, he found a very odd state of affairs. There was a cross on the altar, it's true, but there were also Shiva and Ganpati, the Elephant God, and half a dozen others of the Hindu pantheon. And most of the service consisted of dancing and drumming with elaborate chants in Sanskrit and all written to the tune of 'Champagne Charlie is me Name'. I suppose nowadays he'd be regarded as an ecumenical pioneer, but in those days, so the story went, they simply shunted him off back to England with the suggestion that he was off his rocker. All the same the India that my Great-Uncle Charles had impressed upon me turned out to be a truer one than most Western versions. In spite of the fact that all his introductions later turned out to be to people who'd been dead for twenty years, India turned out to be very much like the old man himself: ancient, holy, immensely tolerant, detached, sentimental and enjoyably dotty.

My Aunt Minnie and I joined the ship at Marseilles. In those days the French were tremendously hatted and spatted and cravatted and about ten times as foreign as they've since become. In our over-dressed hotel what seemed to me a particularly French object was a light minded lift made airily up of brass wire like a bird cage which shakily swooped up and down at great speed. My Aunt had found an old friend in the bar, so Marseilles belonged to me for the night. It was early September and very hot and the streets smelt of tar and of dust laid by water carts and of coffee and black cigarettes.

In the blazing little zinc bars people shouted as they played dice for rounds of drinks and what drinks—dreadful drinks like Gentiane, doubtful drinks like Byrrh Citron; I settled in the end for a fiery red wine called Cap Corse Sec, much drunk at the docks, and finally went off with a pack of Italian sailors to the Old Port, which lived up to every centimetre of its reputation. I clambered up the ship's gangway in the morning as in a dream, drained of all money and feeling and looking out at the world through my little red eyes as if it had just been invented.

It was a dull little ship, a British one, and had a very representative passenger list in those days of the beginning of Imperial anxiety. Almost before we'd got under way, they'd split up into their natural groups. The most solid of all these groups and the only one which didn't arrange itself around a portable record player was the saloon bar group—solid middle-aged men in solid British suits—all called Mr MacPherson, and Mr Moir, and Mr Grant, and Mr Hamilton and other dependable names like that. They were all in engineering firms or the Indian Public Works Department, in charge of all the technical devices which kept the British Raj going. None of them was ever seen drunk, but not one of them was ever quite sober after eleven o'clock in the morning, and one, a very fat man from Yorkshire called Mr Gunnersbury, used to say every night at eleven when the bar closed, 'Just put me out a dozen Guinness and a glass, George, then, will you.' He kept up this routine all through the Red Sea and across the Indian Ocean, as he'd done for years and years, and he didn't have a stroke until the day before we landed in Bombay. All their talk was about work done and promotions gained for work done and their contempt for people whose heart and soul were not in the job. But they were tiresomely aggressive all the same. One of them grabbed me by the shoulder as I came into the bar one night.

'You were asking just now, Mr Hamilton,' he declaimed rhetorically, 'what's the matter with the young of today. Well, now we can get a straight answer. You don't give a good goddamn about the whole damn set up, do you?' he said to me, shaking my shoulder. 'Nay, I want an answer. You don't care a damn if the Empire goes bust.'

'Well, it's nothing to do with me,' I said.

'There you are,' said Mr Hamilton, 'it's nothing to do with him—it's all sex and sitting on your arse playing the ukelele.' I resented this, since they were all far more fully equipped in the matter of what they sat on than I was.

'If my father,' said the fat one, 'had ever heard me say what you've just said, he'd have thrashed me within an inch of my life.' And the best of luck to him, I thought, though I didn't say so.

The Army Officers, ranging from second lieutenants to a major, and a couple of girls who were going out to India to be married, formed another group. They lived on lilos and deck-chairs around the gramophone. From morning to night it played their song, Noël Coward's 'Mad Dogs and Englishmen'. The Major, the leader of this group, had a story that he wouldn't leave alone. I heard it at least three times and I didn't mix with this group much.

'Best thing the fellow ever said,' he used to drawl. 'It was in Singapore at one of poor Old Nosey's parties. Of course, Old Nosey, being who he is nowadays, had to invite practically everybody in the whole damn place. "My God," says this fellow to Nosey, looking round the party, "you begin to understand why there's a servant problem in England." '

One of the junior officers became terribly excited one night in the bar about whether people ought to call their fathers 'Sir'.

'Always call the old man "Sir"—wouldn't dream of calling him anything else. He loves it: tickled to death by it. Do you call your father "Sir," sir? Well, what the hell do you call him then?' This conversation lasted a couple of hours and ended in blows. The other gramophone group was three old ladies and their middle-aged daughters. Utterly aloof, arranged in upright deck-chairs, they played bridge all the way to India to a Gilbert and Sullivan accompaniment.

Aunt Minnie had a seat at the Captain's table, so I had to sit there, too. It was very grand at the Captain's table and didn't suit me at all, except that my Aunt discovered someone there with an impossible sort of name like Lady Brown-Postlethwaite-Basset, with whom it appeared she'd been at school. Minnie reverted to type so quickly in the presence of this Lady that she actually played a few bars of the 'Bee's Wedding' one night after dinner, and her startling appearance was modified day by day, until by the time she reached Bombay she looked almost normal. Judging by her conversations, her theories on racial discrimination and sexual freedom had also suffered under the impact of Lady Brown-Postlethwaite-Basset, with whom and a Canon Somebody she spent practically all her time. The saloon bar contingent were at the second table, and at the third and last —the one I wanted to be at—there were two young and very beautiful Indians, brother and sister, and a pretty Anglo-Indian woman, who'd been visiting her grandparents in Scotland, and in pursuit of whom I grudged every moment of time I had to spend at the Captain's table, where she was not allowed, of course. The two Indians mixed with nobody, but the girl shared a cabin with the Anglo-Indian girl and disappeared most tactfully whenever I was there.

I didn't meet the Indians until we were only two days out of Bombay—it had been very hot all day but with a stiff breeze and the sea had been a blinding green silver, moving past us in long banks of brightness and a green-silver flying fish landing with a swoop and a slither every now and then on the deck. And now it was dark except for the moon and you could smell the land ahead, warm and spicy. I went along to the bows to look at the sea, and it wasn't until I'd been there for a minute or two that I realized that the Indians were leaning on the rail looking at the sea, too. I turned towards them, and the young man, said, laughing,

'Excuse me, you don't look very much at home with the ship's company.'

'I can't make head or tail of them,' I said.

'Oh, that's what India's done to them. You'll be exactly the same in six months.'

'I hope not,' I said.

'It's inevitable,' the young man said. 'Inevitable and sad. I've just spent six months in England, and what nice people you are, on the whole, in England. India, you know, creates the spirit of caste. You can't live in India without despising the human race. You've got to be above it, and that is particularly bad for you people, makes you into nervous wrecks.'

'Oh, I think I'll survive,' I said.

'That's impossible; remember, nothing can ever be done, in your sense of the word, about India, but only accepted. I'm Indian, I can do that: you're English, you can't. I live there: you only run the place.'

'Well, at any rate you can take a look at it, that's all I'm going to do,' I said.

'Yes, well, I hope you like looking at it, but it'll change you. Look me up in six months' time—it's a challenge.' And he gave me an address in Calcutta. 'I'm a lawyer,' he said, 'but I'm rich. I don't do anything, really. You mustn't take me seriously.' It was a marvellous night, but the gramophones were still at it.

I thought I'd look in on my Anglo-Indian friend. As I rounded the corner which led to her corridor, I suddenly realized I'd been trapped. Two unaccustomed deck-chairs lay there; one was empty, the other contained Lady Brown-Postlethwaite-Basset.

'Ah, Mr Cutforth,' she said, 'do please sit down. I've been waiting to have a little chat with you for so long. Now

I wonder if you realize just what you're doing when you encourage that unfortunate girl, you know who I mean. Out here we have a duty which we owe not only to ourselves, but to our race and the ideals of the Empire. The purely superficial charm. . . .' This was undoubtedly going to be, I thought, the most embarrassing talk I'd ever allowed myself to listen to in the whole of my life. Even including my housemaster's piece about the perils of sex. But it was too late—nothing could be done. I sat gingerly down and gave myself up for lost—but prematurely; at this very moment, Mr Gunnersbury, the very fat man in the saloon bar, had his stroke. There was a confused tumult in the bar, and then somebody said, 'He's gone.'

'Something terrible has happened.'

'Excuse me,' I said, on the run.

The voice of Mr Hamilton could be heard booming on deck. Something about 'An old and dear friend has passed away,' and then something about 'Showing a bit of respect.' One of the bridge ladies said,

'Oh, how dreadful. The poor man. Emily, turn the thing off.' In the other corner, the Major was shouting,

'What? Who? Well, what about it? Oh, I see. Oh, all right.' And 'Mad Dogs and Englishmen' at last ground to a halt.

And so it was a silent ship with a stricken saloon bar which nosed its way into Bombay early the following morning. Three months later we arrived in Delhi. Dusty and sweaty and boiled in the heat, my Aunt Minnie and I in our ridiculous topees called Bombay bowlers sat in the old Ford car while our bearer fetched the mail from the post office. My letter was not the one which of all letters I most desired to have but was the second on the list; it was from the editor of the famous Indian newspaper. It said, 'I shall be able to use the half dozen pieces you sent me. I thought at first of publishing them as a comic series under the title of "Travels with my Aunt" which I felt might amuse a public very much less innocent about India than you can possibly be. But I find they're very much better than that. I can use another half dozen of the same length, and I have a more ambitious project for you which would depend upon whether you would consider regular employment. Please come to see me as soon as you reach Calcutta. I enclose a cheque for six hundred rupees.'

'Minnie,' I said to my Aunt, 'you're my lucky charm, and I'm going to buy you the biggest drink in Delhi.'

'Make it a bottle of champagne,' she said, 'at a good hotel. I never want to see a Dak bungalow again, and I'm sick to death of this dreadful country.'

A week later I went on to Calcutta on my own. Whether she knew what she was doing or not, my Aunt's emergency operation on me had brilliantly come off, and in the nick of time. Death by Swadlincote was not to be my fate: there were many other houses in the world besides the one that had made me, and Minnie presented me with an order to view.

From then on I was less concerned with my life than with my times, and the quality of life which they imposed in different places, and from now on, so will this book be. Aunt Minnie will not appear again. She went home to live on the south coast of England, and one day, about ten years after her passage to India, came out of an oyster bar and climbed into her little red car and whizzed off along the sea front, on and on in a perfectly straight line through the traffic as if protected by a miracle. When she finally ran into a bus shelter, they found she'd been dead of a heart attack some minutes before the crash.

VI

The Reverend

I should have been a reporter whether I had ever written a report or not, in the same way that it can be said of a man that he is a poet even if he has never written a poem. It was living with my family in Swadlincote that made a reporter of me, whether I like it or not: and travelling around the world as a young man had nothing much to do with it, though I think it is true that tramps and reporters are close psychological kin, and if I had not done the tramping I should have had less to sell as a reporter.

As a tramp I had now extended my beat to include Asia, and this, though I didn't realize it, was stepping out of the main-stream of my times. Swadlincote was relevant to the unfolding of the twentieth century, the British Empire in Asia was not. Its flavour was already over-ripe, and it is in images of decadence that I chiefly remember it.

Even as far north as Mandalay the river Irrawaddy is gigantic, so huge an expanse of motor-oil green that the hump of jungle on its further shore looks as petty as a privet hedge, and so calm that the green-gold reflections of some village in the water can seem more solid than the real, yellow village swimming in sunshine on the bank.

It's a timeless part of the world. Teak rafts come floating down sometimes: they'll take perhaps two months to reach the Delta. Fishermen drowse in boats over their nets and women wash their golden children at the riverside, and every object in sight seems to have been designed by a slightly deranged artist. Birds, flowers, fish, butterflies, even the boats, the fishermen, and most particularly their women, combine an almost insane fineness and delicacy of shape with an equally disturbing savagery of colour.

Every now and again into this hothouse world a prosaic little paddle-steamer like a large waterborne tramcar comes looking for ground nuts and oil and any passengers who have all the time in the world to spare. In 1932, I had all the time in the world to spare, and I joined one of these little ships not far below Mandalay.

I was a first-class passenger, the first they'd had for three years, so I had a cabin and ate my meals with the Captain and the Mate. The Chief Engineer should have been there, too, but the Captain insisted on clean shirts at dinner and the Engineer was a crusted Scot who said he had no use for 'frippery' and dined in his own greasy time in the engine room.

The Captain was a tall, fair, old maidish Englishman of fifty, who looked like a camel. He had been twenty-five years on the river and was due to retire in six months; his Mate, a blackavised Irishman from Belfast with a witty grey eye, was ten years younger. They'd been together for fourteen years on the same paddleboat and the captain called the mate 'Jack,' except when he thought him presumptuous when he called him 'Mister'.

At dinner that night, the Captain covered the table with nurserymen's catalogues of flowers and seeds.

'I thought of antirrhinums for the bit between the dustbin and the rockery. There's a picture of the house; 146 Wakely Road, Streatham. Only six months more and I shall be living there in civilized surroundings and I think antirrhinums in the bit by the dustbin. Here's what the agent says: "A remarkable feature of the house is that it has two W.C.'s, one on the ground floor. Room has also been found for a small potting shed or garage." '

'I wouldn't thank you for it,' said the Mate, 'nothing ever happens in the town, give me a bit of shooting or fishing in the country.'

'We shall have small bridge parties,' the Captain went on. 'I expect the vicar will call. Drink, yes. But no beer; nothing common. No pink gin. A little sherry perhaps.'

'Ah, don't overdo it,' the Mate implored him, swallowing a large pink tumblerful, and the Captain snapped back,

'Did you tell the supercargo about those hatches, Mister?'

Next morning we tied up at a little yellow fishing village and started to load ground nuts. In the middle of the morning I found the Captain in conversation with a large military-looking man.

'I cannot, as you know, order you to do so,' he was saying, as I opened the cabin door. 'I can only hope you will see your way to avoid tying up at Tegina. I don't want a murder on my hands, but I will not put up with him for another day and the Government is paying his passage home.'

Since it seemed to be a private conversation I went out and closed the door. Immediately the Mate gripped me by the elbow.

'Boys, oh boys,' he said in a gleeful whisper. 'We've got the Reverend.'

'What's that?'

'We've got the Reverend as a passenger.'

'Who's he?' I said.

'Did you never hear of the Reverend? Oh, he's a desperate character. He used to be some sort of a missionary; in fact, I think he still is one officially: oh, he's a character. He's the boy who pulled a knife on Freddie Fox when Freddie was baiting him in the club one time. It was he who fell down in the middle of the Armistice Day parade. Wait. Come here till I tell you,' said the Mate, piloting me into his cabin where he shut the door.

'The great thing about the Reverend,' he said, 'was, he couldn't keep clear of the Burmese girls. He had a whole congregation o' them, and they'd fight each other in the streets. Finally one of 'em became his permanent Burmese wife—that doesn't mean married by European standards: it's a highly convenient arrangement, until the time comes when you want to get rid of the girl and go home, and then comes the big row because her family take a hand in it, too.'

'At this very moment,' the Mate said, thrusting his face close to mine, 'at this very moment, the Reverend's girl friend's brother is waiting on the quay at Tegina, where we should be tying up tomorrow morning. He's waiting there with a bright new dah in his belt and an urgent appointment with the Reverend.'

'Well, it's time we had a bit of fun or I'll go quietly mental like the skipper and begin to boast of my antirrhinums.'

At this point, the voice of the skipper could be heard bellowing, 'Mister, mister, where the devil have you got to?' and the next half hour was filled with the bustle and clatter of our departure.

We were steaming down the river in the blazing afternoon when we saw the Captain again.

'I haven't made up my mind what to do,' he said. 'I have my duty to my owners, Jack.'

'Never mind the owners,' the Mate said. 'They're not backward in looking after themselves. If you tie up in Tegina, you're no better than a murderer. Ah, give the horrible feller a run for his money,' he pleaded.

'I shall want you to relieve the Quartermaster, Mister!' was all the skipper said, and he pointed out to me a fantastic bird which had alighted for a moment on the rail.

'Look at that thing,' he said, 'you probably think it's beautiful, but when you've been here as long as I have, you'll curse it every day. Why can't it be a decent ordinary shape? Why can't it be brown? What does it have to be green, white and pink for? It's mad, like everything else here. I think it's the redundancy of everything that gets you down. It's all so unnecessary.'

We met the Reverend at dinner. He looked like the ruin of something impossibly noble. He was a tall, thin man with long greying black hair and a pair of hot spaniel-brown eyes deeply sunk in a ravaged face, which all the same was just a little too much stricken and over-tragic. He had long wet hands which shook so much that his knife and fork clattered in his plate continually, and he had two shots at carrying his large whisky from the table to his mouth. The Captain had spent some time in preparing a few sentences of cold courtesy which he had thought appropriate to the occasion, but the Reverend dashed the first one aside with a gesture so expressive that nobody could have used it on any stage, and said, 'Pray do not bother to pretend to be my friend. It disgusts me. The hypocrisy of it. But you are all alike, all alike.' He then drank an enormous draught of whisky and wept for a few moments, then suddenly looking very proud and stern, he announced:

'But there shall be a day of reckoning. We need not endure for ever, mocked, scorned, rejected—our day will come.'

That shut the Captain up completely, but the Mate was not daunted.

'D'you anticipate a day of reckoning in this country,' he said reasonably, 'or d'you mean that the balance will be restored in another world?'

'And why should I answer,' asked the Reverend in apparent high good humour, 'when every word you utter is a trap.' He suddenly turned a villainous sneer upon the Mate. 'What does such a thing as you know of grace?' he asked.

After that there was some heavy breathing all round the table for twenty minutes, and then the Captain played his ace.

'Are you interested at all in antirrhinums?' he enquired.

'That's my business,' said the Reverend, and began to pant like a dog. And shortly after that we went to bed.

I suppose I'd been in bed about three hours—it must have been about two in the morning—when I woke up suddenly. I was under the mosquito net and could hear them pinging about in the room. My cabin had a dim night-light fitting near the door which couldn't be turned out, and stink-bugs were making a squalid buzzing around this single brownish light. And suddenly I realized what I was looking at beyond the netting. It was the Reverend, stark naked, standing as still as a statue with great, brilliant eyes popping out of his head. He was grinning at me, and in the instant of knowing himself observed he raised a huge service revolver and fired. I think perhaps only the Reverend could have missed at five feet. I felt the wind of the bullet on my face and I felt the impact which shattered the wooden panel behind me, and before the short ringing echo of the shot was done, the Reverend had vanished and bedlam broke out in the ship. I heard the Mate go flying down the corridor shouting, 'Get down on the floor, you fool,' and then in another part of the ship:

'Steward, steward,' he yelled.

'Yes, sir,' came a muffled voice.

'Did you take whisky to number four cabin?' screamed the Mate. There was a long pause and the steward's guilty voice replied:

'Yes, sir, two bottles.' The Mate began to curse him, and as he did so the second and third shots rang out, apparently from somewhere near the engine room, and there was a scream.

'Anybody hurt?' the Captain shouted, and after a while a voice came back,

'No, sir, he miss me.' After that there was a very nasty silence for a long time, while we played hide and seek in total darkness, for someone had switched off the passage and night lights. After about half an hour of it I was suddenly seized violently from behind and flung on the deck and then the Mate's voice said, 'Oh, it's you. The Captain's on the bridge with a gun to guard the man at the wheel,' he said. 'So don't go up there.' Nothing happened then for another half an hour and then there was a frightful scream and someone shouted: 'Sir, he's in the galley.' But when we reached the galley it was empty. It must have been about half past three in the morning when the fourth shot went off and we saw the flame of it on the lower deck. This time someone was hurt. We heard the shocked grunt of the wounded man, and presently, scouting about, we found him crouching in terror behind a packing case and we tied up his leg in the dark, in silence.

It was a frightening game we played for the next hour or two, because everybody became very good at it. My main rule was never to be silhouetted against the moonlight or starlight, so I kept to the middle of the ship where it was cluttered with pumps and ventilators and housings and packing cases and donkey engines, any one of which in the dark might either have been, or have sheltered, the Reverend. Once I kicked a bucket over and a dark, almost silent shape came after me round the funnel. By this time, I thought, as I flattened myself behind the donkey engine, the Burmans will have their knives out. My ears soon learned to discount the throbbing of the engine. I could hear that the whole ship was full of softly padding feet and the intermittent breathing of intent listeners.

In the end, *I* found the Reverend. I was sidling round one of those big ventilators which stuck out of the upper deck like horns when suddenly I heard a sound from *inside* it. I pushed my head in and listened. Someone at the other end of the tube was singing softly and savagely to himself one of the fiercer psalms.

It might conceivably be the Chief Engineer, whom I didn't know, but it sounded to me like the Reverend. I abandoned my policy of caution and moved on to the gangway where by great good luck almost at once I bumped into the Mate. I put my hand over his mouth and stuck his head in the ventilator. Then we moved round to the back of it and the Mate said: 'This way,' and began to lead me very fast through the darkness, down ladders and along passages smelling of oil. At the head of one companionway he stopped and let out a great yell, 'Mac,' and from somewhere in the ship's intestines, the voice of the Chief Engineer said, 'Aye.'

'Keep your ears skinned for my next shout,' screamed the Mate.

'Aye,' said Mac, and we went on down the companionway, down another, into the hot stuffy bottom of the ship. Finally, in the pitch black, I felt his hand on my shoulder bidding me stop, wait, take care. And then I was alone. And then I realized I was not altogether alone. Someone in front of me was breathing. I held my own breath. Even above the engine throb I thought I could hear the watch on my wrist ticking away the time. The ancient ship's timbers creaked: water lopped. And then the appalling noise of the Mate's voice exploded in front of me.

'Mac; light,' and the lights went up, and I was at one end of a narrow wooden passage, facing the goggle-eyed Mate at the other, and between us, a dreadful sight, crouched the Reverend, with his back to me. As the light flicked on the Mate charged him: the Reverend raised his huge revolver, but when it went off the Mate had a grip on it, too, so the fifth shot crashed harmlessly into the monkey nuts in the hold.

Half an hour later the Reverend was sleeping, locked in

his cabin: his revolver was in the Captain's pocket. The Mate and I were drinking thick coffee with rum in it, dawn was breaking over the river and we were in sight of Tegina.

By mid-morning, with the brilliant birds flashing ahead of us across the green water, we were approaching the jetty. We had no trouble in identifying the girl friend's brother, for he stood theatrically, arms folded, dressed ceremoniously, with a gay pink gombong and a dah conspicuous in his waistband. He was the centre of a circle of friends and behind him stood about a hundred excited Burmans, most of them women.

The Mate was angry with the Captain. 'You can't do it,' he said.

'Go and fetch him out, mister,' said the Captain sharply, and a few minutes later the Reverend appeared shambling along the deck. He was a ruin, but sober. Even at this crisis in his life he could make himself no sympathy. He began by lolling on the rail in an attitude of exaggerated pride and unconcern, waving a cigarette like a girl smoking her first. Then he decided on another act.

'What is my little life to you?' he boomed, using a gesture of such nauseating affectation that only the most innocent of men would have attempted it. Then he said:

'I apologize,' but threw that away at once with: 'I am all humility. I throw myself upon your mercy.'

The Captain was wearing his camel expression.

'I shall be tying up in Tegina in twenty minutes,' he said. 'I shall expect you to be ready to go ashore in half an hour.' And then, with great courtesy: 'Perhaps you had better have your revolver back.'

The Reverend limply took the huge weapon, fiddled with it for a moment, looking at none of us, and then shambled slowly away.

'You can't do it,' the Mate said. 'It's murder. You can't do it,' he said as the ship gently bumped the jetty, and at that moment we heard the crack of the Reverend's sixth and last shot. The Mate and I looked at each other and raced for the cabin.

The Reverend was sitting on his bunk wearing an odd, superior smile. It took us a minute or two to realize that he was under the impression that he had committed suicide. He had used his last shot on his reflection in the looking glass.

'It was the only way,' he said; as he spoke, the ship began to move again and the Captain appeared like a tall iceberg in the doorway.

'The District Commissioner will not allow us to tie up,' he said. 'He is expecting a riot. You will keep this creature locked in his cabin, Mister, for the rest of the voyage. If he stirs out I will have him in irons.'

The Reverend raised his noble head. 'When I reach the United Kingdom,' he said, 'I shall see that this vile persecution is brought to the notice of the proper authorities. That is all. Leave my cabin now.'

The Mate put his head on one side with a grin of pure enjoyment.

'Didn't I tell you,' he said to me, 'isn't he a daisy?'

VII

The Battle of Gondar

Pointlessness was the flavour of the lazy Burmese sunshine, and it was the flavour of the time. Whether on the Irrawaddy, or in India, or Thailand, or Ethiopia, or in Europe, and particularly back home in England, the point for me about the thirties was that there was no point. It was as if everything you looked at was flashing the subliminal message, 'it is later than you think.' A strong smell of thunder: it made everybody restless and uneasy and irritable, and, as the War closed in on us at the end of the decade, England looked and felt like a self-absorbed mad-house with a bomb under it. The statesmen were going through the sort of motions appropriate to 1910; even their clothes were Rip van Winkle. The upper and middle classes, particularly the intellectuals, were addressed sternly to their task of de-romanticizing sex, and couldn't spare a moment to look out of the bedroom window. As for the Left, these self-styled realists refused, until too late, to lift a finger against Hitler. 'No rearmament,' they said: it was going to be enough to alert the proletariat and a great peace would ensue. Still immersed in all our favourite fictions, we were suddenly all in the war by default.

After a brief period of pure farce when I drove a huge pantechnicon labelled 'Female Intake' around the streets of Derby in case of a gas attack, I was in the Army, and on my way to the only place left on earth where war still looked romantic.

There's something about the ancient grasslands of Africa which has a profoundly disturbing effect upon white men. Something in the sting of the early morning sunlight on their skin reawakens in them the childhood sense of summer, of their own life and power, the unlimited possibilities of their own wills. They feel like kings, twice life-size, and this often leads them to disaster. The peoples native to the high plateaux carry off their royal temperaments with much more grace and aptitude. In Ethiopia they even look like kings. The Ethiopian independent fighting man, Shifta they're called, is a long rangy individual dressed in a white polo necked shirt called a Shamma tucked into riding breeches, with long leather boots. A belt, full of brass cartridges, in which a short sword or long knife is stuck, two more bandoliers of brass cartridges crossed over his chest, and over all that a short black cloak with Salvation Army type collar and a metal clasp. He carries a short carbine slung anyhow, even at meals, even in bed—and he has a high-nosed arrogant face with enormous black insolent eyes, six inches to a foot of black frizzy hair on top of his head, and a little curly beard. He doesn't march, he walks with a graceful lope like some long-legged kind of cat. 'If there has to be war,' I thought, 'this is how it ought to be, like Scottish highlanders out with Prince Charles in the '45!' It was a silly thought, but at least it taught me a thing or two about what it was really like in the '45. There were British officers attached or in liaison with the groups of Shifta. I was one of these at the battle of Gondar.

Towards the end of 1941 Mussolini's Italian Empire in East Africa had only one stronghold left: Gondar, in the Western Province of Ethiopia, still held out, whether from conviction or simply because it had never been attacked, nobody knew. All communications with the western region, called the Gojjam, had been cut long before, so the Italians at Gondar were not dangerous, and there was time for a pause and a conference or two to decide how the last battle for Ethiopia could best be presented to the world: who, in fact, had better be allowed to win it.

Naturally enough, the choice fell on the Emperor Haile Selassie, and the word went around that as many as possible of what were called 'the patriots,' that is, the Shifta, should take part in the battle. And so, at the end of the year, thousands of fierce, heroic and almost totally undisciplined fighting men were massed in the peaks thousands of feet above Gondar, which lay on a lower step of the mountain staircase, while, lower down still, plugging along through the heat of the plains, the King's African Rifles were separated from the fastness by one of those diabolically ingenious minefields the Italians were so expert in devizing.

I'd already seen the patriots in action, and it was a sight which still makes my blood run cold when I think of it. They had a set form of attack against Italian positions: they would creep up during the night to within a quarter mile or so of the Italians, and there in the open, in the dark, they built themselves a drystone wall, two or three feet high, behind which they lay and waited for the dawn, teeth chattering and shaking all over with nervous excitement: like many madly brave fighting men they were very highly strung. All through the night the tension built up in their nerves, until by the first light you could hardly describe them as sane, and their charge when it came was a thing almost unbelievable in its speed, its ferocity, its complete disregard of cover or field tactics of any kind. It was as if a long line of leopards suddenly saw their prey. The Shifta had their rifles, but their preferred instrument of slaughter was the panga, a sort of broadsword two and a half feet long. One thing only was certain about a panga charge: that one side or the other would all shortly be dead. The Shifta didn't use white flags, and disregarded those of others, giving as their reason the undeniable fact that, early in the campaign, an Italian outpost had flown one, and then, when the Shifta had walked well within range, turned the machine guns on them.

In view of the Shifta's reputation, it was felt by the British Command that a solid force of less glamorous and more stolid soldiery, of the sort that obeyed orders and drew regular pay and wanted to go home at the end of the war, should get into Gondar along with the Shifta, in case a restraining influence was required, and that was why the King's African Rifles were ploughing about in the minefield down on the plain.

That was the plan. It didn't work. The general in the minefield was in touch by radio with the British officers attached to the Shifta on the heights, and his instructions came through loud and clear. 'On no account must your forces fall upon Gondar until I am through the minefield. Hold them back until I give the order.'

For three days and nights the Ethiopians held back, fretting and fuming, leopards on a leash. There was Gondar, spread out below them around its superb stone fort built by the Portuguese about the time Columbus discovered America, and with every stone still as hard and smooth and sharp-edged as if it had been built last week. Three thousand feet away, almost straight down, the city glittered clear and bright in every detail. On the third night an Ethiopian captain put his boot through the radio set. At dawn they were off.

The first thing I came across on the way down was recognizable after a minute's inspection as having once been a horse and cart and two askaris—Ethiopians in the Italian service. This must have been the first object of the Shifta's panga-charging mood as they came down the mountain. The mess was littered all over a hundred yards of road, literally torn to pieces.

The fighting in the city was one long bloody fury, like a football crowd gone mad. One of the suburbs was all on fire by midday. By three o'clock in the afternoon nothing was left in Italian hands but the great stark Portuguese fortress. The rest of Gondar was one huge sprawling fight. No one, it seemed, was in control of anybody. Most of the patriots were already drunk, and in the middle of this swirling confusion General Nasi, the Italian commander, who had done his own share of hand-to-hand fighting that afternoon, suddenly surrendered the city to a British officer he came face to face with on the steps of the Banco d'Italia at half-past three in the afternoon. It was a wise move. Nobody else had any chance of preventing a general massacre. The General had to yell to make himself heard above the frightful din. 'I surrender,' he shouted, three or four times before it penetrated, and then he said he was sorry he had no Union Jack to fly over the town. Quite rightly, the flag which presently mounted drunkenly up the mast on top of the Banco d'Italia was the flag of Ethiopia.

But that happy moment, which should have been the

finish, marked merely the end of the prelude. The first thing to do was to get hold of the Ethiopian equivalents of Sergeant Majors and tell them to round up a force of Shifta still inclined to obey orders, and get them to the entrance of the fort so as to stave off the rush when the gates were opened. This took some time, and while it was going on I spent an uncomfortable half hour arguing at rifle point with a couple of drunks who wanted to take me prisoner. This was a new thing for the Shifta—prisoners—but the word had already gone around that there was to be a grand parade after the victory, and since the Italians had always made a habit of parading their prisoners, they wanted some prisoners to parade. 'In chains,' they ecstatically chanted. And anybody would do.

In the fort—and we only got in by the skin of our teeth and had to shut the great gates slowly, heaving and straining against the mob outside—the Italians had collected, in addition to their general staff, all the Italian women left in the city, and it was cheering, like the promise of a new world, to see the mateyness which a day among the Shifta had inspired between the colonels' ladies and the inmates of the local brothel—a genuine female solidarity against the world of men, which was turning out to be just what they might have expected. The Italians also had five armoured cars and their crews in the fortress, and all the petrol in Gondar, in jerrycans piled up in a mountain which overtopped even the high outer wall. A British officer was rash enough at nightfall to mount the pile of petrol cans and make a speech to the screaming mob outside. This was a mistake: they all let off their rifles at once, and though the officer wasn't hit, there were casualties among the drunks, as we could hear, and one of the petrol tins was pierced. This was a grim moment. We had cooking fires at the far end of the compound, and the officer who had been shot at reported that the square outside was lit by flares, and men were holding flaming torches. We'd hardly received this information when one of the flaming torches came sailing over the wall, but somehow the petrol, which smelt so strong we hardly dared to breathe, didn't explode. We doused the torch, and from then on stood by with buckets of water in the deadliest game I have ever played in, as the mob outside caught on to the possibilities, and threw their lighted brands up the wall towards the petrol. Only three got over. Why the petrol didn't blow up, I shall never understand.

At midnight the Italians had a message to say that the Convent of the Sacred Heart, three miles away, in which a dozen sisters had elected to stay, was besieged by a drunken mob with rifles. So we did what we probably ought to have done much earlier, co-opted the armoured cars with volunteer Italian drivers, opened the gates and fired the machine guns over the heads of the mob as we drove into it. It took a long time to reach the Convent of the Sacred Heart and bring the nuns back in an armoured truck in convoy. They had not been harmed. The Shifta had broken all the glass in the place, but had baulked at the entrance. Nobody had dared set foot inside. The nuns were cheerful and sensible. 'What heads they will have in the morning,' they said, looking about with interest at the bulging eyes, the open mouths, the staggering dance routines of the conquerors.

And with the dawn, peace arrived.

The benevolent sun shone only on recumbent forms: but in their thousands. The dead, and the dead drunk, indistinguishable. The Ethiopian Sergeant Majors moved off with leather whips an inch thick. 'They will parade at twelve o'clock,' they said, 'and they will be very sorry.'

At four o'clock that afternoon the top-brass Ethiopians, the British officers and the Italian general staff drank coffee together in the ornate lounge of the CIAOU Hotel. It had been looted, but the fabric still held together. We had discussed the battle, the general course of the war, the Italian problem, the British problem, the Ethiopian problem. We had been polite and tolerant. In this rare and precious pause, a piece in brackets, you might say, sandwiched between bolts of bloodiness and beastliness, we had loved each other, the British, the Ethiopians and the Italians. We had demonstrated to each other our high civilizations and our humanity. Now the door burst open and a Rhodesian voice yelled, 'Get on your feet, you sons of bastards, get up on your feet and salute your betters. Come on, get up, you wops, you're finished here.'

It was a sergeant of the King's African Rifles. The Army had arrived.

Even the grand parade was peculiar. The Prince of Harar, heir to the throne, took the salute. Other forces passed him at the usual semi-trot. But in Ethiopia you treat royalty properly. As each file of Shifta passed the Emperor's son it bowed to the ground. The parade didn't finish till about midnight.

VIII

Prisoner of War

It ran through the Eighth Army like an epidemic in early 1942, but we could never get hold of it quite properly—not to sing it for ourselves. Everybody could hum a bar or two of it, but there was no getting at the words. But after the authorities in Cairo had posted a notice in the messes saying that it was strictly forbidden for all ranks to sing or to listen to this enemy song, thus putting it in the heroic, behind-locked-doors, category like 'McCafferty', the rebel Irish song, it became a matter of pride and prestige to know the words in German.

'You can't tell the Eighth Army what not to sing,' said the Signals Officer to me. He and the doctor and I were among the first to commit what afterwards became a common crime: we delayed an enemy prisoner of war on his way to the cage, we sat him in my tent, and prevailed upon him with huge quantities of beer and cigarettes to sing.

'Singen sie, es, "Lili Marlene,"' I suggested in my dreadful German. He was a slap-happy blond youth in the first slap-happy stage of being a prisoner of war: that he was alive he now fully knew, with joy and surprise, and he obliged at once with a full chested teutonic bellow.

'Ja, ja, aber nicht so fort, und nicht so schnell, bitte. Wir wollen es schreiben,' and we picked up our pencils.

With the expression of a man waking up in the mental home of his dreams, the youth leaned forward on his chair, engulfed a tin of English beer and began to croon out 'Lili Marlene,' line by line. And he went on all the long hot desert afternoon to the bagpipe accompaniment of the swarming flies. And then we put him, drunk, in his truck.

And now, three weeks later, I was still whistling it, between my teeth, screwed up in my little hot shallow grave in the rock while the shells cracked along the top of the ridge in front of me, and dotted along the slope were the broken odds and ends of a hundred British Army units from all over North Africa, driven in here off course and piled up like leaves before an Autumn gale. That ridge smelt of disaster. Nobody knew anybody else. Each unit seemed isolated in its own little failure. We had a brigadier, only nobody knew anything about him.

'It's the bloody end'; everything seemed to be whispering it—shouting it whenever I remembered one picture: the looted beer truck and the British platoon rolling about dead drunk in the sun, the sergeant too.

'The Brigadier wants all officers in the hollow,' a voice sang out along the ridge, and I waited for the next shell to burst and got out quickly down the reverse slope to a sort of quarry-shaped inlet at the far end, half filled with great chunks of rock, the size of grand pianos.

The Brigadier had a lined, calm face and his calm was genuine. He was so tired that his jaws moved stiffly when he spoke, as if under instruction. We sank down on the various bits of rock which lay about, and he wasted no time.

'Gentlemen, the position is, we are surrounded and rather closely; in fact we have been by-passed. We have the sea to the north, the Germans to the west, the Italians to the south-west and south, and now the Germans again to the east of us. We must save what we can to continue the war, and the first consideration is the armour. We are sending all tanks and armoured vehicles out through the Italian sectors in three columns, one hour after sunset. They will rendezvous at Fuka, and with ordinary luck will live to fight another day. The rest of us . . .' he paused and looked up and around at us, as well he might '. . . the rest of us will break out in soft columns of trucks without armoured support, along ten pre-selected routes, at intervals during the night. Pass the sketch maps around, please . . . hurry up please.'

'Crack,' went one of those ratty little shells, right above our heads and we all bowed slightly as to passing royalty. Somebody handed me a piece of paper. 'Route C,' it said, 'depart 20.00 hours.' Route C. Good God, this was a bit of the desert I knew quite well and a very horrible bit it was.

If the Germans were down there, it was not so much a route as a bloody massacre.

Mine was the fifth truck in a column of twelve. My unit, of Arabs, was crammed into that one and the two behind it. My driver was an Englishman, from somewhere in the North by his voice. At eight, I climbed in and told him, 'No lights, and follow the one in front,' and we were off. It took us about two hours to get to the bit of the route I had recognized, and in the pitiless moonlight we must have looked like a glow-worm creeping along the map of Africa. But here, for five hundred yards, the left side of the track made an appalling drop, a sixty degree slope, and there were the twin humps in front where I expected the German guns to be, and the soft sand coming up.

'Look,' I said to the driver, 'turn off the track and down that slope, quick.' Poor chap, he had looked happy, nothing had happened for two hours. Now he slowly said, 'I don't like the look of that, Sir,' and at that the column stopped. The soft sand.

'Turn off and down the slope,' I said. 'Keep your engine running.' He did nothing and I grabbed for the wheel, and at that moment a violent crash and flash went off in the cab with us.

The driver slumped over the wheel and my arm came away from him, streaked black to the shoulder with his blood. I grabbed my Sten and jumped out into the moonlight, waving an arm to get the men off the column before it was pasted, and at that there was the most tremendous crump and a gale of fire which blew me like a feather across the track and crashed me down on a pile of stones.

When I woke up again, the moon was still pumping out her seas of enchanted light, and turning my head with difficulty, I could see a dozen dead men on the track, and the soothing, crackling sound turned out to be the column burning, now almost burnt out. And then a German corporal in a long-beaked Afrika Corps cap put a gun in my guts and said 'Bist gefangener, versteht?'

'Ja, prisoner,' I said and he said, 'Prisoner, ja.' And that was it.

Behind the hump I could hear them singing 'Lili Marlene'. There are four main stages in a prisoner of war's progress.

There's the first stage of release from the tension of battle when the new prisoner talks all day long at top speed, and has nightmares all night long, and after that guilt and resentment take over and he spends six months plotting to escape, and after that he plays ping pong and learns Russian and hates the sight of everybody, and after that he does nothing at all: he lies about. He doesn't even read. There's no point in moving from A to B because, not only is B just as unpleasant as A, it is also exactly the same as A.

I was at the talking stage all across North Africa from Two Hump Pass to Benghazi including a month in hospital at Barce. The prisoner finds out pretty soon that there's a difference between the front line soldier and the administrators in the back blocks. The soldiers at Two Hump Pass took our watches and all the papers we had but gave us cigarettes, and I got a swig of Schnapps and the promise of a doctor further down the line.

'For you it is the end of the war,' they all said, with perhaps a touch of envy. At the next stop, though, they were not singing 'Lili Marlene', but howling the Horst Wessel song like a pack of wolves. And here we were flung into a stone fort for the night with no blankets and when our senior officer asked for food, he was knocked flat on his back on the floor.

At Barce, where I spent a month in hospital, everything was Italian, and there we were formally handed over to them. In a way it was like getting back to civilization, but all efficiency perished in the process. We lived on three-decker wooden beds, stifflingly close up. The heat was shocking. There were no drugs except morphine and very little water; bugs were plentiful. But there was also devoted nursing by the Sisters of Charity.

The thing to remember for ever about Barce was the demon surgeon. The operating theatre was next to the small prisoners' ward, and at a quarter to three every day a huge bearded man, the surgeon, would appear in the surgery, washing and disinfecting himself, robing himself, tying up his hair and his beard and inspecting his instruments. At three o'clock a bell sounded once, the huge surgeon loomed in the doorway and pronounced in a thunderous tone the word 'Comminciamo'—'Let us begin.'

At this, two strong plug-uglies in surgeon's white and rubber gloves entered the Italian ward at the far end of ours at a run, to bring out the patient, whom they hustled onto the operating table still at a run, if they could manage it. Sometimes it took a quarter of an hour to get a patient onto the table, and then one assistant lay on his stomach, the other immobilized the afflicted arm or leg or whatever it was. Morphine for amputations, but not for anything else. The butchery stopped at six o'clock, when the surgeon removed his rubber gloves and prayed for five minutes in his glorious voice before disrobing, while the sisters stood around with lowered heads.

'It's barbarous,' I said to the ward sister.

'It is,' she replied, calmly. 'And God will not forgive the Germans for stealing all our anaesthetics as they arrive at the docks.' Few of my nightmares since then have lacked two or three hundred feet or so from the 'Demon Surgeon' picture.

But I survived him, and went on to Benghazi, where I rejoined some of my friends, all looking about ten years older than when we first met. We were all in poor condition now, from general privation, dysentery, the filthy food. The deepest pain of a prisoner's life is a constant, faint, trickling sound at the back of his mind of the sands of his life running out. Sometimes it becomes a roar like an avalanche. I heard this avalanche for a minute or two in Benghazi when five of my teeth came out one morning.

They flew officers to Italy. We had an elaborate plot to take over the plane on the way. It involved dressing up an R.A.F. pilot in Army uniform and swopping his identity with an Army officer. Very dangerous for both of them. In the event it never came off. We were half-way across the Mediterranean and all ready to spring into play when a man came out from the front end of the machine and shouted 'Spitfire!' Men sprang into action along the flanks of the aircraft, manning machine guns, opening flaps. We could hear the Spitfire droning about. It was a lovely day over the Med with great mountains of cotton wool cloud in a deep blue sky. Into one of these clouds we disappeared promptly.

My morale has never been lower than it was in the next ten minutes. The very idea that an Italian could beat an

Englishman at any military enterprise, particularly after I'd seen them at their military enterprises, was really too far fetched. But this Italian pilot totally bamboozled the Spitfire, flitting from cloud to cloud, and even began to play a rather elegant game of mouse to his cat, popping out and popping in again. After a very long ten minutes the Spitfire suddenly roared off in the direction we'd all hoped to take ourselves, towards Alexandria, and not long afterwards, we began to zoom in on the instep of Italy, towards the City of Lecce.

As I looked down on the ancient, honey-coloured face of Italy, so sculptured with habitation, with the uses of man, so complicated, I felt like weeping. I suddenly realized how much I had hated the brutal and sublime simplicities of the abominable desert.

An hour later we were being dragged very slowly in trucks through the city of Lecce so that every one of the twenty thousand or so population which lined the streets and filled the windows could spit on us. It's the only time in my life I've been drenched from head to foot in saliva. When we finally reached the camp, every one of us was shaking with fury.

During his first two months of life in the bag, a prisoner, if he wakes in the night, wakes in a room full of noise. Yelpings and moanings and harsh altercations, and craven pleadings resound on all sides. The unconscious is giving out its version of the war. It had been quiet at night for nearly three weeks. That night in Lecce it was like pandemonium. The spitting had triggered it all off again.

And in this sort of way, in fits and starts, over nearly six months, we came at last in November in the snow to a settled camp, near Sulmona, in the mountains of the Abruzzi.

Fonte D'Amore, the Fountain of Love, which still has a warm stone Venus at the head of the sacred spring, but now incised with deep lines of drapery upon the stone to make believe it's the Virgin Mary. It's a small poor mountain village. Ovid was born there, and all round the splendid peaks rear themselves up and the barbed wire of our camp made scars across their noble shapes. It was a camp you ached to be out of. A day in the mountains, just one day, would cure everything.

It was here that we plunged into our second stage and spent our energies on plans to escape. At one time about half the camp was either on shift down some tunnel or other, or keeping guard. Our method of shifting the soil was ingenious. The senior British officer had leave from the Commandant to construct a tennis court. The tunnellers had a man at the entrance to the tunnel whose job was soil disposal. He would tuck his trousers into his socks, haul up the bucket of soil, and pour it into his trousers down the waistband, then, as another man took his place, he strolled out on to the raw surface of the would-be tennis court, and by pulling his trousers gradually out of his socks, could in five minutes or so, spread the whole load evenly over the area. At least one tunnel succeeded, and six men, I think, got out. We got postcards from some of them from England.

But in Italy, especially in the summer, because the Italians were so civilized, it was easy for a day at a time, but not for a day and a night, to pretend your existence was bearable.

For instance, we could buy wine from time to time, and one evening when we had soaked up a good deal of Marsala we began to discuss Italy and Italians, and I said I thought the most typically Italian thing I could think of was opera, and particularly *Rigoletto*, whereupon we all tried to sing the most Italianate chorus in it. Even if we'd been sober it would have been a dreadful noise. But suddenly we had to stop. In front of me now appeared the Guard Commander, a corporal, who said with authority, 'Inglesi. Non cosi. Momentino,' and disappeared. When he came back he brought half a dozen guards with him. Heavens, we couldn't have been making all that noise. We weren't as drunk as that. The little black and lemon Southerners who guarded us at that time propped up their rifles, anywhere, without any thought, stood in a semi-circle, and at a signal from the corporal, let go with the chorus from *Rigoletto*, marvellously sung. Then they stayed to finish the wine.

But we were moving on. One night one of us, a correspondent, Edward Ward of the B.B.C., lit one of the strictly forbidden little grease lamps that we all had, made of pyjama cord and a cheese tin, and brought it across the open window. Immediately the sentry yelled 'Luce, luce.'

('Light, light'.) Eddie put his lamp down, leaned out of the window, and gave out a tremendous raspberry which rang across the camp.

There was silence.

Two minutes later a small reasonable voice under the window said:

'Signor Maggiore, non ho detto "Duce" ma "luce".' I didn't say 'Duce,' I said 'luce'. An odd thing for a serving soldier to say, and within a fortnight, the Duce's day was done, and we were streaming up the Brenner Pass to our final destination at Offlag 12B near Coblenz on the Rhine.

That was the camp where I gave up. It was a mock schloss in grey granite Gothic with tin gargoyles. It had been a Catholic girl's school. It had a double row of wire, and dogs. There was no getting out of it. One man did, but virtually it was unbreakable.

I was there nearly two years. I began to go round the bend, I think, after the great 'Hitler in the Lavatory' parade. This was after twelve months in the camp. The R.A.F. had been over and bombed the railway, and incidentally smashed the window in a little dark lavatory on the ground floor. It was a window blacked-out with paint, and now it was gone a very stark portrait of Hitler on the gallows was revealed. It was highly obscene and very lovingly done in crayon, by the Poles, as it happened (not that it mattered) who'd been there two years before we'd arrived.

In dealing with totally irrelevant trivialities such as this, the Germans were always highly conscientious and meticulous. The Commandant decreed a punishment parade.

At 6.30 next morning then, we were barked out of bed: ''Raus, Heraus, 'Raus, Heraus, Heraus, 'Raus . . .' and paraded at attention. It was February and there was snow on the ground. The dismal landscape could be heard dripping all around us. Hauptmann Foerster strutted about in front of us. What a mess. He must have been one of those jolly fat Germans you drink with all up and down the Rhine. And he still had his bright blue eyes, his hair, his mouth full of gold teeth, but his jolly flesh hung in folds like an old overcoat, his complexion was Gorgonzola but with crimson veins; you could smell his despair from twenty yards. We were in poor condition and ill fed, and every three or four minutes one of us would measure his length on the snow. And at each fall, the Hauptmann felt obliged to say 'We are not of sugar made.' 'For God's sake,' I thought, 'Can't he find any hole or corner to hide his ruin in but male arrogance? Someone ought to tell him.'

And at length, at first light, the Commandant appeared, preceded by a little man wheeling a sort of soap box on wheels which the Commandant mounted. What a comedian. He looked a bit like Conrad Veidt in some super drama and moved as if he wore glass stays. Everyone knew he was a blameless Austrian water colour painter in real life.

His speech from the box was very funny. It began:

'I am asking myself this morning how komt your nation so uncultural to be.' Weary cackles of laughter followed this flight of fancy and one of the batmen—we had Generals, so we had batmen—yelled out 'What-ho.'

At last the Commandant finished his speech, saluted our Colonel gravely and handed over the parade to the third member of this sketch, who now came stumbling on as usual ten minutes late. This officer was known to us as 'the man who died at Stalingrad'. He was covered with medals. He never looked at anybody or took his eyes away from the ground. Everything he did was a mere rude sketch of what was intended. He now, as usual, flapped his hand at the Colonel, ran like a partridge down the front rank and ran like a partridge up the rear rank, ran around to the front, mumbled 'Appel be-endet,' flapped again and shambled off. Well, there they were, and what other way was there to play it, I asked myself. Becket hadn't written his plays yet. Of the three I preferred, for style, the man who died at Stalingrad. What is the alternative?

Shortly after this parade I took to my bed almost totally. In about a week I'd forgotten how to talk. It wasn't that I'd nothing to say; I had some very deep and involved concepts to expound, but some other time when I could find the words. I was round the bend, and that's the time when prisoners very easily fold up and die, usually of pneumonia. I didn't get pneumonia. I got tuberculosis of a gland, and it was decided to move me to a prisoner of war hospital to have an operation.

A German corporal aged about sixteen with long yellow hair was to be my escort, and one fine morning we set off in a truck through the ruins of Germany, some of which were still smoking. That part of the journey was easy; like watching a film, cold pictures of ruins and people walking about. Nothing much to do with me. Cold and irrelevant pictures with too much space around them. But at Limburg we had to get out of the truck and go by train, and this meant walking down two hundred yards of street to the station. It was one of the most difficult things I ever had to do. I stood shaking on the brink of the pavement in terror. Everything and everybody seemed three or four times life-size and full of violent movement and power, and nothing to do with me. And the daylight suddenly seemed blinding white and hurt my eyes, as if I were going snow blind.

Somehow the corporal managed to steer me under the great flapping banner which said 'Sieg oder Bolchevismus' and through the clanging and devilish station and into the train.

There were women on the platform, the first I'd seen for two years. They looked very large and unsafe, I thought, not easy to avoid. Avoid, avoid, avoid, avoid, the train said as we moved off. Avoid, avoid, avoid, ridiculous word, means nothing. So much the better. I'm all for nothing, all for nothing, all for nothing, all for nothing, and so sometime in the afternoon I reached the hospital and went to bed.

The prisoners' hospital was the biggest army hut I've ever seen, and crammed with two-decker beds. I was the only officer there and the only human being whose native tongue was English. Because I was an officer the Germans had allotted me a little iron bed of my own with a partition along one side of it which screened me inadequately from the rest of the enormous room which was loud with bickerings in half a dozen languages. About half the patients were Russians and there was a tough contingent of Poles, who fought with them continually, a good many Frenchmen, and some wretched Italians who led dog's lives among their former enemies. There were Yugoslavs, Scandinavians, Dutchmen and even one man who said he was a Turk.

Twice a day, the German guards, a collection of old cripples from the Eastern Front who still had two feet and a trigger finger, moved apathetically around the room making vague smiles and gestures of goodwill which were ignored. And twice a day the Polish doctor made his rounds followed by his two medical orderlies, a gigantic Russian called Ivan and a Frenchman called Marcel, both of whom hated him, theatrically flashing their eyes and spitting from time to time as they walked behind him. Ivan used to argue with him in loud shouts at the side of every bed he stopped at, and Marcel would usually contrive to upset the tray of instruments on the floor at least three times during the evening tour. A very good-looking German officer called the Liaison Officer, in the insolent cap that army wore, leaned every night on the door, dangling a cigarette and watching this scene with a superior smile. Every night as the doctor went out, he managed to trip him up, and then he would look slowly round the room, like a schoolmaster, consciously superior, but not unwilling all the same to collect applause.

There were about three hundred men in this enormous room: about fifty of them were too ill to move or take any interest in the life of the place, and the rest were organized into various maniacally suspicious groups: the Communists (they were Russians, and some of the Frenchmen), the Poles who hated everybody except the non-Communist French, and the Italians, who formed a close group like a single spitting cat, and were on the defensive day and night. The rest might be compared to floating voters whose self-imposed task was the spreading of scandal and rumour, hatred and malice among the other parties.

The air was full of plots. There was a plot to kill the doctor outright and various more subtle ones to manufacture evidence that he was involved in stealing the medical stores. One of the Poles industriously took note of every Russian conversation, and these were to be handed to the Germans as evidence of a Communist plot. Two of the Russians took notes of practically everybodies' conversation 'to be used at your trial, comrade, after the war,' they said to the various people involved.

The doctor's departure every night was the signal for a tremendous performance from Ivan, a medical orderly and the leader of the Russian contingent. He would throw his tray of instruments on the ground and begin to shout in 'Lagersprach,' the camp language, a sort of basic ruined German with bits of French and Russian and Italian in it.

'That dirty Pole. Soon I kill him. I cut his throat. One tin of cocoa in the store comrades, only one and who gets the cocoa? Six stinking Poles and one useless Frenchman, while twelve good fighting Russian comrades are dying of starvation.'

His peroration was always the same. When the comrades reached Germany there would be a tremendous massacre in the hospital.

'Alle Deutsche, alle Polski macht keput. Ein gross machtkaputkeit werde sein.'

After this evening speech the Poles and the Russians would start to fight, and the French would begin their normal evening's recreation of baiting an hysterical old Italian sergeant-major until he wept and screamed; and then round about eleven o'clock the British bombs would begin to drop on the railway five hundred yards behind us and anybody who cared to do so got out of bed and lay down in the shower bath which was a concrete basement three feet lower than the floor. It didn't seem worth getting out for, so I stayed where I was.

I had my operation one morning and very unpleasant it was, since there were only local anaesthetics in the prisoners' hospital. The Polish doctor had done his best to cheer me up. He spoke to me in English.

'De doctor which shall operatink is good doctor and good man. He iss German but iss not animal. Good lucky for you hopink.'

The French orderly stayed behind too, to tell me that all the surgical gut in Germany was now of ancient stock and full of tetanus.

'Bonne chance,' he said, in a meaning way.

I couldn't have cared less for either speech. And back in the enormous room after the operation nothing seemed to make much sense either. I lay there while the squalid blue-bottle life of the hospital buzzed around me.

Ivan used to come in sometimes to tell me that his comrades had not yet made up their minds whether I was a

German stooge or not, and he catechized me on my politics. He reported to his party in the end that I was a nihilist and a Fascist intellectual.

The old Italian sergeant-major used to visit me too. He would sit on my bed and drone out his miseries.

'Noi altri italiani son abandonati da tutti,' and then he would weep and as he wept he would put his hand in my cigarette box and abstract one or two absentmindedly.

One evening the German Guard, a corporal and two men, stopped in their rounds at my bed. It had been an irritating day. Hot and humid. An old Frenchman called Marius whose top bunk overlooked my partition, had suddenly woken from the coma of days to give a running commentary of the scene. It lasted all day and consisted almost entirely of one word, the name of the substance which he found most prevalent in the universe. One of the Poles was supposed to have stolen a piece of bread belonging to a Frenchman. Ivan had made at least three public speeches about this and had reduced the doctor to a shaking ruin by handing him his tray of instruments and then snatching it away again before he could take what he wanted. He'd prolonged this game for nearly half an hour. They'd made the old Italian into the slops orderly and when he was loaded with six buckets, a ring of men had surrounded him, pushing him from one to the other until all the buckets upset on the floor and he sat screaming in the middle of the mess.

And now the German Guard. What were they up to?

The corporal, a man of fifty with a fair blank face, smiled at me and gave me a little bow.

'Komm with me please. You will komm with me. In the guard house we wish to speak.'

'Komm please,' said the other guard and held out for me a sort of dressing gown.

Everybody in the enormous room stopped talking for a moment and stared, and then they began talking very fast looking at me out of the corners of their eyes.

I could think of no formula for refusing the guards' request, so I tottered down the passage with them to the guardroom. Six soldiers who were sitting around the table in the guardroom rose to their feet and saluted. One of them pushed a chair up for me and the guard commander, an old sergeant with a big black moustache, said, 'There is big news. Before you sit, let us drink.' He put a glass of schnapps in my hand and said, 'To the end of the war.' It was my first drink for eighteen months and I knocked it back like lightning before they could change their minds. They filled up the glasses and sat down.

'For us and for you,' the sergeant began portentously, 'there is great news. Yesterday a great armament to the shore of Normandy has come. So many ships they cover the sea. So many aeroplanes they fill up the sky. Many divisions with guns and tanks are already past the beaches. There is nothing can stop them. It is the end of the war. Let us drink that it finish quick.' So we drank some more.

'It is impossible to speak with our officers on the subject,' the sergeant said. 'So we ask you. What will be for Germany? Will you be here first or will the Russians? I have been on the East Front and I say those Russians will kill us all, each man.'

I discussed this prospect for hours with the sergeant and his mates and in return they gave me all the information they had about the landing. It wasn't much but it was enough.

The lights were out in the enormous room when I returned, but there was a tension, a restlessness, a faint noise as of rats in a barn.

'Qu'est qu'il y a?' asked old Marius as I passed his bed.

'Ils ont debarque,' I said.

Instantly the dark was full of movement, rustling of straw palliasses, pattering of bare feet on the floor, whispering. Somebody lighted one of the forbidden, the strengst verboten, little home-made grease lamps, and a ring of faces grew out of the darkness. Rail-thin, hollow-eyed, with black shadows on their yellow prisoners' skins, they were intent and hungry.

I began in Lagersprach but I went on in French which I knew better, Marcel translating. And each sentence was carried away in different languages by different voices to new corners of the crowd. It took a long time. Finally I said, 'That's all I know.'

A Frenchman broke the silence with a wild yell. He began to sing one of the most strengst verboten songs in Germany to a tune which everybody knew and which in a moment everyone was yelling.

> '*Ta ra rarara rarara*
> *se croirent les maitres de la terre*
> *mais leur premiere difficulté*
> *est d'arriver à débarquer en Angleterre.*'

The door at one end of the room burst open, and in shot the Polish doctor, his arms held wide open as if to embrace his love.

'We shall a beveritch,' he screamed at me and vanished, reappearing a moment later with an enormous glass carboy of medical alcohol. The singing grew into Bedlamite shouting as we handed up our mugs and the spirit was slopped about, and then the French song faded into the great swelling roar of the Russians singing 'Stenka Razin'.

We had finished a couple of verses of this when the other door opened and there was the German Liaison Officer. He marched up to the doctor and began to scream at him, square-mouthed at six inch range. Then he hit him across the face. There was an instant's dead silence and then Ivan let out a great roar, 'Keep your dirty hands off my comrade the doctor . . . .' The rest of his sentence was drowned in a great shout of laughter, and the enormous Russian took the Liaison Officer by the shoulders and began to shake him; and as he broke free and made for the door while the Russian song rolled round the room in waves, the bombs began to fall on the railway outside.

We all spent that night in what cover we could get and we carried the bed-ridden sick down into the showerbath on their palliasses. It was the first time anybody had thought of doing it. It was Ivan's idea. We lay on our palliasses singing till dawn while the bombs came sizzling down.

When I got back to the schloss I was much refreshed and had spirit enough to finish my term. It was not to be for very long. The news had given everybody a new lease of life, and at long last we had a wireless set. The parts, from wrecked planes, had been collected piece by piece over the years by bribery or forged out of milk tins or paid for in cigarettes and coffee through the guards at terrible prices. It was plastered into the wall, but if you leaned on one little strip of old wallpaper, it came to life. The first voice we heard was Stuart Hibberd's on the nine o'clock news. He said, 'Unless the situation in the Ardennes greatly improves during the next few days, it is feared that the war may last for another two years.'

One day in early spring I was walking in the exercise yard and a man walking with me said, 'Listen.' I listened. Nothing. 'Listen again.' This time I caught it—not a sound so much as a vibration in the air.

Guns. Big guns. On the Rhine. They're here then. But it was a week later that they aroused us early in the morning, barking like dogs. 'Raus, Raus, Raus.' They told us to pack what we could carry easily and throw the rest away. I took almost nothing.

The first twenty miles we did by truck. Then we marched for a day through the desert which Germany had become until we came to an open plain with a high embankment stretched across it end to end. A railway line, and on top of it, as we watched, a train came sidling along it and stopped.

We were formed up in columns. The Commandant came forward.

'We shall now embark on the train.'

'Not on your bloody life,' one of the colonels burst out. 'Look,' he said to us, 'anything but a train. Trains are death traps. This must be about the only goddamn train left in the Reich.' A tremendous argument followed. At the finish the Commandant said:

'I shall now command you to enter the train.'

'We're not going.'

'Very well.'

The guards raised their guns—and—this is the only time such a thing has happened to me, just like a film—at that very moment the air was torn in half with a sound like riven oil cloth and we all fell flat on the grass as a British aeroplane came racing along the top of the train. It disappeared. Raced back. Disappeared. And this time when he came back he was going quite fast and suddenly produced a quite impossible noise of violence and hate like the stripping of gears.

The old engine seemed to sink down on its wheels as if begging for mercy and blasts of steam came whistling out of it in unexpected places. The plane then gave an encore, smashing up all the carriages. It then came over and looked at us, waggled its wings as if taking a bow, and departed.

In the silence the Commandant said: 'Then we march.'

We marched.

Three days later, four days later, we were on the outskirts of the town of Lollar, near Wetzlar, where they make the Leica cameras. The guards were now very polite. There were friendly exchanges.

'Aus from which part of England are you coming, Colonel?'

'What's that to do with you, you ape?' and so on.

At Lollar, we asked the Commandant for his sword and he handed it over.

'But,' he said, 'the S.S. are behind us and they are very nervous. You had better still appear to be in our charge.'

We watched the S.S. cross the bridge at Lollar and 'nervous' was hardly the word—they were in ugly rout. Everything they had was broken, but they pelted on regardless. The Russians were twenty miles up the road, the Americans five miles behind them.

The war ended for us by a stream. Two men from the camp heard a rustle in the bushes across the water and looked up to see a tank on the other side nose its way to the edge. Its gun came hard round on them but immediately a head popped up through the turret.

'Who are you?' it said.

'British prisoners of war.'

'Got any Krauts over there?'

'Yes, prison officers and guards.'

'Well, send them over.'

That was the last we saw of the Commandant, Hauptmann Foerster, and the man who died at Stalingrad—up to their chins in cold water, stepping gingerly into captivity.

The Americans had come and gone in a flash. They stayed about half an hour. After sending their tanks through all the barbed wire and shooting up the prison camp guards, they had released about 250 thousand slave labour prisoners in the area and twenty thousand POW's and then they zoomed on down the road.

'Sorry, boys. We've got to go. Got a date with the Ruskies just a few blocks up.' What they left behind was in fact total chaos.

I shall always see the end of the war not as VE Day in London or even my return to England but as Hermann Goering Strasse in Lollar at seven o'clock that night.

Huge bonfires were lit from end to end of the street and fed on the good solid furniture dragged from the citizens' houses. The Hermann Goering Strasse was lined with ornate silvered lampstandards, very solid, and with cross-pieces to put the ladders on for repairs. The lamps were out, but from each cross-piece dangled a nasty corpse—they were the camp commandants, commandants of the Russian women's slave labour camp, the Polish women's slave labour camp, the Russian Prisoner of War camp and all their officers and head guards. Between the bonfires the overstuffed mattresses of the German rich had been dragged into the street and on these in the red light the rescued Russian and Polish girls, stark naked, were giving of their best to all comers in a sort of frenzy of giving rather than a frenzy of sex. In the side streets the comrades and the Poles, already armed with guns, were exchanging rapid fire from windows and from behind pillar boxes. Corpses littered the H.G. Strasse. A great ring of Russians at one end of the street had pushed into the middle a soldier in a singlet with a great round shaven head lolling like an imbecile's. He was dancing like a genius whilst in deepest bass and shrill falsetto and with a complicated pattern of hand clapping, all of them concentrated intensely on giving him the music for the ballet called 'The End of the War'.

The other end of the street was Polish, and here a manic figure with rapt face and streaming hair had claimed as his loot a huge grand piano. It was chocked up on an island in the middle of the street, and there all night among the bonfires below the corpses, the mad Pole played on.

IX

Changing Gear

In the spring of 1945 I was sitting on a ration box under a piece of corrugated iron jammed across the angle of two ruined walls, all that was left of a customs shed on an airport in East Germany. I don't know the name of the place—I don't think I ever did. I'd been sitting there for about a week. The Canadian paratroopers who ran the place sent me enormous meals of eggs and bacon and beans and bread and tea about six times a day. I fell on each new dixieful like a ravening wolf. My stomach wasn't hungry, but I was. Partly because I had just finished three years as a prisoner of war, but mainly for some deeper-seated reason which I didn't care to examine. Eating seemed to me to be the only activity that was safe to get involved in. Everything else seemed to lead backwards or forwards. Backwards to my life before the war which I wanted no part of—I disowned it—or forwards into the sheer irrelevance of life in the British army and a future of name, rank and unit, orders, conversation in the mess, and finally no doubt the imbecilities of economic competition in civilian England. A trap. Life was a series of traps. Childhood first, trapped in a family. Then a meaningless school. Then the irrelevant rituals of social behaviour, trapped in a job. Then the army, and then, as if to underline the lesson once and for all, the prison camp I had got out of ten days before. The lesson was not lost. That was going to be the lot. No more traps for me, and in case anyone insisted on confronting me with one, I had, tucked into the waist-band of my old khaki battledress trousers, a heavy Mauser pistol and ten of its great savage slugs. I was wearing one of those American Air Force jackets with a fur collar which I'd stolen from a de-lousing dump (how rich the Yanks were). I had about a foot of beard and very long dirty hair and I still wore my old desert boots although the soles were flapping away from the uppers. I must have looked like a tough proposition: in fact, though, as I sat there in the early summer sunshine I'd reverted to a technique of my childhood when confronted by a strange hostile dog. I had believed that if I stayed very still it might go away.

Three or four of the paratroopers came across to eat their elevenses out of the wind in my shelter. They'd brought another great dixieful for me and as I was wolfing it down, one of them began shaking his head from side to side and kept this up for a long time.

'I don't get it,' he finally said, since I took no notice.

'What.'

'You've been sitting here now for a week and before that you were wandering around loose in occupied Germany. What is keeping you? Why the hell don't you go home?'

'Don't want home,' I said.

'Well, what I have to tell you is this, Bud,' the paratrooper said, 'and it's straight up. The station commander thinks you're a nut. "I can't have that nut living in this shelter," he said. "One day some general will look in on us and raise hell about him." '

'When he does, I'll leave,' I said.

'Oh yes, you'll leave for the nut house with a posse of psychologists, or there is another thing. You're a deserter' he said. It had never crossed my mind.

'Oh hell, I am through with the war' I said.

'Yes, but is the war through with you? Now look, you see that dirty old kite over there? The old Dakota? Now that takes off in half an hour. It lands in England four hours later. That's what it's there for, picking up fellows like you on the loose—for one reason or another. All you do is go and sit in it. Well, I have to go. Been nice knowing you. Give it a thought, fellow.'

I gave it a thought for twenty-five minutes, then I walked over and climbed into the Dakota with all my worldly possessions and five packs of Camel cigarettes. There were a dozen other men on the plane, all very dirty and most of them asleep. Nobody talked much and at 3 o'clock in the afternoon, we came down on a runway in a field full of buttercups in Oxfordshire. I had been away four years. It was England all right. There was that special kind of early summer light calming down the romantic distances, and turning the hedgerows into dark blue mists.

Sweet reason was the prevailing atmosphere on the air strip. Soothing girls gave us tea and rock cakes and cigarettes, and asked soothing ridiculous questions such as 'What's it like over there now?' They took down our names and units and addresses, doctors wielded their stethoscopes and beat on our knees with little rubber hammers, and took blood samples. Quartermasters of a new kind to me, young and deploying a winsome charm, issued new underclothes and shoes. Orderlies showed us into bedrooms with beautiful white sheets and bathrooms attached. The first bath for three years was such a revelation for me that I made it last nearly two hours. Then I hacked off my beard and shaved.

They're softening you up, I said to myself from time to time. It's a trap. My neighbour in the next room, a bald major, put his head round the door with another version of events.

'I can only suppose,' he said, 'that the man who runs this place wants to get into Parliament.'

'I'm not stopping here,' I told him, 'no matter what they say or do. If I have to bust out I'm taking off tonight.'

'Oh I don't know,' the major murmured, 'might give the bed a trial,' and at this innocent speech such a fury rose in me that I had to move away from the major at a run in case I fell upon him tooth and claw, so I went into the assembly hall where there was to be an announcement.

'Won't waste your time with speeches,' the Commandant was saying. 'The sergeants sitting at tables down both sides of this room are experts in cutting red tape. They're here to see you get your advances on pay, temporary identity card, ration books, coupons and all the bumf you need nowadays in the quickest possible time. Only one snag. Nobody leaves here until he is past the psychiatrists. The examination will take some time. There are twenty five of you and three psychiatrists, so some of you will be staying the night.

Any volunteers?' To my amazement and contempt he got twelve.

The psychiatrist was Viennese and cat-like.

'Now I want you to stay here,' he said to me, after an hour of chat. I am not at all sure that you're fit to take your place in the civilian world. I ask you to stay. Will you stay?'

'No,' I said, 'I'll break out.'

'That would be very foolish, but also of some inconvenience to me,' the psych said. 'Then have you a permanent address, a telephone number, somebody to look after you during your first three or four weeks?'

'My wife has taken a flat in South London,' I said, 'and she is expecting me.' Quite suddenly I had to put on an absolutely blank face over one of those appalling rages which had been invading me, visitors from inner space, ever since I got free from the camp. Defeat was the only thing. Bluff your way out. 'Oh, I think I'll be all right,' I said easily.

'Very well, you get three months leave,' and he filled in a card. I hadn't taken him in, though. I saw the card later. 'Very depressive type,' it said, 'educated, high I.Q., possibly disturbed. Marked aggression,' and then two red asterisks.

'Have a drink,' said this abominable man, and I drank a large whisky, very slowly to deceive him. Twelve of us left for London by the 9.30 train, and if I was madder than most of them, there wasn't much to choose between us. By midnight seven wives had a job on their hands once more for better or for worse, and for the first time in history, their dramas were being produced by the War Office. When I first heard this I was so furious I thought I was going to have a stroke.

'Do you mean to say,' I yelled, 'that the bloody army gave you lessons in how to be married to me?'

'Well, they told us what we might expect.'

'To hell with that,' I roared, and went off to the pub and stayed away for three days. When I got back, I said, 'I took off because I will not have my life interfered with.'

'Oh yes,' my wife said, 'they told us about that, too.'

We were settled between Forest Hill and the Crystal Palace, where miles of crumbling old mansions which had once belonged to the carriage folk of Queen Victoria's reign now cowered beneath the jungle growth of their enormous derelict gardens. Vast trees lined the roads and marked the garden boundaries. At the bottom of these gardens it was as dark as night, and from the black musty-smelling soil forests of roses and rhododendrons grew and smothered little greenhouses made of glass and cast-iron. It was like a science fiction tale of the triumph of the vegetable world, but quite apart from the effects of the last five years of total neglect, England was almost unrecognizable. This sedate suburb in crumbling yellow brick did in fact parade among its vegetation a grisly set of war wounds made by fire-bombs and doodlebugs and V-2's. But there were more interesting casualties. For one thing the ripe old British horsey class nonsense seemed to have gone for a burton. Literally gone for one, in the local. Nobody had any manners any more. And since for years anything anyone really wanted, such as a gallon of petrol or a pair of silk stockings or a bottle of whisky, had been within the grasp only of the dishonest, the famous English respect for the law had sunk to an Irish level. Oddest of all, the place was gay. The people in that suburb had a bright-eyed, slap-happy gaiety and friendliness born of the resource they had to exercise hour by hour in a world where the ordinary tramlines of daily behaviour had vanished. In between the bombing raids, the doodlebugs and the V-2's they'd improvized a splendid life in S.E. 20.

The only strangers in this bright new world were the few odd servicemen who were beginning to trickle back from Europe and Africa. It wasn't that we were cold-shouldered by the civilians. It was just that we were out of it. We couldn't understand half the conversation in the pub about the night the big one fell on the railway station. We hadn't fought their battle. We were wonderful chaps, no doubt, they seemed to say to us, but from another unit.

My particular friend in the pub was a red-haired Squadron Leader who looked about nineteen, but was covered all over with ribbons and rings around his sleeves. He was suffering from another variety of the disease which afflicted me. What lay in wait for him was the bank. Five years before he'd left the bank as if propelled by jets for the R.A.F. He had fought his war and won his gongs and acquired a twitch in his face, and learned to drink a bottle or two of the hard stuff every day, and now he was back in S.E. 20 waiting, or so he told his wife, to go quietly back into the bank again. His wife didn't play it as well as mine did. She used to come down to the pub to protect him from his friends, and sometimes when the Squadron Leader wasn't roaring 'Knees Up Mother Brown,' or launched on one of those almost incomprehensible stories, he stood brooding with the look of a man who was avidly waiting for something. But not for the bank. For a miracle perhaps. And then he would shout at me in gruff tones 'Hey, snap out of it,' and he and I would order drinks of enormous size for anybody in reach, because by this time we'd conceived a lively admiration for the jungle people of S.E. 20.

The Squadron Leader had been at the dishing out end of the war. Week after week he'd flown his sorties and loosed his bombs and then there was the run-back with home and safety as the objective. For all this desperate danger and tension, it had been in a way like a game. He'd had luck, but he'd also used resource, technique, cunning and sheer effrontery. First he'd been the hunter, then he'd been the fox. I'd been on the ground, and when in the normal course of events bombs had dropped near me, so long as they were not too close, I'd never given a thought of where they had dropped. They were not my bombs in any sense, just bombs. And anyway, I was away next morning to some other place where there might or might not be other bombs. And it occurred to me that in S.E. 20 they'd lived with it for years, with no means of retaliation, no game to play, sitting right smack in Hitler's path to London. They had not been ironed out. They had instead produced a new kind of people who'd thrown away all the inessentials in favour of a huge increase in the survival qualities of resource and resilience. So we bought them drinks.

But we would never have been embraced by the rich life of S.E. 20 simply by buying drinks for the natives. We were foreigners, back from boring lives lived in uniform. It wasn't until we needed them that the jungle folk were prepared to accept us. The Squadron Leader and I decided to give a party. What the Squadron Leader called a proper whizzo party with marks on the ceiling. The first thing was how to get the drink, which was by now, like gold, a high form of currency. We confronted Fred, the landlord behind the bar, and put it to him.

'I'll give you my oath,' Fred said, 'if I had an extra bottle you should have it, and I'd see it didn't cost you no more than four quid, but I can't serve my regulars and you know how things are. But about how much are you looking for?'

'About three of whisky and three of brandy,' I said.

'Three of—here, have you gone barmy?'

'We want about twelve guests,' I told him. Fred stood blowing out his lips at us for nearly a minute and then he said solemnly, 'In your serious position there's nothing to be done but apply to the Fiddler. Here, Ron.' A group at the bar parted to disclose a dark vivid man of about thirty, who looked as if he had a permanent secret joy. He looked clever, competent and generous. He had a long subtle curly smile, and he moved towards us playing on an imaginary fiddle what was evidently a ravishing tune.

'Now, can I be of any assistance?' asked the Fiddler. And at that point a very tall melancholy looking man with a large moustache who stood apart at the end of the bar began to shake his head slowly to and fro and chant 'Don't do it, don't do it, don't do it, don't do it,' and he kept this up throughout the whole of the conversation.

We put the facts to the Fiddler and he pondered for a moment.

'Well, I might be able to do something. I don't know. I'm in the motor trade myself.' At this everybody in the bar gave a short laugh. 'I'm in the motor trade, but I know a lot of people who know about a lot of things, and I believe in having a go, see, so long as there's some fun in it, see. And a little bit of lolly for the Fiddler. And always so long as I don't get mixed up with anything criminal, understand. Right, then we'll go. Can't talk in here. Come round to my place. Take no notice of him,' he said to me in a loud voice, nodding towards the tall man who was still chanting 'Don't do it' at intervals. 'He's a copper's nark.' The bar fell suddenly silent at these words and the tall man drank up his stout and left in a hurry.

The Fiddler's place afforded some evidence that he was, in a way, in the motor trade. For one thing there was a notice which said he was. And the wrecks of various cars lay about on what had been the front lawn of a large Victorian house called 'The Hawthorns'. From the window of the basement where he led us we could see a vast expanse of dripping lawn, bald nearly all over and patterned with double V's from the feet of ducks, geese and chickens which were pottering about in wire-netting enclosures. Two goats were tethered to posts. A couple of turkeys strutted under the long wispy trees. And the basement itself had cages full of rabbits in one half and all the mess of a motor mechanic's workshop in the other. There was also a churn, a cheese-press, a box containing about a thousand packets of American cigarettes, some very fine pieces of antique furniture and rows and rows of good motor tyres. The Fiddler sat us down on one of these, a huge specimen which must have belonged at one time to an American army ten-tonner.

'Now,' the Fiddler began earnestly, 'what is this party?' Who is it on behalf of? What liquor do you want. What will you pay for it? Come on, I'll have to know the lot else I don't play.' We told him we hadn't even started making the arrangements yet, but we wanted a party for about a dozen people. Something that might go merrily on until it fell apart in the dawn.

'Well now,' the Fiddler said, 'it's easy enough to get hold of the drink right here in this house. Arthur can always get hold of it, but he charges six pounds ten a bottle and they give it to him. Paddy makes his own in the shed at the back and even in these days he hasn't the nerve to charge more than a pound for the muck he turns out. It's murder and I mean that literally.' He ruminated, sucking his teeth. 'Now look here, I think we can do it, but you'll have to do it my way. Got it? I'm in command of this operation, else I don't play, see. Now first you have your party here in this house. We've got a big room upstairs, proper big fire, give you the choice of goose or turkey properly cooked, too. It'll cost you roundabout the same as the West End but it won't be the kind of muck you get up there nowadays. The bottles will cost you four pounds ten apiece. Second, me and the Missus will get invites to the party, and we might bring one or two friends. Agreed?' We agreed and fixed the date three weeks ahead. And the Fiddler took us upstairs to see the room where the party would take place.

It was an enormous rambling house, and on the way up he introduced us to various other residents in The Hawthorns, every single one of them on the wrong side of what was left of the law, right up to the top attic where we met old Dr Yellowstone. He must have been over eighty years old and was dressed in the professional clothes of forty years before. He had food on his waistcoat which had been unobtainable for years. And he sat over a gas-fire and never stopped talking.

'This used to be my father's house. Yellowstone and Co., Sugar Brokers, Mincing Lane. My father's house. Carriage and pair. A good-class neighbourhood. Six servants. The best of everything. All gone. All gone. Over-run by this accursed riff-raff. And everything grown over like a forest. No one left to cut the grass, to keep things decent. No one, and no one ever will again. Civilization is over, my boy. I thought it would outlast my time, but I've outlived it.'

'Wonderful old fellow,' the Fiddler said. 'Of course by riff-raff he means Paddy, and he's right. He gets on best with Arthur.' He pointed through the window. 'That's Arthur's car down there.' It was a huge Rolls Royce. 'One of these days,' the Fiddler said, 'I'll take you to see Arthur at work. He's worth watching.' He slapped his knee and laughed. And the day before the party we climbed into the car and went to see Arthur at work.

It was about eight in the evening. The Fiddler chuckled as he let in the clutch. 'London's a different city since you went away,' he said, 'and tonight I'm going to show you one of the cleverest operators in the business.'

'What business?' I asked.

'Ah, now you are asking.'

Our first stop was at a huge glittering Tudorish pub of the sort I don't care for much as a rule. The Fiddler strode to the farthest corner of the bar, where we sat around the table, screened from the door by the crowd. The Fiddler seemed to be trying to shrink out of sight behind a large bushy plant in a pot. He spoke very low.

'Now if I'm right, in just about five minutes a very tall man will come in through the door. He'll have a pinstripe suit and black hat and floppy briefcase, and that's Arthur. I want you to watch what he does. Don't let him see you watching, though.' Sure enough, almost on the word a tall black-suited man did come in, and I realized with astonishment that I'd seen him before, at that famous wine bar in Fleet Street before the war. He used to be a sort of failed minor poet with a prodigious capacity for champagne whenever he had the money, which wasn't often because he scraped up a living by writing beautiful paragraphs about the country for such papers as still used those things. He now looked extremely prosperous.

'I know him,' I said.

'Does he know you?'

'Not to recognize,' I said.

'Well, watch what he does.'

The tall man ordered a double scotch and when it came, instead of putting in the soda, he took from his pocket a bottle, a pen, a label, and a small glass instrument with a rubber bulb at the end. With this bulb he sucked some of the whisky into the tube, held it up to the light, wrote on the label, poured all the whisky back into the bottle and stuck the label on it.

'Just look at old Bill,' the Fiddler was giggling. And peering over a glass partition at the back of the bar was the purple horror-stricken face of the pub's proprietor. It vanished, and a second later the proprietor himself came out into the bar, and spoke to the tall man. They disappeared together.

'Oh, it's clever,' the Fiddler said. 'You see the lark. Now half the landlords round here water their whisky. Stands to reason. Couldn't get by if they didn't. In comes this bloke all dolled-up like a ruddy tax inspector, orders his drink, tests it for specific gravity with his what-do-you-call-it. The old man watches him from behind the bar and he knows what the gravity is—not what it should be, neither. So he comes out. "May I have a word with you?" "Afraid I must report." "Worth fifty nicker to me. Have a drink. Come on. Have a whole lot of drink. Have four or five bottles and fifty nicker." "Well, perhaps this once." Got it? Oh, he's a great operator. You say he used to be a little writing man? Well, I can understand that. He's an intellectual, same as what I am myself. Cursed with an imagination. But what a success story. I can see him there scribbling away and nothing come of it, and now he's worth three hundred nicker a week if he's worth a bob. And I want you to look at his briefcase when he comes out.'

Sure enough it was solidly full. One bottle thick.

'Well,' the Fiddler said, 'we've time for a quick one and then we'll go and do our bit of business. I admire that operation. Don't tell me his real name, I don't want to know it. Do you know what we call him?'

'No,' I said, 'what?'

'He is called the Sprinter.'

'Oh, why?'

The Fiddler turned on me his enigmatic look of joy. 'You'll see,' he said.

We had our quick one and got into the Fiddler's car again. In a side street we stopped.

'I'll just do a bit of a recce,' the Fiddler said, and set off walking. In five minutes he was back. 'Right,' he said. 'Get out.' We walked round the corner on which a big pub blazed with light. The street was empty in the saffron-coloured sodium light, except for a Rolls Royce car parked a hundred yards ahead. The Fiddler turned to the Squadron Leader.

'Now you go up to that Rolls Royce car and stand on the pavement looking at it until I tell you to stop. That's all.' Then he and I went round the corner again and stopped. 'When I give you the nudge,' the Fiddler said, 'follow me. I shall walk fast, you walk slow. Drop behind me, not with me, see.' Then he nudged me and set off at a furious walk round the block. I followed slowly. A couple of yards ahead of the Fiddler the tall man strolled with his briefcase. The Fiddler passed him and as he passed he didn't turn his head or slacken his pace, but I heard him say 'Hey, watch out. Bogies.' And then an extraordinary thing happened. The tall man flashed round at me for one panic-stricken instant, then he dropped his briefcase and overcoat in one movement, and raced up the street towards the car like a rocket. He was about thirty yards from it when he saw the Squadron Leader, turned sharply at right angles like a hare and bolted up a side street.

'Now what was up with that geezer,' the Squadron Leader said as we came up. The Fiddler was peering into the back of the car.

'There's sixteen of champagne for a start,' he announced, 'and I see he's got a full tank and beautiful tyres.' He produced an odd-looking key from a leather case and worked for a minute at the car door. 'Now you boys had better trot off home on your feet, as quick as you can,' he said, 'because I shan't be able to give you a lift. Sorry.' He gave us a joyful wink. 'I'll have to ask you to excuse me while I take all this stuff to the police station. See you Tuesday.'

It was one of the six best parties I've ever been at, and two days later, the doom which I'd felt stalking me since I left Germany caught me unawares.

Over the month, powerful influences, such as sex and affection and drunken company, and the whole uproarious pantomime of S.E. 20, had softened me up so that I had not for some weeks had suddenly to adjust a pokerface over a visiting fury from inner space.

On this bright morning in July, as I queued for a bus in Oxford Street, the young man behind me who'd been shoving madly about, suddenly put his knee in my back and nearly brought me down. It was not an unusual thing to happen on the journeys between the prison camps, but when you were there, you didn't turn round, because you knew there was a German gun in the small of your back. As I regained my balance, I had a sort of sudden revelation—no gun this time. And the next thing I knew I was being hauled upright by a policeman. I looked up, and there was a silent crowd around us. I looked down and there was a young man on the floor with blood on his face, who looked in a very poor way.

'Now what is all this about?' said the policeman.

'He shoved me in the queue,' I said.

'Well, and if he did,' the policeman said, 'you don't have to knock him down and jump on him. I'll want all the details. You'll hear more of this.'

And two days later I did, when a strange major from Civil Resettlement climbed up the stairs of our flat.

'Well,' he said, 'we can get you off the charge because you're an ex-prisoner of war. It's assault and battery and it was nearly grievous bodily harm, but that's the end of your leave. Now you'll have to cool your heels in the Civil Resettlement Unit. Can't let you loose on civilians. Can't have officers battering people about while they're wearing the king's uniform. So here you are, sign this, and report to the unit in Putney on Monday. The psychiatrist, I may add, is fit to be tied. He said he knew you'd do some damn silly thing.'

So as the mad year, 1945, changed into 1946 and the armies began to filter back home, and life in England slowly changed towards a new norm, I was spending my time in Putney, where a thoughtful government had provided a set-up composed of psychiatrists and social experts and a few regular officers for administrative purposes, especially designed for those whom the war had knocked slightly off their trolleys; and there I remained until I was pronounced fit for human consumption.

It was not at all strict, but extremely boring at the Civil Resettlement Unit, where group therapy was all the rage. We were all gathered together in groups and talked about our own and each other's problems until the psychiatrist in charge felt that we'd faced and understood them. Well, that was the theory, but in reality, it seemed to me that all that happened was that the problems got ironed out in committee, as everything else gets ironed out in committee, but remained obstinately in the subconscious where arguments don't count.

Nevertheless, we slowly returned to an easiness which felt like normality. Not all, of course: some the war knocked permanently off balance, and some seem to do better slightly off their trolleys than on. There was one very senior, though very young, Air Force officer who was mad with a sort of permanent euphoria. He was a sort of cartoon of the well-known characteristics of the R.A.F. of 1945. The long moustache, the wild overstatements, the loud whooping it up. In bars, when plastered, this officer would always insist on buying drinks all round for everybody in the pub, and when the evening was even further developed, he would press large presents of money on all those in sight, with tears of pure compassion sometimes. They usually took it to save trouble and then gave it back to him in the morning. His high rank allotted to him a relatively enormous cash gratuity, and soon all the psychiatrists in the place were devoting most of their time and attention to keeping some small fraction of his money intact for the day when he would leave for the world outside. He then suddenly announced that he was spending no more in bars. He had laid the whole of his gratuity on a horse to win the Derby.

The psychiatrists at once came up with a plan to certify him insane, so that the bets would become null and void and recoverable, but their straight-forward Viennese minds were quite at sea with British bureaucracy. By some ancient regulation, it appeared, they could not themselves certify him. They needed the connivance of a local doctor in the town. But when he turned up at the unit, they knew the cause was lost. He was a long, blackavised Irishman in riding boots who immediately said, 'I see nothing insane in putting money on a horse.' The arguments continued for weeks. The participants were in full session nearly all day, while their eccentric patient let off Chinese firecrackers from time to time to show that some significant change of direction had occurred in the stream of his psyche, or that is what he said he did it for.

Towards the day of the race, he was letting them off morning, noon and night, and then came the great day, and we all retired to our quarters with our portable radios, which in due course reported through a tremendous bombardment of firecrackers that Airborne had won the Derby, and our friend, who was about a hundred thousand pounds the richer, went on a modest progress through the unit, buttonholing each psychiatrist to ask politely who was crazy now?

But the mad year in England, from the summer of 1945 to the summer of 1946, was wearing itself out fast. What put paid to it finally, was the trial of Neville George Heath for murder. It's strange what superb mirrors of their time murderers often are. You could deduce the whole of life in England in 1910 from the revelations at Crippen's trial. Neville Heath summed up 1946; large, handsome, extrovert, twenty-nine years old, a pilot dressed as a squadron leader, announcing himself as 'Squadron Leader Sir Neville Heath, Baronet,' roaring in the bars of flash hotels, topping up his girl friends with champagne, and carrying at one time in the pocket of his elegant uniform a collection of the nipples of those of them he'd beaten to death. Heath was the epitome of all the sickening charm, boyish gallantry, extrovert nerve, and social arrogance, real or imitation: all that part of the officer mentality which belonged to horrible old England—the Neville Heath syndrome, you might call it. It had served its turn and now it was on the way out. He was tried for one murder, but it was rumoured that there were six or seven.

I went back to S.E. 20 while his trial was on. Already the jungle was thinner, the trees cut back, some of the grass mown. In the pub, Fred's wife was standing listless behind the bar. Like everybody else, we spoke of Heath.

'Isn't it dreadful?' said Fred's wife, smacking her lips. She poured me a drink. 'Squadron Leader's gone back to the bank,' she volunteered, holding the train of thought.

'Is he pleased?'

'No, but his wife is.' Later, she said, 'are you going to the funeral?'

'Who's dead?'

'Oh, didn't you know? Old Doctor Yellowstone's buried today. Yes, died in the attic. Fancy, after all those years. Eighty three years in the same house. It doesn't seem possible.'

'And the Fiddler?' I asked.

'Oh Ron, he's got a job—£30 a week he can get now, you know—skilled motor mechanic, and not put on like it used to be. Runs his own racket as well. Old Ron's laughing.'

Everyone was laughing, it appeared, except me. The free

money had all run out. I went down to Fleet Street to see if anybody I knew there could give me a job. They all said the same. 'You've no hope whatever,' they said. 'You were never on anybody's staff. I've got twenty men coming from the army next week, all with guaranteed jobs, and one double page is my allotment of paper for the day. Better try the B.B.C.'

X

Getting and Spending

It's about three hundred yards to Broadcasting House from Oxford Circus Underground Station, and twenty years ago at ten o'clock on a cool summer morning I was making my way along this stretch, passing at about every ten yards a spiv. These spivs, always stationed at the corner of a side-street, for a quick getaway, were young men with large woolly side-burn whiskers and trays of little toys or cigarette lighters slung from their enormous padded shoulders: in the post-war period the sharply dressed had to look like American gangsters of ten years before. The style was called the American drape.

As I passed each spiv, he said 'Pssst,' and when I glanced sharply round at him he was pulling out of his pocket a pair of unobtainable nylon stockings, or half a bottle of whisky. Or he said 'Pssst. I got petrol.' And if you nodded you could follow him down the side street, and in some murky passage-way you could do a deal in petrol which would have to be siphoned into your tank with the bit of rubber tubing every car now carried from a lorry at dead of night underneath the arches not far from the Elephant and Castle at about twelve and six a gallon. 'Sorry, guv, I know it's murder but that's the price and no arguing. I get five years in the nick for this, see?'

At the entrance to Broadcasting House I paused and drew a sharp breath. I had an appointment with a Mr Donald Boyd, and I was after a job. On the other hand nothing could keep it from me that my presence on the mat, figuratively cap in hand, was a sell-out. I was not a purposeful character, but such purpose as I had had been directed, rather successfully up to that date, to keeping out of the organized activities of my time. My position was perfectly summed up by a docker I later interviewed in a pub for the B.B.C. He was explaining to me his rooted objection to any change in the free-lance status of the dockers, and he said, 'I do a piece of work and I draw the money. If I don't need the money I stay away, and what I do with my own time is nothing whatever to do with them. If I like to spend it assaulting the neighbours, that's my lookout. But once you start signing contracts, mate, they'll have you going to church before you know where you are. You 'ave to watch 'em.' As far as I was concerned he had defined the position, and the only tolerable social contract. Any jobs I had had up to date had been seen either as a joke, like my brief emergence as a prospective M.P., or as a handout in lean times like my inglorious spell as a schoolmaster, or simply as a passport to somewhere I wanted to be, like my job as courier to a travel agency, or a spell of gun-running in Burma, or as a private enquiry into the terrors of our time, like my job in a Birmingham import-export firm. And there'd been the war, when nobody did as he liked.

Only rarely, in between these compulsory chores, had I ever achieved the happy status of the docker, and that was whenever I had written a piece for a newspaper or a magazine, drawn the money and stayed free until it ran out. And now, after the war, there was no newsprint. Papers were one folded sheet. So that was over. There were however lucky people called Richard Dimbleby and Wynford Vaughan-Thomas, among others, who seemed to be able to do just this sort of thing simply by word of mouth. It seemed worth having a go at. So here I was in Portland Place, and I let loose the sharp breath I had drawn on the doorstep and pushed open the door, which in those days did not require the strength of ten, as it now does, and walked into the lobby, to have my worst fears confirmed.

The entrance hall of Broadcasting House, then as now, though it's since been softened up a little, was a monument to an earlier B.B.C. By my reckoning there have been five B.B.C.'s up to date, all quite different like the reigns of kings. B.B.C. the First was the old company, a cross between an amusing gadget and a miracle of science about to unite the nations. Then there was B.B.C. the Second, which seemed from outside to be staffed exclusively by characters from John Buchan's novels, moving about their divinely appointed tasks in evening dress, with orders, in touch by hot lines, which sometimes got crossed, with the Almighty and the Establishment and with nobody else. It was to B.B.C. the Second that the lobby still referred.

Massive horizontals, deeply indebted to the liberal principles of the Egyptian Pharaohs, seemed poised to crush you to the earth. A great slab of blackest Latin shouting Deo Omnipotenti and calling up other big guns, such as Johannes Reithi and the Gubernatores, glared you in the face. A little to one side a rather wet piece of sculpture, representing the human element, seemed to be whimpering meekly under the impact of all this authority. It represented some sort of hominid sowing seed, and was captioned 'Deus incrementum dat'. It would have cheered me up at this moment to know that the staff translated this freely as 'God gives the annual increment'. But I didn't know, and the tableau had done its work. It was a rebellious serf who presently slid upwards in the lift to meet Donald Boyd.

Boyd effectively dispelled the frigid image of B.B.C. the Second. He was sitting in a rather scrubby office with his feet on the desk: if he hadn't been so long in the leg he'd have been a terrier-type man. His hair bristled, his moustache bristled, he bristled all over with personal integrity. Impossible to think of a sell-out in his presence. He spoke very fast in bitten off sentences using standard Southern English, with the short northern 'a' which had the effect of some dandified personal foible, like wearing a monocle.

'So you're interested in broadcasting? What do you want to do?'

'Find out what there is to do, first.'

'Well, what I can put you in for is news, news-talks, current affairs and talks. You want to broadcast yourself?'

'That was the idea, from listening to the war reports.'

'Well, take a look at this . . .' and he passed me three sheets of typed foolscap: it was a news-bulletin with three Japanese names in it, and quotations in Italian and German. Boyd took a large stop watch out of a drawer in his desk and said, 'Right. Read it aloud. Start when you like.'

I got through it all right, rather well, I thought.

'That was three times our normal news reading speed,' Boyd said. 'Try it again slower.' I tried it again.

'Now again, very much slower.' I tried again, but only succeeded in putting pauses between the words.

'No good asking you to read the news bulletin,' Boyd said, and seemed prepared to leave it at that. He stared into the distance twiddling his fingers.

'So I didn't pass,' I said.

'Pass, pass, of course you passed. There'll be something. Don't know what, but something. News, talks, current affairs, something. Get in and look around, that's the idea. You'll have to sit a board, of course, but that'll be no trouble. Come and have a drink.' And he took me round the corner for my first drink in the George in Mortimer Street, a place which was to see me demonstrated like a specimen in a laboratory over the next twenty years.

The Board, when some weeks later I sat in front of it, turned out to be a thoroughly enigmatic experience. The four men who interrogated me were not in the least interested in anything I knew or anything I could do. The questions were designed to give me the chance to assert that I was a good-hearted, socially-minded, active community member, not tooth-and-claw but heart-and-soul. I was so mystified and tongue-tied by this that at one time a three-man team was urging me on.

'You played rugger for your school, you say?'

'Only for my house.'

'For your house, yes, and no doubt you thoroughly enjoyed it?'

'Well, er . . . .'

'You threw yourself heart and soul into the activities of your community,' another one said.

'You worked hard and you played hard,' a third prompted.

'Well . . .'

'Now, about the Army. Not so much the fighting, but, erm, you took part in regimental activities, no doubt?'

'Well, I only saw my regiment for about a month during the whole war.'

'Yes, of course, and that was a great disappointment to

you. You would have wished to identify yourself with your own county, your own community.'

'Well, of course, I . . . .'

'Exactly. Exactly. Thank you, Mr Cutforth. You will be hearing from us.'

A couple of weeks later, as the autumn fogs began, I was a sub-editor in the B.B.C. Home News Room.

I joined the B.B.C. in one of its interim periods. It was still basking in the glory of the reputation it had won during the war. It commanded at that time not only respect but affection, even love. This was B.B.C. the Third, a national hero, in process of changing into B.B.C. the Fourth, which got under way in the fifties. It was the post-war anti-climax. The Welfare State was about to be born, but when it came you hardly knew the difference, since even semi-luxuries were still unobtainable, everything was rationed, and the spivs accosted you at every corner. The people of Britain were spiritually starved by all the material austerity, so that when a trickle of supplies was at last released from the war machine to civilian industry, a cousin of mine, in charge of my grandfather's old pottery in the Midlands, did very well out of bringing out sets of kitchenware in horizontal stripes of white and cobalt blue, the first colour on British domestic pottery for seven years. It was like the war without the danger, and the stimulus of living dangerously. A sagging period, when the industrial machine which had been driven so mercilessly for six years finally bent and cracked, as trains gave up, and electricity blacked out, and houses fell down, and cars refused to run, and fires went out, and most people seemed to live in the pubs. The B.B.C., wondering where to go after its late triumph throughout the world, had one good idea. It shifted Radio Newsreel from the Overseas to the Light Programme. This programme, Radio Newsreel, was one of those wartime enterprises which had commanded the total devotion and the last dregs of energy of a team which almost refused to go to bed. It now triumphantly flaunted a new kind of reporting on the home air.

But on the whole the B.B.C. stuck to wartime formulae and wartime sentiments. It let the public very gently down from the climax of their lives to the grey realities now seeping through the trailing clouds of glory.

But I knew very little of the B.B.C.'s problems. I was in the News Room, a vast space full of little desks with a muffled clatter coming from along the passage, where the tape machines spewed out their messages from the agencies, and tape-boys (grown men, in fact) bore in great foaming trays of paper strip to the duty editors and the copy-tasters, who in their god-like time would deposit a pile of it on my little desk with some such injunction as 'Not more than twenty seconds,' and I would begin the task of reducing the machine-gun style of the agency's six hundred words to a succinct twenty seconds of spoken English. That was the job, and for us the hub around which time revolved was the nine o'clock News.

The trouble was I was very bad at this job. The News Room was regarded as the B.B.C.'s central activity. Every nuance of tone and style and relative value had to speak for the B.B.C. Subs like me were supposed, in time, to take in through their pores the B.B.C. values to the last scintilla. I didn't even get the first scintilla. It seemed to me that there was somewhere upstairs a body which combined the moral confidence of the Assembly of the Church of Scotland with the ruthless, undeviating line of the Praesidium of the Soviet Union, and we were its representatives. This unnerved me. I knew I never would be. I could feel the Thing's basilisk eyes on me all day long; and this was not entirely fanciful. George Orwell thought of *1984* in the B.B.C. canteen, and it is a fact that in that huge, low-ceilinged underground cavern in those days others besides me thought very carefully before they spoke. In the vacuum after the war much of the spirit of B.B.C. the Second seeped back. In the late forties the place seemed to me too full of people who, nominally something to do with programmes, spent practically all their time in political activity: not national politics, B.B.C. politics. They were always forming alliances, blackening names, discrediting so and so, putting a spoke in someone's wheel. 'You heard what he said at the meeting?' they'd say. 'Well, that'll dish him if we can get George in,' and so on. All too much in evidence was that excellent committee man, the smiler with the knife. I lived in dread of the official backhander, and I'd only been there about a couple of months when I had to ask the B.B.C. to bail me out of a police station.

I worked a shift which was supposed to finish at eleven o'clock at night, and if I sneaked out a few minutes early and had luck with Undergrounds and taxis I could just make the last train to Penge from Waterloo. It was the night before Christmas Eve and it had been snowing quite heavily. Even in the middle of London in the side streets at that time of night you could see great stretches of white, and it was freezing hard.

My system for catching the late train was a simple one. I simply used to run like mad as far as Oxford Circus Underground Station, but if I saw a taxi on the way—they were rare in those days—I took that instead.

That evening I caught a taxi. 'Waterloo station,' I said, 'as fast as you can make it.'

'That won't be very fast, mate,' the driver said, 'because the whole of London's one bleedin' cake of ice.' And he set off very gingerly indeed. And when we got to Waterloo the place was empty and a porter was pulling an iron grille across the entrance.

'Last train gone five minutes ago,' he said cheerfully. 'We're shutting up here.'

'How much to take me to Sydenham?' I asked the taxi man.

'I wouldn't take you to Sydenham at this time o'night on roads like this, mate, for a ten pound note,' said the driver. 'I'm sorry but I'm off duty meself very shortly!' And he drove slowly away.

The porter was doing a lot of brisk clattering and banging about by himself among some packing cases behind the grille, whistling very loudly.

He now said, 'How'd Forest Hill do you?'

'Very nicely,' I said.

'Well, I think I can do something for you,' the porter said. 'It'll cost you two quid—cheaper'n a taxi anyhow. Friend of mine's going that way in a car. 'Ang on a minute.'

He disappeared, and there was nothing left in the world

but a dim clanging in the desolate station and the hard silence of the frost. I was very glad when a big battered black saloon car came round the corner and the porter re-appeared.

'Ere y'are,' he said, 'that's ten bob for me and thirty bob for George 'ere. Is it a deal?' We made it a deal, and I climbed into the back over a pile of wicker hampers on the floor and we were off.

There were three men in the car. George, who had my thirty bob, and sat next to the driver, was a tall, flabby man with a very red face and large eyes of forget-me-not blue which seemed to loll out of their sockets on loose springs. He wore a startling overcoat of brown and white checks, and he was a little drunk. He never stopped talking.

'Anything for a pal,' George said, stowing away my thirty bob. 'Anything for a pal. "That's George all over" they'll say—ask 'em anywhere, ask 'em at the Star and Garter, they'll tell you the same, anything for a pal, never let you down, George Baker.'

My companion in the back seat, a scrubby little man in a huge cloth cap, who turned out to be called Nobby, sucked in his breath like a man who'd bitten on a bad tooth. I could see that George's conversation was driving him mad.

'Oh, shut it!' he said. But George went on.

'If you was to ask me what I'm doing 'ere on this freezing cold night in this car instead of warming my toes at the fire,' he said, 'I'll tell you candidly—I'm helping a pal. And 'e won't 'alf be pleased to see us an' all, eh, eh?' he said with a laugh.

Nobby moved his head as if in intolerable pain, and said 'Clck, clck. Come on, get 'er movin', Arthur.'

'I can't get 'er movin' no faster,' the driver said, 'I'm skidding all over the road as it is. If you don't like the way I'm drivin' you can get out and walk. Suit yourself!'

'Less of the bleedin' acid, Arthur,' cried George. ''Ere, 'ave a drink,' he said, and thrust a large flask in my hand. It was half-full of the sort of whisky you couldn't get for love or money. We passed it round.

As we drifted through Camberwell the streets were utterly deserted and full of snow, and now we began the long uphill slope which led on into Kent. The surface was very bad, and I felt sorry for Arthur, who was really driving very well and very carefully. But in spite of his care we skidded continually. All up that long slope George continued his monologue on Friendship.

'Course, when I say we're out 'ere tonight to 'elp a pal, it's not quite right, that isn't. He's a big business gentleman and very well known in Sydenham circles, but all the same 'e's a pal, 'e *is* a pal,' said George, glaring fiercely round at us.

Nobby said, 'Oh, will you shut your great big mouf,' and then, carried away by his fury, he went on 'Oh get on, Arthur, yer drivin' like yer crippled.'

We were right at the top of the hill at that moment, and we could see the whole white shape of it curving away very steeply in front of us. The lights of Penge and Sydenham twinkled far below us, and we could see the beginning of the great steep curve downhill of the overhead wires. It was then that Arthur, stung beyond all bearing, turned in his seat to answer Nobby's insult. His feet slipped on the pedals and the car did a wonderful thing. It took off in a long fast semicircle, completely uncontrollable. With the effortless grace of a champion skater it described a long beautiful curve. We had plenty of time to see what was going to happen. We watched the great lamp standard by the roadside approach us flying as if in a dream, and then there was a great crash, and when we picked ourselves up again from the heap we were in in the car, the world was silent. Two or three snowflakes turned slowly in the light of the street lamp whose stalk now grew, it seemed to me, out of the middle of the car's bonnet.

Then Nobby said, ' 'Ere, watch out. Copper!' and there was a policeman coming up. He looked young and pompous. He said no word at all but walked slowly round the car in the snow, stood in front of it, then walked slowly back round it again.

And this was too much for George's nerves. 'Good evening, officer,' he quavered. He sounded like a pantomime squire welcoming the tenants.

And that was too much for Nobby. 'One more sound and I'll do you,' he said. The policeman made no reply to either of them. He walked majestically round the car once more, asked Arthur for his driving licence, opened the car door next to me, to count how many we were and then said:

'What you got in that hamper?'

There was a four-second silence which even I could tell meant desperation.

'Open it up,' said the policeman. I could see Nobby's cross little face glowering across the hamper in the lamp-light, first at George, then at Arthur slumped in the driving seat like one shell-shocked, then at me. He got no comfort from any of us. He undid the strap.

The hamper was full of bottles of whisky of an almost unobtainable brand. The snowflakes turned slowly in the beam of light, and we could hear George breathing for nearly a minute in the silence that followed.

'Well, now,' the policeman said at last, 'you can all get out and help shove the car off the lamp-post and then we'll freewheel it very slowly down the hill to the police station.'

It took us twenty minutes. No one spoke. In the police station it was warm and comfortable, there was a smell of tobacco and the place was plastered with drab notices beginning 'Whereas.' We sat on wooden benches while the policeman opened the hampers. There were thirty-six bottles of whisky and twelve ducks. Almost before we sat down George had taken upon himself the burden of the explanations, and for once I began to sympathize with Nobby.

'Now before we go any further,' George said, indicating me, 'I want to make it clear that this gentleman has absolutely nothing to do with it.' Here he saw fit to give me an enormous wink which was not lost on the policeman.

''E's nothing to do with it,' George said. ''E's just an old pal we was givin' a lift to.'

'Oh, he's a pal of yours, is he?' the policeman said.

'Well, pal, what I say, 'e's a pal. I never saw 'im before in me life.'

'That's right,' said Arthur.

'Well, leaving that aside,' said the policeman, 'what are you doing with all this stuff?'

I've never heard anything like George's explanation: it seemed to go on for hours.

'Well, it's simple, really, but now I look at it it's quite difficult to explain. It's like this—this pal o' mine, he's a big gentleman, something in the public house line, known him for years, and I'll tell you where he lives, he lives at 11 Roxburgh Mansions, that's in the West End, but I can save you the trouble of going there to find him because he's not there, see, and for why, because he's on his holiday, he's touring in Scotland, to the best of my knowledge, in Scotland, though I wouldn't like you to put that down because I'm not ab-so-lutely sure that he is in Scotland, now let's get it dead right—he might be anywhere, he's that sort of gentleman—I've known his wife since she was a nipper, and he said to me, George, he said, be a pal, he says, I don't want to disappoint Effie, he says, and I've got all this stuff, he says, at Waterloo station, he says, and it's for her brother-in-law's friends, so nip it off down to Forest Hill Station, he says, in time for Christmas, he says, to be called for in my name, he says—just a box of Christmas cheer, he says, lor bless you the sort of party they'll have, they'll polish this off in one sitting. So, o'course, I nips off to Waterloo and I find this gentleman wanting a lift to Sydenham. So o'course I says " 'Op in," and that's it.'

The policeman let this statement fall into a long, twitching silence in which Nobby said, 'Tcha!'

Arthur's statement was a simpler one. He said, 'It's my car, and I said I'd give 'em a lift with some stuff as far as Forest Hill.'

Nobby's was simpler still. He said, 'I say nothing without my solicitor.'

I said, 'I asked for a lift at Waterloo station because I'd missed the last train.'

The policeman listened to all these statements, and then announced, 'My view, what I should call at this juncture my provisional theory, is that you're all in it together. I've noticed how you've all combined to keep one of you out of it. In my view he is the Master Mind.' And he pointed at me.

And even as my heart sank into my boots, I heard a worse horror. I heard George beginning again in my defence. If anyone could turn a provisional theory into a cast-iron case, it was George.

I heard him give a short, phoney laugh. 'If that's what you think,' he said, 'you want your 'ead looked at.'

And the policeman replied coldly, 'Be that as it may.'

The next two hours were a dreadful muddle of speeches by George and curses by Nobby, and my own voice bleating explanations, all perfectly true, but sounding absolutely fantastic. At one time I was given what was supposed to be my statement, all written out in pencil. I read one monstrous sentence. It said: 'I declare that I was not cognizant of the nature of the contents of the packages, nor during the journey did I have cognizance thereof.'

'Hey,' I shouted, 'I never said this.'

'It's the same as what you said,' the policeman assured me, 'in different words.'

'I won't sign it,' I said. But after a bit I did. It was like a nightmare. I could hear George beginning his fifth statement in my defence. This time it was all total lies from start to finish.

'Look,' I suddenly said, 'I want to go home. I've done nothing at all except sit in the car. I can get the B.B.C. to vouch for me personally.' There was a pause while I watched the magic syllables do their work. Then I gave the night duty editor's number and listened while the policeman hauled him out of bed. It was then only about five minutes before I was being shown through the door into a police car. George winked at me and said, 'Good luck, old pal,' but it couldn't touch me. For about the first time in my life I was wearing the armour of respectability, and I didn't like it.

The end came rather later than I had expected. The News Room, which was full of civilized, tolerant and rather extraordinary men, put up with me for a long time. But in the end I only ever got one story to do. In those days stories about the Royal Family were so lush and saccharine as they came in from the agencies that a mere sentence or two was enough to make the stomach heave. And now, day after day, a thick wad of this goo was dropped on my desk with the instruction 'Take the curse off this. Thirty seconds.' The

Augean task was beginning to get on my nerves, and one day after lunch, three of the senior men, all friends of mine, came and sat around my desk.

'We think you are not happy in your work,' said Tom.

'You're a terrible bloody sub-editor,' said Geoffrey.

'This doesn't seem to be your sort of thing,' said Michael.

'All right,' I said.

'You see,' said Tom, 'we had to put in a report six months ago and we gave you the benefit of the doubt. Rather more than the benefit. Now we've got to put in another.'

'And without being immoderately scrupulous . . .' Michael began.

'We can't say we think you're good at the job,' said Geoffrey.

'So we want you to join the reporters,' Tom said. 'It's all fixed up. What about it?'

'Sounds marvellous,' I said. So I became a reporter. I worked for the bulletins and for Radio Newsreel, and any other programmes which wanted a report.

'It was Michael who saved your bacon,' Geoffrey told me. 'We all got together and said, "Well, he's no good at it, is he, he'll have to go." Then Michael got up.' Michael, it appeared, had risen to his full six feet seven, and blushing and pulling the hair out of his scalp, his usual aids to exposition, had made a speech on my behalf.

'He went on for ten minutes,' Geoffrey said.

'He was not to be gainsaid,' Tom stated.

Everything about reporting suited me. It was all done under a frightening pressure of time, to begin with, and you were dealing with your experience, not recasting somebody else's in the light of yet a third person's policy line. And Radio Newsreel commanded a high drive devotion among the people that served it. Like a theatre company, the Reel must go on.

They suffered, though, from having moved from Overseas to the Light, and nearer to the central nervous system of the Thing. Circumspect they had to be, and policy-wise, and po-faced. Stories which would be hailed as aces nowadays were unthinkable then. For instance, I was sent to report the opening of the site of Hemel Hempstead New Town. When

I got there in the rain, nothing was visible but a great sea of mud stirred up by bulldozers, and in the background, half a mile away in the mist, a derelict farmhouse. In the foreground, a velvet canopy, sodden in the rain, sheltered the foundation stone which was to be laid by the Mayor. There was a table and four seats under the canopy, and a row of a dozen or so seats in the front in the rain. Nothing happened for an hour, and I was reduced to recording the P.R.O. going on about the benefits. And then, suddenly, a woman with dishevelled hair came running across the mud from the derelict farm, wailing like a banshee. I recorded that. When she came closer I recorded an interview.

'The bastards,' she screamed, 'they've ruined the farmhouse, churned the farm to mud, and they can't find me anywhere to live.'

'Is this true?' I asked the P.R.O.

'Unfortunately,' he replied, 'in this case, alternative accommodation has proved unsuitable. We have tried everywhere.'

'Very decent of you,' I said.

'You bastard,' the woman said. And at this juncture a coach arrived and deposited twelve men in pin-striped trousers on the wet seats in front in the rain. Officials of the Ministry and other officials. Then filing in under the canopy came a strange procession headed by Lord Reith, and including the Mayor, very belligerent. Lord Reith, who was looking rather like Alistair Sim on stilts and wore an expression of deep gloom, then made a speech introducing the Mayor.

'Ye'll learn to like it,' was the stern burden of his speech, which I recorded. The Mayor of the Old Town then rose, trowel in hand, and announced that he had been going to refer to the stone as a tombstone, 'but that, I'm told, is out of order, so I'll say no more.' He gave the stone a frightful wallop with the trowel, and shouted in a surly voice, 'I declare this stone well and truly laid.' I recorded that. Then a band began to play 'Jerusalem'. I recorded that. Just to fill my cup to overflowing, the P.R.O.'s hand-out was entitled 'Towards the New Britain'. Well, I mean.

It wasn't used, but actual tears were shed. Screams were

heard, men slammed doors, invoked heaven. This, by God, they said, was the end. But it wasn't used.

It was good passionate work on Radio Newsreel in those days, but I had two years to go before they sent me to the Korean War, and a year out there, and six months writing a book about it before I had enough money to leave the B.B.C. and start a new relationship with it under that happy social contract defined once and for all by the docker in the pub.

XI

Reporting the War in Korea

'Well, I think that's all I have to say,' the editor said. 'But the main thing to remember is stories in your head are no good to me. I want them here in the office and I want plenty of them. If you get yourself stuck somewhere for four or five days, I don't care how good your story is, it will be no good to me. And no heroics, please. You're no good to me dead and as a prisoner, you're a positive liability. If I hear you broadcasting from Moscow, I shall disown you. Right? Have some more sherry. Passport, visas, press card, cable card, innoculations, money, air tickets; Miss Crow will look after all that and you'll meet Forbes in Tokyo on Tuesday night. Good luck.'

The Korean War was the first assignment I'd ever had which commanded the world's headlines. Not that the headlines were my job. We had a man in Tokyo constantly in touch with General MacArthur's headquarters. The world's press agencies were feeding acres of coverage into the B.B.C. day and night. The story of the war's general progress would do very well without me. I was a special correspondent. I was there to add to the general a touch of the particular, to be exposed like a piece of film to the sights and sound and smells—the whole impact of the Korean War on the human material engaged in it.

As a piece of film I began to feel over-exposed on my very first night in Korea. I'd heard about the Korean cold. In Tokyo they talked of nothing else, so I was dressed in four layers of wool over a string vest with a fur parka over it all, and when I changed planes at Taegu in Korea bound for Kimpo, the capital's airport, I had just time to notice before

I bundled myself into the small, battered looking aircraft which was to take us on, that I might just as well have been naked. The cold bit right through to the bone in the fifty yards that separated the two planes, and the wind which kept up a low howling like a miserable dog had completely paralyzed my face in about twenty seconds, before I scrambled into the plane which was half full of a great load of machine guns roped down under canvas: it also contained a colonel, an air force lieutenant and three G.I.'s, two of them drunk.

The engine roared. The brown light brightened from Van Dyck to Mulligatawny, and we were off. The colonel took out of his parka pocket a paper-backed book called *The Terror of Bar 71*, on whose cover a pair of gigantic men wrestled for a six-shooter, and began to read.

From the very first that trip did not go well. About ten minutes after we took off, we began to make very sharp and uncomfortable turns. The luggage shifted and rolled on the floor and something fell down 'slap' at the tail end of the plane and brought all our heads round abruptly. At this point a small, dark man came precipitately out from the front of the machine and yelled, 'For Chrissakes get yourselves and your baggage out of the tail and up front a bit.' This order was obeyed almost before he'd finished speaking. We piled ourselves and our baggage into the small space between the seats and the machine guns and the walls.

'The pilot don't want any you to go to the can. We don't want no weight in the tail.'

We waited for the next manifestation. It came about four minutes later. The plane made a long, terrifying, scooping movement sideways through the air, like the swoop and check of a paper dart, but sideways, and almost simultaneously the small, dark man came out from the forward doorway and chanted: 'Get your parachutes.' He added redundantly: 'We're having a little trouble up front and you may have to jump.'

I admired the way the small, dark man whistled as his nimble fingers flew about the fastenings of the parachutes. The lieutenant helped too, slowly, with a reassuring smile, looking into our eyes as he talked.

The dark man said, 'I'm opening the door now, but I want nobody to jump until he's told. When you do go out, go headfirst, fold your arms thisaway, count one thousand, two thousand, three thousand, four thousand . . .' he went on and on. The plane bucked and struggled paper-dart-wise. As the dark man opened the door, we were suddenly drowning in a tempest of freezing air.

The lieutenant shouted to us above the noise. 'Just a minute. The situation is that we've having trouble with the de-icer. We're losing height and we haven't a hell of a lot more height to lose. If you jump now, your parachute won't open, but we'll come to one of these deep valleys in a minute and then it'll be safe to let go. The two civilians, the correspondents, will go first.'

He smiled around at us. He was a wonderful chap. Very nearly he persuaded me that it was all in a day's work. Not quite though. I was so frightened, I had a kind of paralysis. My mind was going so fast that all action seemed to me to be in slow motion. The lieutenant's speech had seemed to me to last about twenty minutes. I had lived half a dozen lives while they were buckling my parachute. It seemed about half a lifetime more before I realized that the plane wasn't jolting any more and seemed to be riding evenly. The engines still kept up their high-pitch screaming.

The dark man came back. 'We're over a deep valley now,' he said, 'but the pilot thinks he has a chance to make Kimpo. So he's not ordering you to jump. If anybody fancies he's better off jumping, he'd better go now.'

There were no takers.

After that we began to sink slowly towards Kimpo with the engines murmuring 'woom-woom, woom-woom, woom-woom, woom-woom.' The dark man came back.

'Fasten lap-straps,' he said, in his efficient voice, parrot-like, and then added as he looked around at us, 'Well, if you can't get a hold of any lap-straps, hang on to sump'n' 'cause we're comin' into Kimpo now.'

It was not a bad introduction to Korea. It had the basic elements which set that war apart from all the others for sheer spiritual abrasion. All over the peninsula, the cold, the wind and the dark conspired to breed fear. Fear seemed to ooze out of the ground. It hung around the terrible skyline which was always much the same wherever you were—row upon row of sharp peaks like sharks' teeth, jagged and very steep, so that the snow didn't lie on their flanks: except at the top, they were black against the snowscape. Whenever you raised your eyes in Korea, what you saw was a threat.

The wind was an enemy you didn't even begin to think of facing—only of avoiding. There was a rotation of wind and calm; after two or three days of ordinary calm, cold weather, when there might well be snow, the wind—a north-west one straight from Siberia—would begin to blow, usually without violence, and it would last for three days. This wind lowered the real air temperature often as much as ten or fifteen degrees, but its effect on the skin was as if the thermometer had suddenly sunk fifty degrees. And it created fear—a quite generalized fear which sapped every kind of morale. I've stood in this wind feeling so small and helpless that I was ready to cry with self pity. It was such an implacable foe. It never let up. It sought you out and wore you down. It was like being nagged beyond endurance. Half an hour was the absolute limit of a sentry's usefulness when the wind was blowing.

Then there were the refugees. At one time that winter, one third of the whole population was out in the snow, moving south day and night, often in 30 degrees of frost. The sight of the refugees, swarming in their thousands down the roads and the railway tracks, was deeply shocking, as if what you saw was humanity itself on the run. And the war seemed suddenly to be nothing rational at all, but a monstrous insanity which had engulfed us all—refugees, allies, enemy—everything. I first saw them on the Han River sand flats at Seoul City, and the first impression they gave us as they approached was one of gaiety. For the women and the children wore the brightest of silk clothes, screaming pink, purple, golden yellow, rose and saffron and acid green. The women carried on their heads bundles as big as baby elephants, tied up in the same gorgeous materials. The little girls also walked erect under bundles proportionate to their size—proportionate according to Korean ideas, that is. I never began to understand how such tiny children carried such loads. Most of the women had babies strapped to their backs, Japanese fashion, with bright silk bands, and the girls and boys of walking age often carried a younger brother or sister. Even children so small as to have to be led by the hand carried their small bundle on their heads. The men, more soberly clad in the wide white clothes of the country or in dark jackets and trousers, had A-frames strapped to their shoulders. These are frames of wood shaped like the letter A with two prongs sticking forward at each end of the crossbar. On one of these frames a Korean peasant can carry four or five hundredweight for ten or more miles a day, more or less for ever. Most of the refugee men were old, or so young as to be barely men at all, for the adults had stayed to look after their farms or been drafted into the army. The procession's air of gaiety faded as it came closer.

They were absolutely silent, the refugees, except for the whimpering of a child, who walked on still, desperately, long after his legs had given up the struggle, and a terrible grunt 'Ugh, Ugh' which an old man gave out at each step. He was bent nearly double under a gigantic load on his A-frame and walked with a stick. His face was streaming with sweat. He wore the baggy white cotton trousers of the peasant, tied at the ankles with a cotton bandage, a black jacket and an American felt hat turned up all round and undented. Every step made his old knees sag and drove out of him the gasping grunt of exhaustion. The children's faces were whipped by the wind until they were as red as polished apples. Tears streamed from their eyes, and the little girls' Japanese haircuts gave them a sturdy appearance which was denied by their flat-footed automatic leg action. It was the gait of the utterly weary.

The Korean War was fought all that winter to the strains of 'Goodnight Irene'. In tents and foxholes and ruined mud-houses and on the snowy tops of mountains, when you tuned in the wireless, that was what you got, take it or leave it. Nearly everybody took it. G.I.'s used to be able to make a kind of mooing noise out of it which lasted them the whole day. It was the hummed accompaniment to every activity. There was nothing gay about it or even sad. It was dreariness made manifest. It, like the wind, was a morale buster.

I'd been in Korea just long enough to assimilate this atmosphere and get used to carrying it around under my belt day and night like an ice-cold lump of lead, when the great story broke: Seoul City fell for the third time. First the North Koreans had taken it, then the Americans took it back, now the Chinese were to have it.

Seoul at that time had a million and a quarter inhabitants of whom 400,000 were refugees from the north. It was bursting with them. Every house was crammed. It's socially impossible in Korea to refuse to receive a relative, and it was a poor refugee who couldn't find some distant relative to claim in Seoul, or indeed anywhere else in the country. About two-thirds of the Korean people share the patronymics, Kim, Pak and Li. To refuse to share your house and food with a fourth cousin three times removed was to lose all face at once, though it wasn't necessary to simulate any joy at the prospect of providing free board and lodging. Wailing was in order.

There were some regulations about overcrowding in Seoul, and the Korean police were having the time of their lives making fortunes out of blackmail, and their other rackets were doing very well too. Black marketeers were flourishing on the material thrown away in the retreats and on leakages from army stores and the police took a big cut out of the black marketeers' ventures. They were not doing badly out of supplying destitute refugee girls to the brothels either, and there were various other enterprises. Middle-class refugees, for instance, hired trucks to drive them south. They paid enormous prices when they were frightened enough for a seat in one of these vehicles. The police had the screw on the drivers because most of the trucks were stolen, and frequently the truck drivers were simply bandits who drove the refugees south onto the lonely roads and cut their throats. If there was nothing else to do, the police could fall back on the old devices which were working better now than ever. Denouncing Communists for instance, a very profitable sideline. People would pay almost anything sooner than be denounced.

I was living in the Biology Room at Seoul University at the time, because the American Public Information Office had requisitioned that building, and I was in the Public Information Office when the great news came through. A French correspondent under the jaundiced eye of the Information Officer, a grizzled old American called Pop, had been saying 'Allo, allo, allo, allo' into the telephone for some time, when Pop took the receiver from him gravely, listened, then jiggled the hooks up and down.

'Operator,' he said, 'operator, operator.' He went on for about two minutes and then flung the receiver on the table. 'Gentlemen,' he said, 'the phone is dead. It's dead because the exchange is closed. You can't get your stories out now so I'm at liberty to give you a little piece of news. We are buggin' out of Seoul. The main part of headquarters has already gone. The rest will begin to move out now. The front line troops in this sector will pass through this evening on their way south and the Chinese are expected to occupy the city a few hours after they leave. You are advised to cross the Han River as soon as possible, for the bridges will be blown up behind the army. That is all, gentlemen. Don't ask me questions, since I have no wish to figure as the father of all the quotes in your stories. Just quote yourselves. I'll tell you one thing more. We are going to Taegu.'

There was an incredulous silence. Taegu was two hundred miles south of Seoul City. It looked like the end. 'Christ,' somebody said, 'it's the end of the bloody war.'

I went straight up to the Biology Room where I was bedded down, to pack. I had two things to do: to get Kim, my Korean stringer, out of the city on a train to the south, and to see that a jeep went to Kimpo airport to meet my colleague, the cameraman, Page, who was flying in that night, if it wasn't too late.

I was halfway up the stairs when the most extraordinary racket broke out on the other side of the compound. All the sash windows flew up as one, and voices began bellowing and roaring and baying to each other like hounds across the square.

'Diddya hear the news?'

'Chinese are just a small piece up the road.'

'It's the bug-out.'

'Well, what are we waiting for?'

'Haul your ass out of there, Murphy.'

'Just get going and keep going.'

'Well, what are we waiting for?'

'Yeah, just up the road.'

'We're waiting on Murphy.'

And suddenly everybody was running about in the compound. The engines of two score of trucks and jeeps began roaring into life, and in a surprisingly short time they slid one by one through the compound gate going very fast. At a quarter past three Kim and I had Seoul University to ourselves. It was by no means a pleasant sensation.

There was nobody in the Biology Room, but the luggage was still there, and a pile of folded blankets showed that Kim had been packing not long before. The beds had gone: they were the property of the P.I.O. There wasn't a sound in the building except the faint moaning of the Siberian wind and the 'ker donk, er donk' of my heavy boots on the bare wooden boards of the floor.

This snatching of the beds so early—by the Korean staff presumably—worried me a little. The Koreans always knew. Perhaps there was some reason for moving out quickly. I felt in my stomach the beginnings of anxiety: fear had not yet bothered to launch a full-scale attack on me, but I could feel in my solar plexus that he had a patrol out, and as usual my mind began to work faster—not better, but faster—and I began to go over the facts of the situation so that no contingency had escaped me. I felt that any minute I might remember some clue to the general situation which would send me roaring down the road to Suwen like a rocket, leaving Page to get out of Kimpo as best he could. But I couldn't see it yet. We packed the jeep with our luggage and I handed Kim about half the money I had with me—about £20—and we set off to catch the train.

The first part of the journey from Seoul University to the railway station ran between rows of little wooden shops with open-stall fronts and flimsy sliding doors of wood and paper. They were middle-class streets, remarkable only for their hysterical show of patriotism. Ever since I had been in Seoul these streets had been one of the sights of the city, celebrated for the festoons of flags—South Korean, Stars and Stripes, Union Jacks—and for the artless inscriptions on thousands of linen banners which used to hang from the eaves of the houses: VICTORY SPEED I PRAY, UNIFY KINDLY! HEARTILY LOVE UNITED NATIONS and so on.

All this was gone. There wasn't a flag left. The street was empty and shutters were locked across the faces of the shops.

Past University Street the road becomes a canyon between eight-storey buildings near the centre of the city. We saw a cat in Town Hall Street, and a little farther on four ragged and dirty children (a very rare sight in Korea, where loss of 'face' as a parent is among the more serious shames) and these were cracking open the shutters of a shop with a wooden pole. They fled at the jeep's approach, except for one shaven-headed, snotty-nosed citizen aged perhaps three years, who stood his ground, gave us an American salute and piped up 'Aw keh'.

At the first bend in Bridge Street, the great thoroughfare where the tramlines run down towards the river and a pontoon bridge a mile to the south, two women were supporting an old man who had, at that moment, died. It had been a sudden collapse, for their bundles, tied up like puddings in enormous cloths, were scattered in the roadway behind them. They were propping him up against the doorstep of a shop, a very old man with a grey beard, a village elder by the country cut of his white clothes. He wore a little black horse-hair top hat tied with a ribbon under his chin.

One of the women, old enough to be his wife, shuffled slowly round under the weight of belongings tied to her back to look at the jeep as it came up. As I stopped it, she raised both her arms and stood extended like a crucifix for a moment before she let them drop to her sides with a smack of finality. The younger woman knelt by the old man's body in the doorway of the shop. There was nothing to be done. Round the next bend in the road we came upon the little band of country refugees from which the old man and his women had dropped out.

In front of us, dropping down a steep hill, lay the last straight three-quarters of a mile of Bridge Street under a powder of snow, and I became aware that there had been for some time past a faint rumble, so indistinct as to be more like a shaking of the air than a definite noise. It was louder now, a continuous muffled thunder, and after another half-minute of jerking the jeep between pot-holes and leaden tramlines, I could see what it was—it was the 'bug-out'. Halfway down this stretch of Bridge Street, the Main Supply Route to the north turns abruptly away to the right, and from the mouth of this street, between tall houses, the stream of military traffic was swinging south to the river, a dark, grey-green stream of tanks, jeeps and trucks, with monstrous bridging and digging machines, guns, troop-carriers and half-track vehicles all jumbled together, pouring out and pounding down towards the pontoon bridge. The American troops, packed upright in their trucks or sitting on their tanks in their conventional panoply of beards and dirt, stared ahead with tough expressions. It was a big moment in the history of the war, but by no means clear in its emotional implications: dramatically, they didn't quite know what to do with it. It was easy to spot the troops who had recently been in action—they had a quite different appearance, tired and quiet, not concerned with drama.

White-helmeted policemen screamed up and down the column in jeeps, cutting out a limping truck here, ordering and fixing a tow there for a vehicle which had cast a track, threatening terrible vengeance on fast trucks trying to jump the column. The faces of the policemen were running with sweat.

It was twenty minutes before they allowed me to join the column, and I talked to an American officer, whose truck on the pavement was the centre of a swarm of mechanics.

'How far behind are the Chinese?'

'Now that's a thing nobody ever seems to know,' said the officer, who was a Texan sort of type—tall, fair, skinny and slow. 'They just seem to turn up in half-millions, anywhere, any time. It's right what Mac says: this is quite a new war, and we've not much idea what to do about it yet. Are you with the British Brigade?'

'I'm a correspondent.'

'I wouldn't ask you,' said the Texan, 'only I haven't had a

drink in weeks and I'm cold, but you boys seem to get all the booze . . .'

I produced my bottle.

'It's strictly illegal,' went on the officer, tilting a good draught of the Korean whisky down his throat; 'we're not supposed to drink this fire water. Does it kill?'

'I'm still alive,' I said.

'No,' said the Texan, 'speaking of the Chinese, I'd say just now their technique has the boys rattled. But not permanently. No, sir. You're a British correspondent, and I'll tell you something. The boys are looking poor now, and they know it, and all this "bug-out" talk and "to hell with the war," that's because they know it. It's like as if looking poor, they gotta make out they're poorer than that. It don't mean much, but it looks damn bad. I know G.I.'s.'

The policeman whistled me back into the column then, and for the next five minutes driving between monstrous vehicles in the deafening din took all my time and attention.

The station squatted, black and hideous, an island in a multi-coloured sea of human beings. The great black Japanese engine, twice the size of an English one, was already letting off throaty hoots from its whistle, and the refugees had rightly assumed that this would be the last train out of Seoul for months—perhaps for ever. About ten thousand optimists were waiting for a place on it. For a radius of a hundred yards around the station they were packed, squatting in the dust, in their padded cotton clothes, the women and children decked out in all their silk finery—three or four layers of it sometimes. Old men, in their antiquated Ming garments and little top hats tied under the chin, smoked 3-foot brass and bamboo pipes, leaning on their bundles. Young men, in Western clothes, stood about talking in high, quarrelsome voices. The children played and cried and laughed. There were little fires with cooking pots here and there, and I stopped the jeep in the middle of the crowd while Kim automatically removed the motor arm and padlocked the gears.

We pushed our way through the crowd towards the American policeman at the station gate.

'Ah dunno why they all sit here' he said to me as I

passed him. 'The train's been full up now for four hours.'

There in front of us was the train, and the huge engine was barely visible through the swarm of human beings condensed upon it. Men, women and children, they were standing on the running plate, sitting on the boiler, on the buffers, clinging not only to every projection but to other people who had hold of a projection. The tender was full of them, and there were three or four on the footplate itself. And behind the engine every one of the thirty-four enormous covered cattle trucks, stretching away far beyond the station itself, was similarly painted with a patchwork quilt of vivid silks. Thirty or forty people sat on top of each truck; there were a dozen clinging desperately above each set of buffers between them.

These were the lucky, the privileged. The mass fought, screamed, and struggled on the platform. Four gisang girls, the geishas of Korea, sat squealing pleasurably on the nearest coach roof, powdered and elegant among the moon-faced peasant women. A hawk-faced crone sat on the engine's running-board, glowering about her and gripping the hand-rail in a grasp that death itself wouldn't shift. (In fact, death itself didn't shift it. Later, I watched that train come into Taegu. The old woman was still on the running board, and she was dead.)

I was fascinated by the sight of an old man who jogged up and down the platform at a slow but frenzied trot, carrying an old woman on his back. Frequently in the press, he was forced to a halt, but still his feet jigged away in 'double mark time'. His eyes were fixed on the train as if it were the Holy Grail.

Under the hiss of steam the prevailing noise was the wailing of children.

It took me an hour to get Kim on that train, and I was shameless. I used every official dodge I knew. I threatened, I lied, I bribed. Finally I begged—from an American sergeant who seemed to have some position of authority.

'What goes on here?' he enquired, pushing in.

'I kept this boy so long doing my packing that somebody's taken his place on the train.'

'No room,' said the Korean Station-Master, spreading his hands, although I had bribed him.

'You a correspondent?'

'Yes.'

'You're the guys with all the booze.'

I handed him the bottle.

'Well, how goes the war?' said the sergeant, inclined to gossip.

'I was going to ask you,' I said.

He handed me back the bottle and put his head in the cattle truck door.

'Plenny of space in here,' he said, 'plenny. In you go, kid.' And Kim dived in.

Even in that hour that I'd spent on the station the situation in the city had grown worse. As I put in the clutch to turn in to Capitol Corner, four deliberate rifle shots crashed out quite close at hand, from the direction of the bazaar by the Mai Ja apartments. I went up University Road pretty fast, but noticed on a wide wooden door, freshly chalked, the hammer and sickle and AMERICANS GO HOME.

And then my tyres were crackling on the University gravel. Standing on the gravel, looking around him with the air of a man who had seen many other and better places, was a British soldier.

I recognized him as one of the R.A.S.C. drivers attached to the British Public Relations Unit.

'Good evenin', Mr Catford,' said the driver pleasantly. 'I bin looking for you. This is Mr Page's jeep, isn't it?'

'It is,' I said, 'and I should be at Kimpo to meet him now.'

'Yes sir, well. Captain Haytor sent me down here to collect the jeep and go and meet Mr Page at Kimpo. He said perhaps you'd like to come up to the billet for a drink, if you were still in town, sir?'

'The billet?'

'Yes sir, you know, 2 P.R.S. Press billet.'

'Good Lord, is Captain Haytor up there by himself?'

'No sir, there's me and another driver and two or three Australian correspondents. We're in a bit of a mess like. We've no transport. No wheels at all.'

'Here, hold on,' I said. 'I'll get my typewriter. Have a drink.'

'I don't mind. Gets a bit parky—well, all the best.'

So it was stuck in the press billet with very little hope of ever getting out of it again, that we watched the fall of Seoul. First a series of brutal explosions shook the little house and panes of glass tinkled on the floor as the petrol and ammunition dumps were blown one after another. And then at about midnight I was roused from a sour doze by the voice of the press officer.

'I don't know whether any of you are interested, but the whole place is on fire.'

We climbed the stairs to the leads again, stumbling in the dark. The wind moaned in the hollows of a stone lantern in the garden and whispered in the fir trees. Seoul was burning. Over the whole of the southern and western perimeter of the city bristled an aureole of crimson light; and nearer, dotted about in the black sea of roof tops, which rolled right up to the base of our pyramid, a dozen islands of orange flame grew—one big one was recognizable by the light it shed on the tiny streets about it as an area near the Capitol building, and, like a small moon above the flames, the scaffolded dome glowed pink. Another big blaze silhouetted the big Chosen Hotel.

At intervals, now of less than half a minute, the rattle and crackle of automatic fire drifted up to our ears with an occasional closer burst like a racing motor cycle engine in the streets immediately below us. One was so close that in the silence which followed it we could hear the click of a gun bolt and laughter and voices in the gully at the pyramid's base.

And then at last we heard the jeeps.

It must have been two in the morning when we put out the fires in the press billet and moved into the street. Ahead of us rows of tip-tilted roofs were silhouetted against a crimson glow. We headed towards the fire. The streets were completely deserted, and for nearly a mile utterly dark. It was a sudden discovery at one roundabout that the whole side of the street ahead of us was dully lit by a red light, low down. A minute later, and we needed no more jeep lights, for a brilliant orange glare danced on the house fronts and made the long shadows move in the gutters, and we heard the roar and crackle of the fire. Three men in the uniforms of Korean soldiers or policemen went slinking down an alley off this street, with their rifles held at the ready and the packs on their backs full to bursting with loot; a great silver cup thrust its bowl out of one haversack and a roll of purple silk was tied to the shoulder straps of another. The men moved off down the orange-coloured ravine of the alley, warily like prowling cats, in single file.

In University Road a quarter of a mile of wooden shops was well alight from end to end, the flames curling upwards from horizontal timbers, and inside an orange sea of flame. Rolls of silk lay scattered on the road all the way to Capitol Corner, and at the crossroads before that, where four streets were burning together, a group of black-jacketed figures fled from the jeep's approach, dropping bundles on the road as they ran. Here the crackle of the fire became a roar and every few minutes a floor or roof collapsed in a shower of sparks with a noise like the delivery of a ton of coal. It was pleasantly warm in the burning street, and we stopped there for five minutes warming our hands at the fire.

Bridge Street was blazing. The dead old man sprawled over the pavement, his white clothes now orange in the glare. At Main Supply Route corner, halfway down the last half mile, the military traffic had thinned to a trickle emerging between blazing cliffs from the north road, and the British Military Police were on duty at the roundabout. The fires in North Road were fifty or sixty yards away from them, so they had heaped up a great bonfire of wood in the centre of the roundabout to keep them warm.

As we left the policemen and moved slowly down Lower Bridge Street a dozen fat rats ran drunkenly across the street. The M.S.R. roundabout marked the end of the fire's progress, and twenty yards south of it the cold and darkness poured over and into us again. Ahead of us the road lay black, but seemed to run between hundreds of flickering lights at ground level, until it reached the long hump of the Han River embankment, faintly discernible as a black wall against the navy blue sky. And hardly had the crackling of the fire died behind us to a murmur when we were among the flickering lights: they were the camp fires of thousands of refugees who had been forbidden to cross the river until dawn. At the end of Bridge Street, where the policemen had stopped them, they had sat down. Moved off the road, they had claimed the pavements, and now upwards of two thousand of them squatted there on each side of the road, two long quarter-miles of packed, enduring humanity. They had broken up flimsy houses on either side of the end of Bridge Street and were burning the pieces so as to keep alive during the night. I shall never be able to think of 'the family circle' as an abstract idea again. Here was the original primitive organization itself. Each family of refugees had dropped its bundles and piled them in a circle, perhaps eight or nine feet across. This kept the wind from their backs as they crouched in a ring round the fire which dug a little tent of light above them out of the bitter night.

A thousand of these little tents reared themselves out of the darkness as far as the base of the Han River Embankment. The refugees squatted there, knees to chin, gazing into the fire, waiting for sunrise. Only the children showed the slightest animation. There seemed to be very few youths or grown-up girls among the refugees here: the most usual family group was an old man and woman with two or three children. They fed their fires with cupboards, window-frames, boxes and ornamental carvings from the middle-class houses of Bridge Street. Brass pots full of rice were bubbling on some of the fires.

And then we were on the bridge. The naked lights slung from a pole in the sand showed a yard or two of olive-green ice beyond each rubber pontoon. Ice and pontoons were all one mass and the bridge did not give an inch to the weight of the heaviest vehicle. 'Ker-donk, ker-donk, ker-donk' went our jeep on the joints of the runway. We mounted the ten-foot slope at the end and we were on sand again. We were south of the river. We ran on for a hundred yards, turned off the track and stopped. I had known it with dread all the time, but hadn't dared realize it before. Without blankets, sleeping bag or whisky, I was going to spend the night on the Han River sand flats.

It took me a day and a half to get down to Taegu in the bug-out traffic. At last I lifted a telephone I'd waited four hours for, and spoke to my colleague in Tokyo.

'I've a hell of a story,' I said. 'Have you got a girl to take dictation?'

'Okay, but it's not the fall of Seoul, is it? That was a nice story the day before yesterday. What else have you got?'

XII

All the Bright Night Long

On a Saturday morning in August, 1953, a far from cosy scene was going on in one of the B.B.C.'s offices off Portland Place.

'What the hell is this?' the boss was saying. He was a big bull of a man, curly hair and everything, and he was up on his feet and shouting. He flourished a newspaper clipping which announced that I was going to South Africa with *Picture Post*'s photographer to do a series of features.

'That's right,' I said.

'Whaddya mean, that's right? You're contracted to me.'

'Only while you keep me working. When not working for you, I can work for anyone. It's in the contract.'

'It is not.'

'It is.'

'It is not.'

'Well, get the contract and have a look at it.' We stood eyeball to eyeball while the contract came. 'Here it is,' I said. ' "... Except when actually employed upon a Features assignment" etcetera, etcetera, "retainer" etcetera, etcetera, "each assignment by separate contract" etcetera.'

'How long have you been doing nothing?'

'Lawrence,' I said, 'I've been sitting in the pub opposite for two solid months drinking my retainer and now I'm off to South Africa.'

'You're not, you're going to the North Pole. Tomorrow.'

We both sat down.

'Yes?' I said.

'Slight exaggeration,' the boss said. 'Not the North Pole but not far away. Queen Louise Land, North Greenland. Equally cold and unpleasant. At least I hope so. *Picture Post*!' he said. 'Well, get a lot of warm clothes and spiked boots and so on, and get off down to Pembroke Dock and ask for Squadron Leader McGuire. I want a damn good feature—about an hour. If you're not back in a fortnight you'll be stopping up there for the winter. McGuire will tell you all about that.'

It took British Railways an unconscionable time to get me to Pembroke Dock. Sunday, it was. A desert—not a cup of tea, not a bite to eat: just clanking and jolting on and on for ever and ever. Squadron Leader McGuire turned out to be one of those Irishmen from the north, a redheaded one. Do you know the kind of Irishman who finishes a folk song with a gay twitch of the head before the pipes stop and the final yell? That kind of Irishman: admirable rather than safe. The kind I'd heard junior R.A.F. men in the war refer to as 'a press-on type'. In the Mess he introduced me to the officers of his squadron and led the way to a table with a map spread on it.

'Now you want a large drink and I'll give you the gen,' he said. 'Well, there's this party of scientists in the Arctic—twenty-five of them—expecting their stores for the winter. They're camped at Britannia Lake: that's in Queen Louise Land, 79 degrees North, a long way up, more than six hundred miles beyond the Arctic Circle. Well, the plan was for a ship called the *Polar Sirkel* to take out of Deptford, nose its way up through the pack ice with all the stores to a fjord called Young Sound. D'ye see on the map here, Young Sound, two hundred miles south of Britannia Lake? She should 'a got there by the 26th of July (it's clear of heavy ice by then) and dumped the stores on shore. We'd have been there about the 3rd of August, when the ice melts on Britannia Lake and we'd have had nearly three weeks to cart the stuff up to the Lake. Well now, the *Polar Sirkel* has broken down in the North Sea. She won't be at Young Sound till the 12th. The lake freezes up again on the 21st, so that leaves us nine days for the whole operation. Since there's only fifty per cent flying weather up there, that's cut to five days with luck. If the lake freezes over before we get out of Queen Louise Land, then we'll have to stay there till next summer, or walk down to the warm water level which might take nearly as long. So ye see the point. We fly tomorrow at nine o'clock. Motto, "press on." Now get your drink down ye and go to bed. Here's to Operation Britannia,' he said, and we downed our enormous pink gins.

Next morning, a hot, brilliant summer day, we took off into a fleckless blue sky for Iceland in five Sunderland flying-boats. They don't make Sunderlands any more, but they were splendid machines, very thick for their length, square-shouldered thirty-ton jobs which could carry five or six tons for hours on end, urbane and equable under almost any conditions. We watched Wales keel over and vanish astern and the Isle of Man come briefly into sight, and then we were over Northern Ireland, and the Squadron Leader called me up on the inter-com to show me, miles below, the lonely farmhouse in County Antrim which was his home, and the rest of the day we zoomed on in a mid-blue sky over a dark blue sea to the Arctic Circle.

The Sunderlands made a loud deep buzzing noise like bumble-bees and they didn't have names: they were called by the signallers' versions of the letters of the alphabet—Able, Baker, Charlie, Dog and Easy. Big, unpretentious, good tempered beasts, alighting in the evening like fat silver moths, exactly to schedule, on the dark blue water of Reykjavik harbour under that odd little town of mustard yellow, sage green and pink corrugated iron.

It was very hot in Reykjavik, but the light had a northern quality, a lack of heaviness, and everybody in the town obviously knew each other so well that we felt like men from Mars. Iceland suffers, as all northern lands do, under dire drink laws. It was impossible, they told us, for us to get a drink in Reykjavik except at one hotel which was designated as the R.A.F. H.Q. whenever there were any R.A.F. men in Iceland. That evaded the law, so that's where we went. And it suits me,' the Squadron Leader said. 'I don't want. you lot stravaguing around the town. Remember this'll be the last night's sleep any of ye'll get for a week.' So we sat down at long trestle tables with dirty cloths to huge clumping platefuls of meat and mashed potatoes and an hour-long sweet course of thick, creamy, treacly pudding and very good coffee, and Aalburg schnapps from Denmark, while the gramophone gave out over and over again the latest Scandinavian top of the pops.

We went to bed in bright sunshine and we woke in a sort of twilight at about three in the morning. Everybody in Reykjavik was up and about. We had an enormous breakfast of porridge and meat-filled omelettes. There was a ragged black sky blowing in half a gale a few feet above the rooftops. We took a taxi to the meteorological station, on a bluff over a raging green sea. It was very modern in the functional way, all polished blocks of exquisite woods and bars of chromium and glass.

The pilots stayed in the waiting room while the Squadron Leader and I penetrated to the oracle's inner chamber, a cube papered with maps and charts and liberally sprinkled with dials and machines which clicked in corners, to themselves, ruminatively. There was a big black-haired man with a Chinese sort of moustache, sitting at a desk in the middle.

'What are you wanting, Mister?'

'Weather up the East Coast of Greenland, to Young Sound.' The Met man telephoned twice and we waited in silence while two girls handed him sheafs of papers from which he made notes.

'When are you wanting to go, Mister?'

'About now.'

'Nice day for suicide, Mister.'

'What's the difficulty?'

'Fog all the way, very thick from sea level right up.'

'Where's your information from?'

'Yes, Mister, you're right. It don't mean much. Three ships and two land stations, none of them very far north, nothing anywhere near Young Sound.'

'Really you don't know.'

'Right, but all the indications, all.'

'Okay, thanks very much.'

'I could stop you going, Mister.'

'It'd take you too long. G'bye.'

'Good luck, Mister.'

'The Denmark Strait is solid fog,' the Squadron Leader told the pilots. 'Beyond that they know very little, but the indications are that's solid, too. So we'll go. I mean to say, there's no point in sitting here on our bottoms waiting for weather reports. We'll go on up there and find out. I think there's a good chance we might find some breaks near the coast. I'll go in Able and have a shufty, and if I can't get through I'll make back to Iceland. You in Dog,' he said to a tall Welshman called Parry, 'take off a half hour behind me, and I'll send back my weather reports, and, if I do find a break, you'll know to come on and follow right through. No, you'd better keep an hour behind—that'll put you 120 miles after me and give me plenty of time to turn round. Right, off we go then, and the best of luck.' He turned to me. 'You can come with me if you like.'

'Fine,' I said, and reaped the blessing of sudden inner warmth that an actor gets when he knows he's brought off a difficult line. It didn't last long.

Able took off into a glass of milk, and in that glass of milk she remained for three and a half hours, flying due north. I shared the pilot's lofty perch with a navigator and second pilot. The Squadron Leader kept up a running commentary on the inter-com.

'Those Met men are scientists you know. That's the trouble. He knows very little more than I do about the Greenland weather but what he does know is scientific. So the faintest scientific indication becomes a great faith when there's nothing else to go on. The real horse-racing odds are about seven to one that he's wrong. Anyway, I've sixteen hours of petrol, so time enough to worry when we're eight hours out.'

After four hours of it, I went down the stairs into the wardroom, a box made of aluminium girders—a cube of about eight feet, where they were brewing coffee. Every inch of the ship except the pilot's cabin was crammed with Arctic stores and equipment. Even in the wardroom you sat on sacks of dried yellow fish like stones. There were huge drums of paraffin, sugar and flour in sacks, two great sledges, a pumping engine, chests of tea and dynamite, hundreds of tins of dried milk, biltong wrapped in canvas, blankets, soap, an army cooking stove, everything roped to stanchions and staples, everything creaking and shifting a millimetre or so as the plane veered. The fog was so thick you couldn't see the end of the wing. On the inter-com the Squadron Leader kept us informed, as we froze and shivered in our metal box, in spite of our layers of clothing, our wind-proof overalls and knee-length fur-lined boots.

He'd tried to get above the fog, he said, but couldn't fly high enough. He'd then flown between two layers of fog roving up and down following a thin seam of comparative visibility. That had now given out into thick fog, and now he was going to try to get under it. We came down to fifty feet and found that we could see.

Above us the fog was a low grey ceiling and below us the sea was like a pewter tray. In the dirty light, the icebergs below us looked like chunks of plaster. Huge, but somehow quite unimpressive, they came and went beneath our floats hour after hour. Where the icebergs were absent, the pack ice filled the surface of the sea with a litter of jagged shapes like a smashed pane of white glass. At one time, in pursuit of visibility, the Squadron Leader came down to about 20 feet. His cheerful voice could be heard on the inter-com bawling out 'up periscopes', but even his optimism was on its last legs when, after seven hours under the fog, all in a minute it cleared. The water and the icebergs glittered blue and amethyst in the sunshine; we sailed between brown peaks up a fjord of Mediterreanean blue with one great green iceberg sparkling in it. There was the supply ship and there, on the low brown shore under the mountains, were three huts in a litter of sledges and petrol drums and boxes of food. The Expedition's Southern Base. This was Young Sound—seventy five degrees north.

The first noticeable thing was the silence: and the second, the air's astonishing clarity. Every detail of the brown mountain in front of us, every rock, every little stream was clear and sharp. I reckoned the Sound a mile wide, but it was in fact seven. It was like a warm December day in England but the water was so cold you pulled your hand out of it as if it had been burnt. Nothing in the whole brown mossy landscape grew more than six inches high.

The Squadron Leader was so impatient to begin his task that within an hour he'd taken off to see if he could make the Lake that night, though the weather reports spoke of thick fog. It was dreadful weather to fly in, and the Squadron Leader was in fact lost in it for a brief time. He came back cursing, but there was nothing to do but wait for the break. All that night in bright sunshine—the sun wouldn't set for another fortnight but rambled around the top of the mountains red as a blood orange—all that night, the work of loading and unloading went on. McGuire's orders were pointed and succinct.

'Doc,' he said to the Medical Officer, 'lock up all the drink. Nobody touches a drop until the job's done. We'll be very lucky if anybody gets as much as three hours sleep in the twenty-four.'

To me, he said, 'Now I know you'd like to lend a hand but I'd be terribly pleased if you wouldn't. You see, everybody knows exactly what he has to do—it's rather like a sort of complicated dance and an extra partner who didn't know his steps would throw them all out. Get some sleep or talk to the trappers or just watch. Anything you like. See you Wednesday.'

I watched the loading for some time, and then moved inland along the shore to where the other two huts, the salmon net and a big scatter of pale wooden barrels broke the tobacco brown monotony of the valley's floor. Two hundred yards, I reckoned: it was more like a mile and a half. At closer range the brown floor was less monotonous. I moved through flocks of birds with long red legs which barely took the trouble to move aside as I passed. The tundra was covered in patches of white, acres of it sometimes, where some little plant six inches high presented to the sky a tuft of cottonwool where the flowerhead ought to be, and there was quite a variety of little blue and yellow flowers among the moss, and brown tufts of what looked like wire.

The net stretched a hundred feet or so across the Sound. You could see the salmon in their hundreds caught by the gills in the mesh. One Dane in a red woolly cap was hauling himself along the net in a canvas boat which he was filling with fish. The other, with a blue and white stocking cap which fell over his left ear, was pressing the fish into barrels between layers of salt. He had thirty barrels filled and nailed up, and about another hundred empty. A mountain of fish guts rose on the narrow shelving beach, down to the water's edge.

'Hello,' he called out, 'I'm Pieter, that is Jens. Your name please.' I told him. 'We'll finish in about an hour, and then we leave the net for six hours to fill up. You want to help? All right, we finish quicker. I gut them—that's a trick you have to know. You pack—like this.'

It was quite easy. You put two inches of coarse salt in the bottom of a barrel. You dipped a gutted fish in salt, spread it cut side down on the salt in the barrel and then another and another until they covered the surface, put in another layer of salt and then bash the whole thing solid with a baulk of timber. Then another layer of fish and so on.

'Something for the ship to take back,' said Pieter. 'Six shillings a pound in Denmark, eight shillings in England.' Jens came ashore and began to gut the fish. 'We've been here three years,' said Jens, 'catching the white fox—you catch him in the winter in traps made of stone. He takes the bait and then a big stone falls down crack and breaks his neck. This is a terrible week for us when the ship comes. We have to make the great decision.'

'What decision?' They looked at each other and roared with laughter.

'Go or stay,' said Pieter. 'Stay another year or go back with the ship. Every year it is the same. Now I say go. He say stay.'

'Next year will be better,' said Jens.

'You don't know that, you just say so.'

'Couldn't be worse.'

'Has it been a bad year?' I asked. They looked at each other.

'Shall we tell him Jens?'

'No, no, everybody will laugh.'

'I tell you,' Jens said, 'but for God's sake don't laugh.'

'Oh don't laugh,' said Pieter.

'Last year,' said Jens, staring ahead like a man with a vision, 'we are catching little white foxes—seven. Don't laugh.'

'Seven,' said Pieter. 'Year before, sixty. Year before that four hundred seventy two—and we are rich.'

'What does silver fox fetch now?' I asked.

'Silver—that's it. Well, the price goes up and down. Fifty

pays expenses: a hundred—all right, I settle. Two hundred very good. Four hundred seventy two, very, very rich.'

They filled a huge wicker basket with fish guts, cut four or five salmon into large pieces and put them on top, added one small whole fish and we all set off uphill to the hut with this load.

In a hollow in the ground out of the wind, fifteen husky dogs like thick blunt Alsatians were hitched to two long cables pegged out on the gravel. They whined and snarled as we approached, and the two Danes threw the fish guts to them.

'All stores finished,' said Jens, indicating a great black patch where the coal had stood, reduced now to a few bucketsfull. 'All the dried fish finished. These bastards are eating salmon now at six shillings a pound, eight in London.' He threw the chunks of fish at the dogs. 'And this little one for us,' he said, and we went into the hut.

A Danish trapper's hut which is built to a government specification is a fine implement for survival. It's a cube of about eighteen feet with a sloping roof, one door and one small double window. Inside there's another cube about a couple of yards smaller, so that there's a three foot wide passage all round the inner cube. The door to the inner room is on the opposite side from the outer door. The passage is full of gear hung on hooks on both walls, so you have to push your way through sideways, and the roof space is filled with more gear, tents and bedding and tarpaulins, extra furs and parkas and so on. The main feature of the inner cabin is a big flat iron stove with an oven and four holes in the top with iron covers. One wall had built-in cupboards and three built-in bunks, with openings just big enough to crawl into. There's a wooden table, two benches, three easy chairs in wood and canvas, rows of cooking-pots, three guns on the wall and a big coloured photograph of a sailing ship.

Pieter put an eighteen inch iron frying pan on the stove, cut the salmon into steaks and put them in to sizzle. Jens wound the gramophone into action.

'My God, are we sick of that tune,' said Jens, 'but we can't get our new stores out of the ship until your operation Britannia, is finished. All the vodka gone, all the whisky, all the schnapps. Nothing but Benedictine, present from a friend, we don't like it.' He sloshed out three mugs full. For the next two or three hours we stuffed ourselves with salmon, oven-baked bread and Benedictine, while the Danes told fearful stories of life in the Arctic winter night. Jens had once lost all his dogs in the second night of a blizzard, and had thereafter lain under snow in a little tent, without hope, for nine days, while the blizzard blew itself out. On the tenth, by a miracle, Pieter found him.

'I had no idea where I was,' Jens said, 'you could see nothing. I must have been driving in circles the first day of the blizzard. In the end I was only three miles from the hut.'

They let me have the third bunk, and when I woke up they were quarrelling in thick voices in Danish.

'Pieter is a damn fool,' said Jens, when I joined them. 'What, leave now, with all our losses!' They glared at each other.

'Fresh air, what we need,' Pieter said, 'fresh air.' He picked up a squeeze box and we moved outside. The world outside was as we'd left it, bright, utterly calm and still.

'We shall dance,' Pieter said, 'to show we are friends. It is the dance of the midnight sun.' Solemnly they capered about on the brown moss like a couple of bears. The peaks, the red-legged birds looked on in silence.

It was not until three o'clock in the morning the following day that I left for Britannia Lake. We circled twice over the Sound and headed straight over the top of the mountain into the sun, due north. Even then, in August, in the height of the short Arctic summer, the country below us was terrifying. The brown, bare mountains were so steep as to be more like cliffs. Seven thousand feet, some of them were. Most of them were capped with snow and their narrow valleys half filled with ice. To our left, the ice cap, a tremendous dome of ice which covers nine-tenths of Greenland, rose into a whitish sky showing no horizon. To our right, the jagged coastline had a rim of glittering icebergs. We crossed the glacier called Storstrom—a thirty-mile-wide river of dull white ice, so rough that it looked as if a sea had suddenly frozen solid at the height of a great storm. And we were lucky enough to spot a herd of musk ox, now very rare and protected game. Even in his hurry, the Squadron Leader couldn't resist going down to almost two hundred feet to inspect the musk oxen, very melancholy looking animals, a sort of mournful buffalo with long hair like weeping willows. To our delight when the plane shadow crossed them they formed up at once in a defensive group with the calves in the middle, and all round them a circle of great horns with their tips less than two feet from the ground waiting for the charge. At last we caught the glitter of the Lake between grey mountains, long and steep and shaped like coal-pit banks in the North of England. Six miles of grey water, opaque like milk, lying between two walls of white ice—the ends of the glaciers which fed it. And there, crouching between the mountain flank and a long bed of boulders, on a tiny grey shore where an iceberg bobbed, lay a yellow matchbox of a hut which was the Expedition's northern base. We scouted round the iceberg and settled on the water which was exactly as cold as ice—thirty-two degrees.

The figure at the rudder of the motor-boat which came racing towards us over the water might well have been Robinson Crusoe himself. He was dressed in filthy rags and tatters, patched in half a dozen colours. A great tangled black beard lay on his chest, and he peered out of a thicket of hair in which he'd cut a sort of window so that he could see. He turned out to be a geo-physicist.

'My word, we were excited when we heard the plane,' he said. 'We all dropped what we were doing and rushed outside, and George had a wash.' Outside the hut when we reached it, forty-one sledge dogs, tethered along a stream, were howling and baying in the thirty-knot wind which blew off the glacier.

They were not all scientists. Some of them, including the commander of the Expedition, were officers in the Services: experts on such subjects as Arctic travel, or dog teams or surveying. Some of these, notably the commander, a naval man, were as neat as their company was shaggy.

They had been in the Arctic a year and by now knew the worst. And the worst had been pretty tough. Now thoroughly aroused by the challenge of unloading the stores in time for us to get out, they threw themselves on the work like a commando going into action. I could only talk to them as they climbed into bed in the few minutes before they slept, or while they snatched a meal of thick stew made from pemmican, which, with coffee, flowed all day and night from the kitchen. Nobody knew much about Queen Louise Land, they said—it wasn't even mapped except by photography. The geology was a mystery—the ice cap was a mystery. Greenland was rather like a badly iced cake with the icing humped in the middle and not quite reaching the edge where the mountains were. On the other hand, bits of it dribbled right over the edge and down into the sea. These were the glaciers. Nobody even knew if Greenland was a land. The ice cap might be supported by islands. They had a team living out under the surface of the ice cap two hundred miles inland, part of whose job was to find out about this with an echo-sounding apparatus. You fired off an explosive charge and waited until the echo came back. That team had been under the ice out there for six months. The rest of them were divided into teams, geological, geographical, wind and weather, biological, glaciological—all sorts. They sometimes stayed out for months at a time. Most of the travelling had to be done in spring and autumn by sledge. In the summer there was no snow, and in the Arctic winter the business of picking your way between the crevasses with dog sledges in the dark was a thing only to be attempted in dire necessity. It wasn't easy, they said, and later some of them took me for a walk out on the glacier, and I began to see what they meant.

The base hut was warm and, in a simple way, comfortable. It was built in the shape of an 'L' and the southern half contained eight very small bedrooms. There were four bunks in each, two up and two down, and a foot of gangway and that was all. Then came the large dining and living room with tables and benches and a wireless set and a gramophone, and next door, the kitchen. In the other wing were the laboratories where the scientists worked, and the wireless transmitter. Oil stoves heated the hut. There was electric light from a little engine inside the back porch.

Every two hours a Sunderland landed on the lake or took

off. From the dining room window, where I sat for a day and a night to waylay the members of the expedition as they came in exhausted from their stint of unloading, you had a perfect view of the arrivals and departures.

Each Sunderland came in over the long pitbank mountain, suddenly appearing, glittering in the sun. Each one did a half turn as it came into sight, came down on the water leaving a wake of white spray, disappeared for a second behind the big iceberg, about three hundred yards from the shore, and then taxied round to the harbour, circumspectly, giving the iceberg a wide berth: and before the plane was at rest, the motor launches would be scuttering out to meet her. But taking off was different. You could get a straight run long enough to take off at an angle across the lake, by shaving the iceberg very close, within about ten yards. And this was what everybody did. From the hut it looked extremely dangerous.

All through the airlift, the thirty knot wind blew around the building, the dogs whined, the gramophone played on. Finally, one day or night or afternoon or morning or evening, the Squadron Leader was suddenly there in the hut, in the middle of a group of tired men with their mouths hanging open. They included the Danish trappers from Young Sound. In a heavy silence he ticked off the items on a waybill, pushed back his cap and made the great announcement.

'All right then, that's the lot then. Is there a drink in the house?'

He'd delivered so remorseless an attack on the problems of the airlift that his assessment of three hours sleep in the twenty-four for everybody had been an overestimate. On 16th August the job was done. With muscles aching and their eyes sunk in their heads, the expedition relaxed. The ban on alcohol was lifted. At Young Sound the Army and the Air Force celebrated all the bright night long among the Arctic poppies and the clumps of golden moss.

By midnight at Britannia Lake a party was in progress which threatened the very structure of the hut itself.

At about three in the morning the whole crowd moved down to the beach to cheer the Squadron Leader on his way to Young Sound. They sang the 'Eton Boating Song' as the boat ferried him out to his aircraft Charlie. They sang 'Will Ye No Come Back Again' as his engine started up. He taxied into position and then across the lake on the short cut across the iceberg's bows and at that moment the iceberg, which had stood like a monument during the whole operation, turned over right in his path and split up. Somehow the Squadron Leader contrived to miss the ice, but he had too much way on to stop. Charlie hit the rocks on the north shore with a noise like a giant trampling on a huge tin tray. Badly holed, she lay there well down by the nose. McGuire emerged, grave but undamaged.

Then began the great epic of rescuing Charlie before the ice set in. First they fixed boats at anchor in the lake. Through adjustable pulleys attached to the boats they ran a long rope from the shore to a ring on the aircraft's tail. The whole expedition pulled and heaved on this rope, hour after hour, grunting and sweating even in the wind off the glacier. The Danish trappers sat all night sewing a great canvas binder to pass round the nose of the aircraft to lessen the flow of water, so that she could be pumped out. The Expedition fitted rubber dinghies under her floats, and buoyed her up with another under her belly. Two sergeants stayed in her on the water for a day and a night, pumping her out and trying to stop the holes. Their arms were plunged for hours in the freezing water. They plugged her with plasticene, oakum and concrete. Finally, after two days, the Squadron Leader said he thought she might take off.

And this time it was a silent send-off. McGuire climbed in and headed up the lake. One of his pilots stood next to me, and during the take-off, he writhed and twisted, and at one point went down on his knees.

'Oh, come on, Mac. Come on, boy. Lift her. Oh, she won't do it. Come up, you bitch, come up. Oh, for God's sake. He's off. Jesus . . .'

It was 75 seconds before she lifted, and she climbed over the glacier at the mouth of the Lake with six feet to spare.

That was it, then. The Danes and I said goodbye to the Expedition. They gave me an iron ration of biltong as a souvenir—dried antelope meat which tastes agreeably like the cedar pencils you used to chew at school.

In the little cold box of the wardroom the Danes argued all the way to Young Sound.

'Will you make up your mind, Pieter?'

'You're a damn fool, Jens.'

We taxied up alongside their hut, and a boat came off for them.

'Toss for it,' the pilot said.

'O.K., Jens.'

'O.K., Pieter.'

'Heads we stay.'

The pilot spun the half-crown. Heads.

The Danes climbed into the boat. Wewatched them land on the sand, push their way through the red-legged birds, over the golden moss into the hut, and presently, before we left, the gramophone came to us faintly across the water.

Thirty-six hours later, it was Sunday, and British Railways was carting me slowly through Wales. All my enquiries about food and drink received the same answer. 'Oh no, Sunday, see.' Days later, it seemed, at Reading, their eyes were snapping with indignation, they were saying, 'Oh no, Sunday!' There was nothing for it. I opened my suitcase and took out my souvenir—the biltong. In the frozen wastes of Queen Louise Land I had not felt the need of it. Here in Great Britain things were different. It lasted all the way to London.

XIII

The Red Roads of Nigeria

I it begins to be felt south of the Sahara—the awful presence of Africa. The first of its flavours is a sense of immense antiquity which has nothing to do with history; nothing to do with cultures or ruins; nothing you an attach any sentiments to. It simply says: 'As it was in the beginning, is now, and ever shall be.'

And the next thing you notice is that Africa was designed by a child. Who else could have thought of a giraffe or a hippopotamus? Only a shilling paintbox could have inspired this sky of ultramarine, the chrome yellow corn straw everywhere, the frank emerald green of the vegetation and the curly roads in crimson lake.

And the humble squalor of Africa is childish, too. In the courtyards of baked mud, the litter of dirty tins with wire handles, old bicycle wheels, and scabby three-legged kitchen chairs. Broken pots, corrugated iron, and triangles of looking glass hung on rusty nails—a slum-child's treasure island, glittering in the sun. And lastly—and this creeps up on you a little later—everywhere, just out of sight, something odd is lurking; something shocking but humble and familiar, something on the lines of a scarecrow. African ghosts have no grandeur, no dignity, no explanation, and they are not tragic; they simply make your hair stand straight up on end. In Ilorin, for instance, there is a cooking pot which walks about at night. This presence, a tinge of lunacy, is an inseparable part of the African experience. Nowhere is it stronger than in Nigeria. The B.B.C. made me free of the red roads of Nigeria for three months in 1959. That was a few years before Independence, and Nigeria was regarded as a showpiece. It was the supreme example, we claimed, of a great, raw piece of Africa now tamed and civilized, equipped with democratic institutions, and at last ripe and ready for its separate life as a nation. My brief was simple; take three months and bring back Nigeria alive and kicking in six long radio feature programmes.

As it turned out, these programmes were never broadcast or even written. What I brought back from this most fascinating assignment now exists only in my head and in a few rolls of tape in the B.B.C. archives.

For me, Nigeria began in Lagos under a sky of frosted glass, so bright that it was difficult to keep your eyes open. Wisps of steamy cloud blew about and the town smelt like an airing cupboard full of old blankets.

I dutifully signed the book at the Governor's residence—stone lions, a stern, off-white façade, the Union Jack and the stamp of sentries' boots on gravel: the official British moment abroad, drab as an income tax form and guaranteed to depress you for the day. 'Though when you come to think of it,' I said to myself as I went out towards the leaden sea, 'these are the people who'll get me out of trouble if there is any.' And since I was already irritated by authority, I might as well get it all over at once, and make the only other official call on my list; on the travel permit office. So I walked along the sea front to the government offices. Lagos had a makeshift look in spite of the modern office blocks and some areas of solid old colonial buildings of real charm and character. It was full of gaps, where shanty towns of mud and corrugated iron only half hid themselves down stinking alleys and mud tracks. The people, on the other hand, the black people that is, had a certain magnificence of manner and attitude, derived, it seemed to me, from sheer health and strength and lack of inhibition. Groups of them were holding hands, laughing, on the pavements—and really laughing; you could hear them fifty yards away. The approved stance among friends seemed to be a sort of laughing arrogance, particularly effective among groups of huge black men like kings in splendid robes of green and blue with their chins held high, lazily inspecting the earth they obviously owned and finding it . . . funny.

The white men, on the other hand, looked harassed and

dyspeptic, sedentary and fat. There was none of that bronzed leanness associated with Africa. Their faces were lobster red or white like boiled cod. And they all looked as if they had been recently irritated beyond bearing and they were still thinking about it.

The permit office was a black hole in a blinding white wall and two flights of wooden stairs to be clumped up. At the top, in a dirty little waiting-room, where on the bare boards a swept pile of dust and cigarette ends and match-sticks marked where the brush had stopped and the dustpan not begun, five or six people were sitting in chairs staring hopelessly in front of them. I sat down, and a great voice suddenly began to bellow in the next room, as if on the verge of tears:

'And he can go on waiting; he'll wait there another six months if I choose. Don't dither, Corporal. Don't dither, man. Come here. How often have I told you the files go on this side, the letters on that? Can you see? Are you blind, Corporal, as well as deaf? Your bootlaces are undone again. Well, don't stand there. Do it up, man. And now send in the next fellow and see he steps up smartly.'

The door opened and a Hausa Corporal came in sweating.

'This way, Sah,' he said to me, saluting, and I lounged into the next room as unsmartly as I was able, and flopped on the chair in front of the desk before I was asked to sit down. An enormous, purple-faced man with an orange moustache from ear to ear filled up the whole of the far side of the desk. He was clawing the air with one hand and for a moment I thought he was going to have a fit. Then I saw that what he was doing was 'pulling himself together'. He was using every atom of his will-power to simmer down. It seemed indecent to watch him. I put my passport and request form on the desk in front of him, turned my eyes away and waited. It was a full minute before he picked up my papers, read them, stamped them, signed them, and said, 'That's good for a month; you can renew it at Kano.' He shook his head and there was a patter of sweat on the papers. He was looking at me now like a big, kindly dog, wrinkling up his eyes, as if he wished to be understood.

'Lucky fella,' he said at length, 'goin' up country into

the fresh air. I've been here five years,' he said, and then, half-crying again, 'Five years in this bloody office.'

I thanked him for the papers and ran down the stairs. Before I reached the street I heard his great voice behind me.

'Oh, will you stop scratching your bottom, Corporal? Just to please me.'

'It's the humidity,' my host said. 'Combined with the heat, it's a killer.' A pale civil servant, he lived in a large suburb of smart, air-conditioned bungalows, well out of the town. 'Old Jack, fellow you saw this morning, was a first-class man out in the bush, first-class. But he did something silly—hit someone or something, so they recalled him to Lagos. He's useless in Lagos. And this new chap they sent out to the bush is useless there. Still, must have some discipline. What'll you drink?'

'Palm wine,' I said.

'Well, I can get it through the servants, but please have a gin instead and then I'll take you to the Island Club.'

'For Heaven's sake, don't ask for palm wine at the Island Club,' my host said, as we drove away, and when I got there I could see it would not have done. This was a club for intellectuals, African and English. *The Times* and *The New Statesman* lay about on tables, the gin was flowing like water, there was Mozart on the record player, and someone was giving a harangue about the Italian novelist, Moravia. It was so exactly like the sort of evenings I enjoyed in London if they didn't go on too long that for ten minutes I joined in the dance, giving out all the old clever answers to all the old clever questions, until the very glibness of it suddenly alerted me. This was not a debate—it was a play. It was a play about how like clever London Nigeria could get.

'You will need to take your gin with you, sir; in this country, for the general public, it is forbidden.'

'What do they drink in the country, then?'

'Palm wine—but you will not drink it; it is horrible.'

About my journey, the comment was Johnsonian rather than New Statesman-like. 'You will see our country, sir, but you will not know Nigeria.' Well, obviously not. 'What you see you will not understand and much will be hidden from you.' No doubt. 'You will pick up many stories from English officials but they will not be the true case.' I see. It had all been settled in advance.

'What do you think of the Island Club?' my host asked me as we drove home.

'Dreadful,' I said.

'You've had a lot of gin.'

'Yes, but it's not that.'

'Don't you find them very much like the same sort of circles at home?'

'Exact copy.'

'Well, then, what's wrong with it?'

'They don't drink palm wine,' I said. 'In London it's not shameful to order a pint of mild.'

'They don't want to get back to primitive simplicity here, they want to get away from it.'

'More fools they.'

'You're romantic,' said my host, lifting his lip.

The next morning the sky was flawless, the sun bounced back at you from the glossy enamel surfaces of millions of green leaves. Lizards flickered on every flat stone like neon signs, a strange bird was whooping in the sky. It was the sort of summer morning you remember from childhood, a picnic morning packed with possibilities. And on the gravel stood my truck, loaded to the hood with bundles and packages, cooking pots and water carriers, hurricane lamps and blankets and a shotgun. Arranged along its nearside the three Nigerians who were to show me their country. They were: Sam, an Ibo, about eighteen, with all the vitality and restlessness of his race, dressed in a singlet and khaki trousers. Broad-faced, awkward and giggling, he was the cook and general factotum. Next Achmet, the driver, a lean Moslem aristocrat from the north who wore his fez very straight above a hard, scornful face. Fulani blood, however dilute, insulated him once and for all from these plebian Southerners, banana-eaters, white men's pets. He shook hands with me in a disapproving way, like an offended aunt.

And rather apart from the others, as if to be included with them or not, as you thought fit, Mr Okara, advancing down stage to meet me with outstretched hands. His English clothes were beautifully cut and pressed. His glasses had so much tortoiseshell in them, they must have weighed half a pound. He had a very large and sophisticated wristwatch and his breast pocket was full of shining pens and pencils with a silk handkerchief in the background. He also carried a flywhisk of red horsehair and a briefcase, and all these pieces of equipment were in perpetual motion as his brief-case changed hands so he could take off his glasses, and his flywhisk was tucked under his armpit so that he could get at his spectacle case, and changed again so that he could get at his watch, which meant that he had to put his glasses back on.

He was perhaps twenty-five years old and spoke English and French and five Nigerian languages.

'Since Achmet is a Hausa and Sam is an Ibo, I ought to be a Yoruba to balance the party; in fact, I am Igbirra; we are an odd, provincial tribe but considered intelligent. Let us find out about Nigeria together,' he charmingly said, and shook hands.

So we climbed into the gaps in the luggage and set off through the litter of Lagos, weaving among the bright chromium bicycles with their three or four bells and couple of windmills, and out past the shanty towns until we turned the corner and left the last scraps of Lagos behind, across a bright green plain with palm trees; and there the road ahead of us was red. Achmet pulled in onto the grass and said something to Mr Okara, who said to me: 'Achmet says this is the true beginning of the journey and here he will say the appropriate prayers for the beginning of a journey.' And so he did, prostrate on the grass, a full fifteen minutes of them. At first we could hear his thin droning, but as the sun soaked into the luggage and into us, and the churring of the crickets like millions of tiny telephone bells swelled around us, concentration slipped a notch, and then suddenly out of the distance in a pink cloud of dust, two buses in the last stages of dereliction came roaring towards us abreast on the road. It was a race. They bounded and swayed with not a yard between them at about 60 miles an hour, the drivers leaning out of the windows and shouting like demons. The buses were full of women in bright head cloths and flaming clothes of shocking pink and acid green and gold and yellow—and what women! Six feet round, ten feet round, like bundles of enormous tropical fruit, ripe to bursting, and all screaming and yelling with pleasure like country girls at a fair.

The first bus, a sky blue one, had 'All Roads' written on its front, and 'Hallelulia' on its tail The other, a luscious pink job, said 'First come, first served' as it approached, and 'The Lord be with you' as it departed.

'Mammy waggons,' said Mr Okara; 'we shall see a lot of them.'

As Achmet climbed back in the truck, we heard the talking drum.

'Probably,' Mr Okara said, 'it is talking about us.' He began to discuss the inscriptions on mammy waggons. 'We have had every kind of Christian missionary here,' he said, 'and one thing they all said was "you may only have one wife". It's all very well for missionaries to say this but what is a man to do who has four wives and knows that he is called to follow Christ? Get rid of the wives, say the missionaries, but this, sir, is very hard on the wives. What are they to do? This is why we have so great a number of sects,' said Mr Okara. 'First we forsook the missionaries in the matter of wives, and then we forsook them in other matters.' He spoke to Achmet and shortly afterwards we turned off the road down a mud track which ended in a large, roofless, mud building with the representation of a bicycle carved in the pink mud above the door.

'This,' said Mr Okara, 'is the Church of Christ Bicyclist. It had at one time five churches and thousands of members. But now that bicycles are common, no religious feeling is attached to them and the churches have perished.'

Slowly we pushed on up the green plain of West Nigeria. Every day, as evening fell, the drumming began. From time to time in the heat of the day, a drum would start up in a desultory way as we passed a village and die away again, but as evening fell they grew more insistent until at dusk, by the time we'd reached our night's halt, and thousands of little cooking fires were glowing in the village square, the drumming would be a steady roar and at about 9 o'clock, the whole population would be dancing. Babies of two danced. Babies of three made music with a nail in a bottle. Babies of four played complicated drum rhythms on old tin cans.

The real drumming, the expert touch which people would flock for miles to hear, is a thing of tremendous sophistication. The great drummer is a folk hero, and since culture in Nigeria is not split into pop and education as ours is, he is an absolute king. He has the adulation and the girls and the money that our pop idols get, and the critical acclaim and status of a Yehudi Menuhin. This is Nigeria's cultural life, religious, social, aesthetic in one, and everyone is in it. The very old shuffle and clap their hands, and babies on their mothers' backs wag their heads in time.

At Ilorin I stayed with the District Officer.

'Very sad case today,' he said, 'clerk in the office, first-class man, been there fifteen years, does a first-class job by local standards, nice house, well educated children, pinched £50 out of the safe. I suppose he'll have to go to jail. What else can we do? But it's not defect of character, he has no debts, no pressing needs; it's just the system.'

'How do you mean?' I said.

'The family system. It's called the extended family. A little welfare state. You are absolutely responsible for about 100 near relations, right out as far as second cousins. It's unthinkable not to help them if they're in need. Now, one of this chap's maternal uncles, silly old man, has got to pay a fifty quid debt or go to quod. So my clerk, being a good man, shoulders his responsibility and pinches it for him out of my safe. No chance of getting away with it. Doesn't deny it. Just sits there and says he's sorry but that's how it is.'

At Ebbe, we met a ghost. It's a tiny village but there is a travellers' guest house—three round pink mud huts with conical straw roofs, perched a mile out of the village on the edge of a steep escarpment, almost a cliff. It's lonely up there and the wind whistles in the grass. One of the huts is the kitchen. The Nigerians had the middle one; I had the one at the cliff edge. I lay on a camp bed under a mosquito net reading very late by the light of a Tilly lamp. It must have been about four in the morning when I heard a piercing yell and a scuffling noise, and Sam came belting into my hut, rolling his eyes and shaking all over.

'What is it?'

'A ghost, sir, oh sir, a ghost.'

'Is it outside?'

'No, sir, inside, with us.'

I seized the Tilly lamp. I rushed over to the other hut. They'd lit a hurricane lamp and Mr Okara and Achmet were sitting against a wall staring with bulging eyes at Sam's blanket, which was humped up in the middle exactly as if a very large football were rolled underneath. As we watched it, it rolled under the blanket from one end to another, vanished, and immediately reappeared in the middle of Achmet's bedding two yards away. Mr Okara's teeth were chattering but he said: 'It appears, sir, we are haunted by a hump.' At this, the hump vanished.

'It must be an animal,' I said. And I rushed outside with the Tilly lamp—and tripped head over heels across—a hump. Same size but in the hard ground this time and right in the middle of the doorway, where it had certainly not been a minute before. The Tilly lamp went out when I fell and when they brought the hurricane lamp, there was nothing there. We relit the lamp and poked about but there was nothing there.

'Hold on,' I said, 'I'll go and get us all a drop of whisky.' While I was fiddling about with the straps of my hold-all, I suddenly saw the hump in the middle of my bed and let out a yell. Sam and Mr Okara came stumbling over and the hump vanished. Shortly after that, we heard very faintly a cock crow in the village below. Sam, who had been trembling as if in convulsions, now sighed and sat down on the ground and stopped shaking. I thought he had fainted, but he said something to Mr Okara, who said: 'Oh yes. At cockcrow they finish.'

Then we drank the whisky, and then we packed the car, and as dawn came up, we left Ebbe behind us, I hope, forever.

An old, old man with a white beard, in the government service, wanted to speak to me. He said, very earnestly, 'Sir, it is impossible to exaggerate the good that the British have brought us. Those who say otherwise are young and have no memories; but when I was a boy it would have been unthinkable to walk by myself in the long grass to the next village. I should have been killed and eaten.'

Now we were getting near Mr Okara's country and as we swung to the west up a narrow mountain track which drove on upwards as if it would never end, Mr Okara began to talk about his country and his origins.

'I am a son of a son of the king,' he said, 'but now the king is deposed and lives in the bush and hunts bush cow and runs free. And in any case the king had very many sons.' We were in time, he added, for the great juju ceremony of the year.

'What is the point of it?' I asked.

'It is the New Year, but it is more like your Hallowe'en when the spirits of the dead return.'

Soon, surrounded by mountain peaks, the Igbirra capital came into view. The houses were like nothing else in Africa, square, two-storied buildings, built of mud and thatch and tree trunks, attached in rows like old-fashioned council houses. The Igbirra agricultural land is miles away, and the people have to get up very early in the morning to get there in time to do a day's work.

'It's a question of belief,' Mr Okara said, when I asked him about this inconvenient arrangement. 'For us, the essential power is the spirit of fertility and there is only a certain amount of this in any one place. Here in the village we are using up all the fertility spirit in increasing the population. If our cattle and crops were using it up, too, there would not be enough to go round. So we site them in another place. This, please, is a belief I do not share.'

We all got up early the next morning for the new year juju ceremony of the ancestors. They were drumming at dawn on the hills set apart for these matters—a deep-throated drum first, followed by a yelping, feverish one, spelling out the message that the hill was now sacred and women must keep away. The drumming and the bleating of rams' horns continued till noon while the crowd grew thicker on the hill-top in the open spaces between green woods. It was no hotter up here than an English June day, and quite suddenly the ceremony began, with the high tenor yelping of the talking drums in quick time. Two young men in white robes with white peeled wands about ten feet long controlled the dancing crowd, until the drums suddenly stopped and something rushed out of the wood and started to dance a dreadful dance by itself while the crowd shrank away from it—and no wonder. My hair stood straight on end, for this was The Thing, the thing that waited for me in the wardrobe when I was four. To begin with, it had no face. It had a kind of straw sconce, and it was dressed all in long rags and tatters, all green and brown. Its sleeves dangled and flapped a yard below its wrists, and, most horrible of all, it was mentally defective. It parodied obscenely the slobbering unco-ordination of an imbecile, and all the time it staggered and swayed, it gobbled in the very voice of the wardrobe goblin.

And then another of the same sort but in a corset of jangling metal plates and covered in gourds and rattles rushed out of the wood to join it and danced by itself a mad clashing dance in which, suddenly, everyone joined in. And then the young men rushed at the crowd, slashing and swiping with their peeled sticks and herding the whole tumult, crazily dancing, down the hill into the village, leaving the ancestor ghosts alone.

'You see, at exactly the time of the New Year,' explained Mr Okara, 'the spirit dies. It does it in the old year and there is not enough power in us to make it continue so we have to call on the ancestors to help. For a second or two the universe is dead and then with the ancestors' help, it lives again. Please, I do not believe this.'

But it was Mr Okara who was the most shaken when we played the tape back. At the moment of the old year's death, the tape faded gently out for five seconds and then came back again.

And now we went up into the North, Achmet's country. He was delighted to be able to exchange dignified Moslem greetings with people on the road. He became quite affable. We moved into a land where walls fifty feet high crowned with battlements marked the palaces of the Emirs—direct descendants of the Fulani chiefs who, a hundred and forty years before, had fallen upon the Hausa, giving them Islam at the point of a sword, and then swept on down to middle Nigeria, where they were only halted by the tsetse fly and by the British coming up through the southern swamps to trade. Vegetation was sparse here in the north. There was sand underfoot. The desert was not far away. At a water hole we met a group of the Fulani surrounded by their beasts. A beautiful people, copper-coloured and slim with wavy, dark hair, great eyes, noses faintly aquiline, and a conceit beyond all bearing. Some authorities think they're ancient Egyptians who've been wandering through the ages across the Sudan from water hole to water hole, living on the blood and milk of their cattle. Whatever their origin, their fusion with the Hausa has produced a race of famous warriors and wild horsemen. I went to see one of the Emirs, the pedigree princes of this racial mixture. The man who took me to see him was a British official, a very young, blond and offhand man. We passed under the battlements and ten soldiers in scarlet saluted us with their long swords. The Emir sat in council, facing the door of the council chamber, bolt upright upon a throne while his councellors were seated on benches along the walls, old reverent men in turbans, with grey beards. A boy brought in two chairs and two cushions and we sat facing the Emir, whose face was half-hidden in a head cloth. He looked like a bad-tempered eagle. Even his eyes were golden like a bird's. The young English civilian asked him, for my benefit, various questions on the state of his dominions. The Emir replied in the grand manner, barking out 'It is so.' 'It is not so.' 'Would it were so.' 'Praise to God,' and 'Curses be upon them.' He didn't look at us but straight ahead with his half-hooded eagle's eyes.

'God knows what use these Emirs are to anybody,' the young man said as we made our way out, 'but he's a decorative old piece and very grand. Naughty, though; we've just caught him out trying to pinch the education tax for himself; that's why he was so snappy.'

The North is Arabic in feeling and culture, and Kano, a splendid pink city, walled and crenellated and battlemented, a maze of arched, narrow streets and passageways, is altogether North African, a product of the Sahara like the old cities of Morocco, and civilized—a coffee-drinking, hookah-smoking, text-quoting civilization, firmly stuck in the Middle Ages. Unmovable, it seemed to me.

'Kano is the place,' all my fellow countrymen had told me as we travelled through Nigeria. 'You'll like Kano. Dignified, proud, great horsemen, you know.' And then they'd look around them at the frenzied vitality of the dancing and drumming tribesmen of the South with a pitying smile. Certainly the dancing tribes were not elegant. It's not an elegant position to be straddled uneasily between the primitive and the twentieth century, and often they have the aggressive bad manners of the insecure.

But they'd spoilt me for Kano. 'Dead and proud of it,' I thought ill-temperedly as we pushed on north through the city and out into the sparse bush, green at a distance, but near at hand you could see that each bush stood in its own little fifty foot desert of sand. The horizon line was a drab yellow. We had reached the Southern shore of the Sahara, and one of the outposts of the world—the Grand Salutation and Gold Help Us Hotel, the start of the desert crossing, the end of the camel trail from Timbuctoo.

The Grand Salutation and Gold Help Us is a long, low shack with a verandah and tables, the biggest refrigerator I have ever seen and a Liberian hostess with gold bangles in her ears and a red, spotted headcloth. Six feet across the beam, she must have weighed thirty stone.

Three Arabs and a Frenchman were arguing at one table so we all went and sat down with them, even Achmet, while the Liberian girl brought us icy lager which we drank in quarts, even Achmet, and we stayed there till the sun went down and then turned round and headed once more for the steamy south.

Onitsha market is the biggest in Africa—a square mile of market stalls where you can buy anything from a love potion to a Rolls Royce.

'Avoid the meat stall,' the District officer said; 'last year someone bought a human leg and ate it before he found out, so, if you must buy meat, buy it with the skin on.' Flintlock guns, the flints from Suffolk, were selling like hot cakes that day, and the middle tubes from Chevrolet steering wheels which make exceptionally good gun barrels. Cloth of gold with silver cowrie shells. Gramophones. Dried frogs to make magic against your enemies. A pennyfarthing bicycle. Bows and arrows, and knives of every murderous kind. Nose rings, necklaces of turquoise and silver. Little tins of embrocation to stir into your tea. 'It give power,' the stall-holder explained.

In the great airy store of the United Africa Company alongside the market, it was comparatively cool and quiet. I had my tape recorder open on a table and I was talking to the manager. 'Unprecedented sales of Lifebuoy soap in the upper Benue River,' he was saying, 'it took us weeks to find out why. It seems there is a large fish in the river up there which can only be caught with a rather rare kind of pink worm. Well, what do you think? They were pressing the soap through perforated tins to make pink worms to sell to the ignorant fishermen. Then it was discovered that the fish would take the soap worms, and then we were in business.'

At this point we were interrupted by a chief, an enormous man, dressed very simply in a red bikini and a scarlet ten gallon stetson hat. A draggle of wives were following him about in the store. He was swaying drunk. He came over to us and looked long and vacantly at the tape recorder, then he pointed at me, 'Na, who dis fella?'

The manager explained me. 'You savvy dem box, you switch um, you turn um, dem queen speak for London. Dis fella he go fill up dem box for London.'

'Oh ho,' said the chief, and staggered away. He was holding a couple of steel-shafted golf clubs.

Five minutes later, the manager, who'd been recording an interview for me about fashions in cloth, stopped, and said to an assistant, 'The chief's gone, I see. What did he buy?'

'Steel-shafted golf clubs, one dozen.'

'Well, you never know what will take his fancy. Golf, eh? More at home at the nineteenth hole, I should have thought. Golf clubs . . . steel-shafted golf clubs—he's going to make a still! Why did you let him have them? You know the regulations about metal tubing. Oh, my God!' the manager shouted and rushed away.

That was the beginning of the great scandal of the bootleg rum called 'King of Clubs' which presently penetrated to the remotest villages all along the Niger.

South, farther south into the dark of the rain forest. In a company launch puttering along creeks of poison green water at the foot of great cliffs of trees, sixty feet high to the first branch. Hardwoods, mahoganies. At Sapele they make them into plywood and this factory, miles deep in the forest, is the bright spot of Nigerian industry. They were felling a 150 foot mahogany that morning. It stood in a clearing criss-crossed with beams of sunlight as from cathedral windows, and clouds of huge black and yellow butterflies flopped about in the glade. This is the deep forest where nobody has ever lived, and this is the wealth of Nigeria.

At Lagos they seemed pleased to see me at the Island Club.

'Ah ha,' they said with glee, 'you have seen Nigeria. We heard of your progress. You danced in Ilorin, yes, and you recorded the Igbirra juju, yes. You saw a ghost at Ebbe and the juju crocodile at Mokwa and at Onitsha you heard the tale of the human leg.'

'How well informed you are.'

They laughed a great deal.

When I was leaving, full of gin, one of them, almost unable to speak for laughing, said, 'I think you are going to have a surprise.'

I got the surprise as the aeroplane came down over London airport—a message from the captain to say would I kindly not leave the airport until I had seen the B.B.C. officials who were waiting for me.

We met in the bar.

'Bit of a shock for you, I'm afraid; none of your stuff is going to be used.'

'What?'

'No, we can't put out any of it. Have you see the *Lagos Daily Times*?'

He produced a copy. 'Yesterday's,' he said.

The leader, a full column, was headed 'Cutforth's Follies.' 'Mr Cutforth,' it said, 'has certainly worked hard. But instead of interesting himself in our penal settlements, our model prisons, our educational structure and our progressive outlook, he has chosen to immerse himself in folk law and magical practices.'

'I see,' I said, 'the Island Club.'

'They've made such a fuss with the Colonial Office that the whole thing is shelved. Indefinitely postponed is the formula. Have a drink,' they said.

XIV

Waiting for the Dalai Lama

Until 1959 when the Chinese overran it, Tibet shared with the headwaters of the Amazon that place in the Western subconscious from which it seemed quite possible that something immensely old and completely new could emerge to put mankind on the right track. Shangri-la has now been shifted, of course, to some wierd planet in a remote galaxy, but in March 1959, when the news came through that the Dalai Lama was riding hell for leather across the roof of the world, through the blizzards and the Chinese, for the Himalayan passes and sanctuary in India, it was obvious that for hundreds of millions of people who didn't care a damn about world politics, this was a tremendous story.

'It's all very vague,' my editor said. 'Nobody will say where the Dalai Lama is, in case the Chinese get to know. The Indian Government has some information of course, and when they think he's safe, they'll let you know where to go and meet him. I've booked you as far as Delhi, and you can book yourself on. Get away as quick as you can. Wherever and whenever he comes down the mountain, you'll be there to meet him.'

Unless the city of New Delhi is frying in the midday sun of the hot weather, when every object in sight appears to be an incandescent white, with a short, dense, black shadow at its foot in which lies a dog or a cat, the best thing to do is to leave your luggage at the air terminal and walk—for at least the first half mile; it's a marvellous way of dropping the English load. You can take your pick of architecture from the 'Ceremonial Imperial' done in red sandstone with the trailing curves of art nouveau—if architecture is frozen music, this is frozen Elgar: or you can go straight up the avenue towards the towering white office blocks and multi-storied, air-conditioned hotels of Middle Delhi; or you can take off sideways into an older tradition of Colonial buildings with eroded cornices covered in weeds, and rows of wooden shutters with flaking paint where the monkeys dance along the edges of the balconies and bright rugs are hung out. And from there into the trading streets—packed rows of little open shop fronts and the full blare of Indian salesmanship, with gramophones. Whichever way you go, the pace is the same—an unchanging one-mile-an-hour: the exactly proper pace to show off the languid splendour of a sari and how beautifully heads can be carried on necks, and hands on supple wrists. How absolutely inessential it is to get from A to B, let alone to get there at any particular time.

All along the edges of the pavements, the neem trees were in flower—feathery trees rather like acacias, foaming with a sort of meadowsweet blossom and with a heavy scent of the same sort but darker in tone—and this, with a touch of curry, a whiff of burning cow dung and a tang of water on the dust is the smell of India.

I breathed down great drafts while the sun unbuttoned my spinal column and settled me down on my hips and the gramophones drugged my ears senseless, and the glare, my eyes. I was as relaxed when I reached my hotel as if I'd spent a week in a nursing home.

Delhi is dry, which means an embarrassing fiddle with the lift man who will put a bottle of Scotch in your room at a price. He was bringing it in when the telephone rang. It was a correspondent I knew well in London.

'I heard you were in Delhi,' he said, 'and I suppose you're on the Dalai Lama story. Well, so am I. We seem to be the only two in from London so far; the Indian Government's in a tremendous flap about it, and Mr Nehru himself has called in the *Times* Correspondent for a conference which is going on now. I'm going to meet the *Times* man when it's over. I'll pick you up if you like and we'll all go along to Viceregal Lodge together. In half an hour.'

Nothing anywhere in England that I know looks half so English as Viceregal Lodge, New Delhi. The wonderfully kept lawns, the huge English trees throwing long shadows in the waning sun, looked as though they'd been there for a thousand years in a wet climate, only instead of rooks, the kites wheeled overhead in a flawless sky.

The *Times* man came out as we were strolling on the grass and said, 'The Prime Minister says he wants to see both of you since you're here.'

Mr Nehru gave us whisky and then said, 'If I decide to allow the Press to meet the Dalai Lama on his way down here, I want you to understand that it will be under the most strict regulations. The line you may not cross will be well south of Tibet. There will be armed sentries and they will shoot. Anybody found north of the line will spend several years in jail. If anyone flies an aeroplane across, it will be shot down. You understand? I mean it. It will be a very serious matter. The Press Office will let you know what arrangements have been made.'

And a day or two later the correspondent and I were flying in a very old Dakota into Tezpur in Assam, with strict instructions that the north road out of it, to the Himalayan foothills and Tibet, was strictly out of bounds except in government vehicles under escort.

Tezpur is an ancient city with traces of past grandeur and more than traces of present squalor. It has an antique fort and presents on one side a fine, dramatic skyline where the old fort and a group of great trees on top of a very steep hill are enfolded, together with half the city itself, in a great calm sweep of the River Brahmaputra which, by the time it reaches Tezpur, has crossed the whole length of Tibet, turned a huge hairpin bend and still has half its length to run before it reaches the sea.

The first thing we did was to hire the only hireable car in Tezpur—about fifteen years old—and make a survey of the place. It didn't take long. There was no hotel in the Western sense of the word. There was an Indian hotel, clean little rooms like monks' cells with a string bed, called a charpoy, and a bowl and a jug in each. But they didn't want us there. We were all very uneasy thinking of the sanitary arrangements being so different, the caste rules and the elaborate social routine which we didn't know properly. It wasn't until late afternoon that somebody told us about the Planters' Club.

It was a mile or two out of the town, a large, shambling structure of blackened wood, like a very solid Noah's Ark. It must have been built by the tea planters around Tezpur round about the early nineteen hundreds, to judge by the interior.

There was a long bar of teak, and in one corner a mouldering billiard table, long abandoned to fungus and termites. There were some old-fashioned heavy teak Public Works Department armchairs and ordinary chairs and tables in good repair, a clock with a Big Ben chime, a bathroom with a zinc bath on a cement floor, a lavatory which worked, and the walls were covered with the pale yellow ghosts of photographs of King Edward VIIth leading in a Derby winner, the Tezpur Planters' Association Cricket Team for 1909, and hundreds more, nearly all pre-1914, most of them just decipherable; and there were cartoons and sporting prints by the dozen, badly foxed and mildewed.

And there wasn't an Englishman left. Nearly all the planters were Indians, but there were a few Anglo-Indian heirs of the founders of the club, and I suppose it must have been these who decreed that nothing should ever be changed.

Then came the negotiations. Could they put us up at the Club for a day or two? Well, a member could hire a room but must provide his own bedding. Were we eligible for membership? Well, we were not of course Tezpur planters, but nothing could be discovered in the rule book which said we must be. If we would care to wait until about 8 o'clock, there'd probably be a quorum to vote on the matter—meanwhile we could be made honorary members simply by signing the book.

At 6 o'clock they said that if we wanted anything to eat, we could send the boy down to the bazaar for some curry, only we ought to send him now before the rain began. 'At half past seven, it rains,' they said. So we paid the boy and we ate the good, black devilish curry with chapatis and dal and bottles of beer. And at half past seven, prompt, just like pulling the chain, the skies opened and for eleven hours, that night and every other night we were there, a deafening downpour thundered on the tin roof; conversation went on unevenly in shouts and the only sound which came through loud and clear against the storm was the chanting of the frogs outside. At half past eight, there was a quorum; some of them had driven a hundred miles. At 9 o'clock, we were life members of the Tezpur and District Planters' Club. At a quarter to ten, we were buying drinks for the Committee; at ten o'clock, we had a room and at half past ten, we'd found a very ancient horned gramophone in the cupboard and were settling down to the first evening of waiting for the Dalai Lama.

At half past six in the morning the rain was promptly turned off, the sun shone, steam arose, birds sang, somebody started to play a flute outside. The old man who looked after the Club made tea, very good tea, as you'd expect from a tea planters' club. I noticed a telephone, a collector's piece screwed to the wall; its earpiece, a fluted cylinder of ebonite weighing about three pounds, hung on its own wire separately from an ornate hook. I jiggled it. To my surprise it worked, and in less than half an hour, I was through to our man in Delhi.

'Any news about the Dalai Lama?'

'Not a word. All they're saying is "the nearest you can get to him is Tezpur." '

'But who are they saying it to?'

'Well, there are sixteen Indian correspondents who think it's too early yet; the two big British popular dailies are due in this afternoon—whole teams of them. A big American group day after tomorrow, two Frenchmen from *Paris Match*, and, I hear, some Germans and an Italian.'

'Shall I send a piece about Tezpur?'

'No good. Everything is embargoed by the Government.'

So I rang off.

'Now then,' I said, 'the whole place is going to be bung full of correspondents with money to burn. First thing to do is hire this old car for a month, paying in advance and getting a receipt. Then we want blankets, tins of biscuits and fruit, and we'll go and have a look at the Telegraph Office.'

At the Telegraph Office, we aroused with great difficulty an elderly man with a large grey soup-strainer moustache who was sleeping on his back on a bare wooden bench. When he opened his eyes, they were bright crimson. We showed him our cable cards, and it was clear he'd never seen their like before.

'Telegram,' we said, 'to London.'

'London,' he said, 'London,' as if he recognized the word. He held out a form. With luck you could have got twelve words on it.

'No, no, four hundred, five hundred words.'

'Four hundred words impossible.' He groped in his mind and found the formula. 'No cable facilities.'

We didn't waste his time.

That afternoon five more correspondents turned up, three British and two American; agency men. By half past eight, they were life members of the Tezpur and District Planters' Club. By quarter to nine they were buying drinks for the committee. By nine o'clock they were in despair, talking to the Anglo-Indian secretary.

'Well, where's the nearest cable station?'

'Ooo, Shillong, there's one in Shillong.'

'How far's that?'

'About ninety miles.'

'How long by car?'

'Ooo, you can't get to Shillong this time of year, all the rivers are flooded, man.'

'Can a plane get there?'

'It could, I suppose. There are airstrips. There is no service.'

The next night the club was full, and the night after that it was bursting. In the Indian hotel, Indian correspondents were sleeping six to a cell. Anybody in Tezpur who owned a verandah had a dozen correspondents sleeping on it. One correspondent came in so late that there wasn't a place for him at all—there was not a square foot anywhere, but in the yard at the back of the Planters' Club there was a sordid little structure of four poles and a low straw roof, under which a goat normally spent the night. He appropriated this shelter—whether he turned the goat out or shared with it I don't know, but in the morning an Indian, who went out to wake him with a cup of tea, came back in great agitation and signalled us all to come outside. Round and round the shelter, pressed deep into the mud, were rings of monstrous paw marks. An old, white-whiskered, bright-eyed Shikhari was borne into the compound from the town by a great crowd of people eager to see the sight. It took him about two seconds to make his diagnosis.

'Tiger, Sahib,' he said.

So the correspondent spent the next night on a verandah.

That day, no doubt in response to all the frantic telegrams and telephone calls which every correspondent had been sending day and night since his arrival, the Indian Government announced that we would be permitted to go up in Government transport with a military escort to the line south of the Tibetan border where we should, on the appointed day, meet, we hoped, the Dalai Lama. It was about fifteen miles north of Tezpur at a place called Foothills. The road to Foothills turned out to be a country track between banks of bright green jungle with a stifling green smell. Every leaf glittered as if varnished and the vegetation was piled up on steep hillsides on either side of us. The road, too, led steeply uphill and had a surface of broken rock which reflected a kaleidoscope of glare from the sun. It was a surprise, after about an hour in which our old buses made twelve miles, to come out in an open space where the jungle had retreated a quarter of a mile on each side of the road. Here there were grass and flowers and long, low huts of bamboo and thatch and we could see in front of us the foothills, considerable mountains, thinly clad with jungle and behind them an even more considerable range, rather more thinly clad. Wisps of steam-like cloud moved along their flanks. The air began to smell damp and cool and still our red-hot old bus engines ploughed on uphill in bottom gear, until suddenly we made a right-angled turn and there they were, the Himalayas. They rose from the foothills like trees from grass and they were utterly alone and remote. They might have been ten miles from us or a hundred. They made scale seem ridiculous. The sun shone placidly on the calm snow of their upper halves and we could see dangling like a thin, twisted fly-paper from a ceiling the track down which it was hoped the Dalai Lama would eventually arrive.

And now the road turned another abrupt angle and right across our way was a barrier, one of those poles with a weight at the end, and at that end was a Gurkha sentry, with a great grin, standing at ease with his rifle.

It was a company of Sikhs who'd been given the job of superintending us and now, jovial, bearded, immensely obliging, they jumped off our buses and their trucks and began to explain the lie of the land. They had a bamboo barracks a hundred yards behind the sentry, and their discipline was obviously ferocious.

There was a monastery, they explained, some six miles up the track from us, hidden from our view by a spur of the hillside, and there they expected the Dalai Lama would stop for the night, and they would know about this and bring us up here in the early morning to meet him. They were terribly pleasant. They soothed us as if we were children. 'But not past the barrier, oh no, sir, oh no. Ha ha ha ha.' They laughed the whole time. I wouldn't have tried to pass them for anything on earth.

So we all stood around, looking pretty squalid with the Himalayas behind us, and smoked in the silence. We said very little, and after about half an hour we got in the buses again and went back to the club.

If you included the stringers and the stooges and the pilots and the drivers and the interpreters, there were now about a hundred newsmen in Tezpur and it was possible to take a look at the runners and assess the form. First, the heavy stuff: the two great British dailies with enormous circulations had each brought its own circus headed by a correspondent whose name everybody had heard of. Each of these had an aeroplane, a pilot, a car, a driver, an immense stock of hard cash, a couple of interpreters, a secretary or two and a few angle men and assistants. If sheer weight of money and supplies could do it, they were most likely to get the story. By now all the correspondents knew where the real story lay. Anybody with eyes in his head could write some sort of piece about the actual physical descent of the Dalai Lama in the Foothills. That didn't matter. The real question was who was going to get from either the Dalai Lama or his escort the first-hand story of their escape from the Chinese in Lhasa.

On form, it looked as if the lesser of the two big dailies had the best chance. They were equipped with the cars and aircraft and interpreters that the other had, but in addition they had brought off a very smart stroke, they'd hired Heinrich Harrer. And there he was, a mythical man, who'd escaped from a British prisoner of war camp during the war and walked across the Himalayas all through Tibet to Lhasa, where he'd become a personal friend of the Dalai Lama, learnt Tibetan and became a sort of adviser to the Tibetan government. He's written a very good book about it. And here he was, amongst us, a haunted figure in fact, followed about everywhere he went by a formidable female journalist on the staff of the paper which had hired him. She was there to see that his special knowledge of Tibetan affairs should not be used to swell the colour stories the correspondents were all busy writing, against the day when the embargo would be lifted. The only place you could talk to Harrer was in the Gents, and even there not for long.

'You writing anything?' I asked him in there one day. He turned a hunted look on me.

'I write long pieces every day, good solid information about the foundations of the Tibetan way of life, and every day they are taken from me and when I see them again in the evening with my name on they are not at all the same.'

'Oh well,' I said, 'it's not your fault and you must be making masses of money.'

'Not all that money,' said Harrer.

'Look, I wonder if you could tell me,' I said, 'the present Dalai Lama was discovered when he was five. Isn't that unusually old?'

'Certainly,' Harrer began, 'in old times it was usual . . . .'

'Mr Harrer,' came an imperious female voice, from just outside the can. 'Can you spare a moment, please, most important.' And he bustled out, rolling his eyes.

On form, I thought, Harrer would probably pull it off, but there were plenty of dark horses. The agency men were keen, deadly operators; the Indian papers had a pull; most of their correspondents spoke half a dozen Indian languages;

the *Times* of India correspondent, an Englishman, was playing it very cool, something up his sleeve, watch him. The Frenchmen from *Paris Match* I thought had little chance. They were a sharply contrasted pair; the cameraman was a bright, very modern Frenchman with a crew-cut and a cool look. His companion, who was about fifty and did the words, was a long-haired literary romantic. The prolonged absence of the Dalai Lama hadn't worried him at all, and he'd practically given up the story in favour of one about the British in India. He roamed about the Club, noting down the captions under the sporting prints. He stood for hours in a reverent attitude with his head cocked up in the air before the photograph of King Edward.

'What a race,' he would say to me, 'what a race. Here on the confines of the habitable earth, the billiards champion and King Edward's horse.' When he first heard the clock he was in raptures.

'Ah, même a Tezpur, le carillon de Westminster!' He didn't even speak Hindustani. Not a hope, was my assessment.

The only other one who had a hope was a Canadian girl correspondent; she was pretty enough to get herself anything she wanted.

It was round about this time, when we'd been waiting for the Dalai Lama for ten days or so, that the correspondents began to go a bit mad. It began with the malicious spreading of rumours.

'Well, we got the story then.'

'What story?'

'We know where they are.'

'Who?'

'The Dalai Lama and his party.'

'Well, where are they then?'

'Mean to say you haven't heard? They're up at the monastery. Been there a week.'

'How d'you know?'

'I have my sources, old boy, which you wouldn't know a thing about.'

'Well, it just could be true.'

'I'm flying over it tomorrow.'

'You'll be shot down if you do.'

'Who told you that?'

'Well, if you want to know, Mr Nehru.'

'You can't believe that, old boy.'

'What?'

'The Indian government shooting down a British civilian plane.'

'It's an Indian civilian plane.'

And so on.

But in the end everybody believed the monastery story. Everybody made plans which they chewed over in corners by themselves. I had my plan. I hired an elephant.

It's extremely easy to hire an elephant in Tezpur. There were elephants all over the town carrying great bales of firewood, or loads of hay, and I simply stopped a driver who was ambling along by the side of his elephant and said:

'I should like to hire an elephant.'

He looked all round him several times and then put his finger to his lips, rolled up his eyes and moved on. Later that night he turned up at the Planters' Club with a friend who spoke English and we did the deal.

My plan was to take off through the jungle, north-east of Tezpur, and join the Dalai Lama's track four miles or so beyond the Gurkha sentry, take a good look at the monastery for an hour or two through field glasses and—I might have a story.

'All right,' the elephant driver said, 'that'll be a hundred rupees a day for the elephant and me and fifteen rupees for the elephant's food which we'll have to take with us. I'm not taking you in European clothes, but I will provide you with Indian garments for another ten rupees and some dye to rub on the bits of your skin which will show. Meet you by the fort at 6 o'clock in the morning.'

I cannot think now why I ever assented to such a mad plan, but at the time, after nearly a fortnight mewed up in the Planters' Club with a trip to the Foothills by bus once a day like a school outing, it seemed not only enterprising, but sensible.

I did have a qualm as I climbed on the elephant; I was dressed in a very voluminous dhoti with a long shirt and a lot of cloth to cover my hair, which was the wrong colour, and the elephant driver had anointed my hands and face and legs with a brown preparation which stank. The elephant was carrying about a ton of hay, and in front of that, me, and in front of me, its driver. It had only just stopped raining and everything on the elephant's back was sopping wet. I hitched up my dhoti and tried to find something to catch hold of and suddenly the elephant climbed off the track and lolloped into the jungle with a loud crashing noise.

I think we'd made about a quarter of a mile, when somebody ahead of us blew a shrill whistle and went on blowing it in an hysterical sort of way for about two minutes. And then all of a sudden a Sikh Major with a revolver in his hand came bounding out of the dense shrubbery and stood in front of us. When he saw me he began to laugh. He laughed till I thought he would injure himself, and then he had to sit down against a tree and laugh all over again. Finally he said, 'I see you, Sahib. Come on down.' I came down, clutching my finery about me, and the Major led me through the undergrowth for about a hundred yards to a bamboo hut. Five Sikh soldiers inside it were laughing their heads off. The Major sank into a chair and when he got his breath back, he said, 'Taking into consideration the entertainment you have provided, I fine you one hundred rupees to be paid on the spot. I shall then provide you with an escort to the road.'

And so he did, but to a very special piece of the road: the one that runs the whole length of Tezpur market before it reaches the taxi rank and the road to the Planters' Club. The brown stuff was still brown, but not so stinking when I landed in London weeks later.

It was at this juncture in the correspondents' bitter lives that the Indian government sent down a representative to talk to them. I have never admired a man more than I admired Mr Chowdri—I think that was his name—that morning. The correspondents were like mad bulls; there were actually placards hung out saying: 'To Hell with the India Press Office' and 'Nehru, Wake up. The World wants the Story.' The Americans were making most of the noise.

Mr Chowdri arrived in a splendid car. He was a slim, elegant, very good-looking man in his thirties. As he got out of his car, he was surrounded by a dense mob of correspondents who bore him along to the big table off the bar and sat around him shouting and screaming and shoving their great red faces under his chin, while they banged on the table with their eyes bulging out.

'If India don't get me to see the Dalai Lama then India's going to have the worst American Press that India's ever had,' roared the loudest voice.

'Oh, I don't think we should care about that,' Mr Chowdri said. The noise redoubled. During the tumult, Mr Chowdri glanced appreciatively around the Planters' Club, waved at me, I can't think why, but I waved back because I liked his style, and when they were all exhausted he said, 'I came down here to say, but it's been a little difficult, that the embargo is lifted from 3 o'clock today. You will have cable facilities here in Tezpur tomorrow morning and we believe you should meet the Dalai Lama inside three days.' He then rose.

'Nice to have met you. Don't drink too much—it's dangerous in this climate. Goodbye.' He climbed into his car and drove off back to Delhi.

We all spent the rest of the day rewriting the sheafs of irrelevant colour stories which we'd all been working on for weeks. We all telephoned our principals in voices full of emotion and alcohol and then we spent most of the night on whisky.

It was about half past five that morning, I suppose, when I was awakened by a rough shaking and a voice which said, 'Sahib, Sahib, Dalai Lama come.'

Out into the pelting rain with my recorder, and then, stuffed into the bus with thirty or so competitors, I jolted for the last time up the track to Foothills. There it all was, the glorious sun, the glittering leaves, the mountains from another, grander planet, the giddy track like a narrow, twisted fly-paper hanging from the ceiling. And now I could see on the fly-paper a group of minute dots.

From where we first caught sight of them until they passed through the Gurkha soldiers' barrier it took the Dalai

Lama and his party nearly five hours. And then the big, jovial, sturdy Tibetans in their fur hats and fur coats, their faces crimson, dismounted from their little tough horses at the barrier in a ring of Sikh soldiers, and in the middle was the Dalai Lama. A great surprise. Like a large handsome specimen of American college youth straight off the campus, with his round, intelligent face, his round intelligent glasses, his large size and his expensive Western suit. As he emerged smiling from among his followers, the press leapt on him like a single carnivorous animal. He was borne very slowly along in the middle of an almost silent mob, except that one of the interpreters in a low whining voice like a beggar, besought him in Tibetan all the way to the Sikh major's house to say something—anything. In the scrum I somehow managed to keep my microphone close under his mouth the whole time, but during the 150-yard journey, while moving his hands like a Bishop blessing his flock, the Dalai Lama said absolutely nothing, but kept up a sort of wordless murmuring, too low to be recorded on my tape. 'Ulla, ulla, ulla, ulla,' that's what it sounded like and that was all. Then the Sikhs snatched him and his attendants inside and the door shut. That was all we got.

Later in the day when he left on a special train from the railway junction, we got even less. He remained locked impenetrably in the train and this time the journalists meant nothing to anybody. The station was crammed. It was almost collapsing under all the Buddhists in North India who'd been able to get there. For hours the train puffed away in the station unable to move for the throngs of worshippers prostrate on the railway line. Tibetan horns mooed in concert on the platform, women held up children to be blessed and men, weeping on their knees, turned prayer wheels, chanted, prayed and beat gongs. It was a marvellous sight, but it was all we got.

It was all we got, all except one of us. The *Times* of India correspondent had had a cool look. He had also concealed in Tezpur a Tibetan youth. At Foothills, indistinguishable among the drivers and interpreters and secretaries, this youth had slipped into the jungle and changed into his native mountain clothes. Then he had mingled with the horsemen from Tibet and spent two hours in the Sikh Major's house, chatting the story out of them.

So the *Times* of India scooped the world on a story which must have cost the press round about, well, half a million. It printed it two days later at the length of three paragraphs, nearly at the bottom of an unimportant page.

XV

Agadir

In Algiers, which rose glittering out of the deep blue bay like a three-tiered wedding cake, a dense traffic of luxury cars screamed along the terraces and round the hairpin bends like a whole city-full of escaping crooks. But there was no escape, and the furious tirades of weeping patriots in the cafés, the stone-throwing mobs of youths in the streets, the ferocious slogans daubed in black on every white wall, 'Death to de Gaulle,' 'Death to Communist Traitors,' 'Death to the Socialists,' 'Death to the Liberals,' 'Death to Defeatists'—all these things were beginning to be seen, even by the slogan painters themselves, as the protests of the damned. From time to time above the scream of the traffic you heard the loud 'thump' of another bomb going off, and then the sirens, the trucks full of gendarmes racing in, and the fierce concert of motor horns in unison. Taa . . . te . . . taa . . . taa . . . . taa . . . Algérie Française.

The bombs were usually planted in big stores or restaurants or on the tops of buses. Eighty per cent of the casualties were women and children, and the only result, some counter atrocity.

By this time you were searched as you entered any big store and on the conductor's platform of a bus. It was the only thoroughly committed society I've ever lived in, and it was a very wearing experience. Nearly all the correspondents had gone; there were only three regulars left; the *New York Times*, the *Associated Press* (another American), and me, from the B.B.C. We'd all long since ceased to go out on the grisly expeditions offered by the French Press Office to lonely farm-houses full of horrors committed by the Algerians; women tied up to chairs and their children left on their laps to die slowly of knife wounds. That was the usual centre-piece in scenes carefully contrived and meticulously produced—scenes inconceivable except by the insane or the committed.

Because these filthy exhibitions had failed to commit us to the cause of Algérie Française, we of the foreign press were extremely unpopular. The night before when I'd made my broadcast by land-line to London, from the radio station, a young officer of paratroops had lounged in the doorway throughout the session with his submachine-gun pointed in the small of my back.

'I want you to know,' he said, as I sat down, 'that I understand English perfectly,' and when I'd finished, he said, 'The usual load of British hypocrisy—you gave away your Empire, so now we've got to do the same to keep things equal.'

So this morning, after breakfast at the Aletti Hotel—and when would the next bomb go off in this dining room?—I picked up two messages at the desk; one from the cameraman said: 'Will shoot the introduction at Bay Point. Meet me there at 10.30'; the other from London, said: 'Ring London without fail, 1 o'clock.' So I went out into the yard to find my car, and there it was, all by itself, with all four tyres slashed and D.P.E. written across it in white paint. All countries furiously committed to an ideology go through the same process. Thought is the first casuality; it is degraded into cliché, and after that the clichés are degraded again into sets of initials. Algeria had this disease badly. D.P.E. meant 'Défaitiste de la Presse Etrangère,' and as I stood and looked at it, I thought it was not a bad description. At that moment 'Defeatist of the Foreign Press' exactly summed me up.

I took a taxi to the cameraman's rendezvous. It took twenty minutes and £5 worth of francs to persuade the driver, who was a French-speaking Arab, to go.

'I do not care to go out of the town.'

'It's only two miles.'

'A mile is enough these days.'

And so it proved. About a mile out on the cliff road, a rattle of rifle fire suddenly broke out around the corner about a hundred yards ahead. The taxi driver promptly drove his car into a deep ditch and down a sort of tunnel made by an overhanging tree and we got out and lay under the taxi. For about an hour we listened to the battle until finally a truck full of gendarmes came screaming out of the town and we heard their machine-guns going into action; then gradually the noise of the fight moved away from us down the road and then there was silence.

'I shall wait,' the taxi driver said, 'for half an hour.'

'Oh come on, it's all right now.'

'I shall not in any case take you any farther. My principle is to remain alive, monsieur.'

So in the end I walked. It was very hot. Round the corner was a French corpse and a blown up telegraph pole which lay in a cradle of wires. Six corners farther on, Bay Point, and there was the cameraman crouched over his equipment.

Bay Point was a favourite spot with cameramen. On the edge of the cliff a big white wall, twenty feet high, had been breached by a bomb. Through the gap you could see, hundreds of feet below, a large picture postcard slice of Algiers—all white icing and blue sea and golden sunshine. The rest of the wall was covered with furious slogans and drawings, particularly one of General de Gaulle dangling from a gibbet, and the legend 'De Gaulle au Poteau'. There were the two black footprints of the settlers' Fascist organization, the 'Pieds Noirs' and under that, 'Merde aux Pieds Noirs Assassins'. Death, of course, to practically everybody and 'Merde' to all the rest. A kind of text book of ferocity. The point of the rendezvous was that for a television news report, if you posed your commentator with the picture postcard view on his right and the savage picture of de Gaulle on his left, you'd already said a good deal about Algiers before the commentator opened his mouth.

'Hello, Bill,' I said as I came closer. The cameraman held up one of his leather cases which had a neat bullet hole right through the middle.

'They shot at me,' he said without rancour, 'and now we're out of business for two days.'

He was a big broad man from the North Country and

wore a flat tweed cap. He stood for a minute or two contemplating the view of Algiers, the hideous wall, and finally he summed up.

'I'm that fed up,' the cameraman said. 'I could write bum on the wall.' An hour later I was through to the B.B.C.

'Anything interesting?'

'No,' I said, 'bombs, atrocities, gang fights, no news, and nothing's going to happen.'

'You've been saying that for a week. You're very lucky to be on the Mediterraean in March, let me tell you. It's snowing here.'

'Nothing's going to happen,' I said. 'Since the government actually arrested all those leaders, there's a new spirit. Nobody thought they'd dare arrest them. Nothing will happen.'

'You honestly think that?'

'Yes,' I said. 'I'll bet on it.'

'All right then, you can get a plane to Casablanca in Morocco and go to Agadir. There's been an earthquake. That's all the hard news we've got so far, there's been an earthquake. There are rumours that it's a big disaster. You're the nearest, get there as quick as you can.'

At Casablanca it was rumoured at the airport that nothing could land at Agadir, so I hired a car and a French-speaking Arab driver, since I couldn't understand a word of the Moroccan Arabic. I had a chat with the chief engineer at the radio station, a Frenchman, got a promise of lines to London, stocked up with food and water and set off down the main road to the south. Not the coast road: that was too slow, the driver said. We could get on to that for the last ten miles where you had the best view of Agadir. 'The inland road is a fast one,' the driver said, and he certainly made it one. We did eighty miles an hour for stretches of fifty miles on end. All the same my first view of Agadir, on a wide bay with a sandy beach running for miles until lost on the horizon, was at dusk, with enough colour still in the sky to silhouette a huddle of masonry all across a broad hilltop, the Kasbah, and below that, back from the beach, roads in terraces up a gentle slope, one great towering building like a London office block and a muddle of indistinguishable shapes in the dark hollow enclosed by the crescent of hills. When we reached the town it was dark. The driver turned a corner uphill between low banks of rubble, drove a hundred yards and stopped. Stopped for a full minute. Tears ran down his face. He said in a whisper, 'Monsieur, the town has disappeared.'

We had stopped at the edge of a small cliff. Ten feet below us in the headlights the road continued, flanked by banks of rubble and plaster with here and there the top of a car poking through, or half a lamp standard. When we switched the engine off, it was absolutely silent in Agadir; a dim moonlight on white plaster, the hills black against the stars and that was all. Later as you sat there you picked up the faint lazy washing of the sea.

Agadir had been a new town on its way to a reputation like that of Tangiers—the sort of city where anything goes. A gay, international resort, where sixty thousand visitors, mostly from Germany, Scandinavia and England, could enjoy the kind of holiday that's based on a lavish allotment of sunshine and total permissiveness. In the background a stimulating hint of drugs, smuggling, orgies and international layabouts. It had been a brassy, vulgar town, but it had been alive. The whole point of its existence was its claim to be more alive than other places. The shocking thing was not so much that it was dead, but in how short a time it had joined the remote past. It might have been one of the cities of the plain.

The driver wept with his head in his hands, and presently he began to mourn the vanished city. It was his home town, he said, and that was why he'd been chosen to drive me there. It was to have been the greatest town in Morocco and one of the great seaside resorts of the world. Since before dawn that morning, he said, all communication with Agadir had ceased and the rumours had begun to grow. A man had met a man who'd driven up by car; an aeroplane had flown over and reported back. There'd been a wireless message from Inezgane up beyond the airport.

'So I came to see for myself,' the driver said. 'All in a minute,' he said and snapped his fingers. 'We're all in the hands of God.'

The silence was suddenly broken by a loud rumble and crash as some great piece of wall collapsed somewhere in the town, and this brought the driver and me sharply back to the practical world.

'The thing to do,' I said, 'is to try to find a way through the town to some other place not far away which has not been destroyed. Can we get through to the airport?'

'Up to Inezgane,' the driver said.

'That's it. We can try.'

We spent nearly half the night looking for a way round or through the wreckage of Agadir. Nearly always we were brought up short by a cliff up or a cliff down, or sometimes by a section where the road had twisted like a ribbon until it stood almost vertically on its edge. We walked for miles among the rubble heaps, tracing roads which had disappeared, tracks which might be passable. We discovered that we were not alone in Agadir. On one great mound near the lonely skyscraper which turned out to be called the Mauretania Hotel, guided by a faint clink of shovels, we discovered a dozen French sailors digging.

'There's a live man down here,' they said and, with our ears to the ground, we could hear him, groaning.

'Half an hour ago he was talking to us,' the sailors said. 'He's about twenty feet down and can't move at all, but he can hear other people trapped down there.'

They were from a French warship anchored a mile or two out.

'We anchored well out,' a Petty Officer said, 'because when we came to take the soundings, one place was only ten feet deep. Well, on the chart, it should be fourteen hundred, so we anchored, and the boats brought us in. We've been working in parties all day. So far,' he said, 'we've got out about twenty people. It's very slow digging—and as you dig it collapses with you.'

This was our first contact with the real horror of Agadir, and it took a little time to sink in. Of the thirty thousand inhabitants and sixty thousand holidaymakers, the only ones left alive in the city were buried underground. And as we stood there in the starlight, the silence suddenly took on the quality of a nightmare. We were rooted there in a trance of shock, and for the rest of that night we moved about like people in a dream.

The moon came out and bathed in its dispassionate silver wash a First World War scenery of mounds and banks and hillocks, utterly silent, under any of which, we now knew, a dozen human beings might be boxed up alive. Not under all of them, though. On the tops of some a ghostly blue light wobbled and flickered where the gas from broken mains had been set alight. And once, just before we found a way out, we heard the long howling of a dog a long way off.

The driver found our way out. There was a hundred yards of quite impassable rubble and then beyond that, in the middle of what had been the street, an abandoned car, quite undamaged, with a tank full of petrol. So in the end we humped our luggage across the bad patch and stowed it in the abandoned car and drove away. This operation, three days later, would have had us shot as looters, but we never thought of that, and we put the car back before we left.

'I'll find a way out for my car in the daylight,' the driver said.

It was half past three in the morning when the driver's superb piloting brought us out on an unblemished main road, uphill, with a signpost to Inezgane, and three miles along the road we came upon the first of the refugees. On a grass patch by the side of the road was a small squalid encampment of handcarts and furniture, draped with curtains and blankets. There was a fire with cooking pots around it. Twelve members of an Arab family were bedded down there while a young man lay watching the fire.

We stopped. And after he'd inspected us closely, he invited us in and we sat by the fire and he told us his story.

By the greatest of good luck, he said, nearly all the family had been out in the street, saying goodbye to a couple of guests and pointing out their best way home, when the earth began to shake and at the first tremor they'd dived in and got the children out, just before the house fell down. It was about two in the morning, the young man said; suddenly the earth rose up a little and shook and paused and all the lights went out. And then the whole street leapt up, turned half round and fell down again, much farther this time than it had risen. There'd been a deafening noise, a long, creaking groaning sound like an enormous tree coming down and then the long crash as the town fell down around them. Then there were a few seconds of silence and then all the dogs in the town ran yelping out of Agadir. And then the human cries began.

There was a thick fog of dust and for a long time you could see absolutely nothing. You could only hear the crowds of people running past, running anywhere out of the town. Most of them took nothing with them—they just ran. These people in the camp had stayed because they'd lost one of the children and they could hear her crying somewhere. In the black fog it took hours to find her, and then the grandfather was too old to run or even properly to walk. They were still there when dawn came up and by that time the town, or their part of it anyway, was completely deserted. So they collected three handcarts and loaded them with household furniture, and, with the grandfather and the youngest child on top, walked until they were too tired to go any farther.

'We have water,' the young man said, 'there's a stream down there; and we have some loaves of bread, but very filthy, from under the wreckage, and after that, we're in the hands of God.'

Long afterwards, we learnt that in that second shock, when the earth rose up and turned round and dropped again, twelve thousand people died. Thousands more were injured or trapped and eighty per cent of the town was destroyed. It took ten seconds altogether.

At the airport there were lights. Not from the mains but from a generator, and there were men with bulldozers working furiously to patch up the runway which in any case was not badly damaged. I could have flown in. There were American Marines there from a ship anchored in the bay. The Americans had now been at work in the town and on the airstrip for about twenty-two hours. They'd landed only about an hour after the main shock, while the streets were still full of distracted people. They had worked themselves practically to the point of exhaustion, but a sergeant told me: 'In the town there were no lights. There was no water, there was nothing but total darkness. People wandering around, trying to find out where their possessions and their families were. From some buildings came the cries of people who were trapped in the wreckage. Rescue crews led by Colonel Williams immediately broke into these wrecked buildings and homes attempting to take these people out. They were successful in many cases. The condition of these people was deplorable. It was hard to realize the human misery that was present there that first night. Everybody, including ourselves, after a while, really were perhaps in a state of shock because—in twenty-six years in the navy myself—and two wars and many many other disasters, I've never seen such a vast amount of misery as was there that night.'

'By now,' the Marine said, 'the whole world knows the news. We've been sending radio messages all day and the first plane with food and medical supplies should be here at daylight.'

'Is there any means of communication at all?'

'No sir, only ship's radio. There's no mains electricity. The wires are all down. The roads are all cut except the one you came in by. No, sir, nothing you can do.'

'Then,' I said to the driver, 'I think a large drop of whisky and sleep in the car.'

'Purely as a medicine, you understand,' the driver solemnly said. 'I would accept a mouthful of whisky if you offered it to me.'

The American planes were the first to come in. It was the sort of operation which Americans do superbly.

Shortly after dawn the first one—an enormous machine—circled the airport and then reappeared from the north, seeming to leap down on the inadequate runway from the top of the hill where the Kasbah, the old walled city of the Arabs, lay like a heap of broken pots. They brought doctors and nurses, medical supplies and blankets and they went back to Casablanca loaded with wounded.

'Can I get a lift back to Casablanca?' I asked. I was thinking of my story.

'Are you wounded or a doctor?'

'No.'

'Well then, you can't.'

It was the classic nightmare for reporters. I had got a magnificent story and I'd recorded a tape early in the morning which even by then was momently getting more stale and irrelevant and which, by evening would be hopelessly out of date. The nearest telephone was about a hundred and fifty miles away *if* we could get through the town again: the nearest radio station—Casabalanca—five hundred miles and more.

On day three in Agadir, some of the refugees returned and nearly all the dogs. The dogs ran yelping about the streets lost and hysterical and maddened with thirst. The refugees sat wailing on the mounds which represented their homes. I spent most of the day helping to dig out a Frenchman buried nearly thirty feet below the wreckage of a small hotel. During the whole operation he kept up a running fire of jokes and repartee. He was an irrepressible man. When at last he was hauled to the surface, as he lay on his stretcher, I asked him about his experience of the earthquake.

'Well, Agadir,' he said, 'is one of these brand new towns put up in a hurry and the plumbing is terrible, simply terrible. Every night before I go to bed, in my hotel, I go to the lavatory, and every night it is a struggle. When you pull the chain, it either fails to work or the top of the cistern falls off or the chain breaks or the pan floods. It's chronic. Every night I curse the thing. Well the night before last, when I pulled it, the whole damnedt own fell down.' He was still laughing when they carried him away.

On day three I was so desperate that I gave three recorded tapes to an American pilot to get to Casablanca radio station for me if he could. He said he would try. None of them got through. Spanish planes were flying in now and I made a very hurried recording, especially for a Spanish officer, who said he thought he could get it to London through Gibraltar. Curiously enough it did get through, two days later.

It was on day four when the flies began to swarm in Agadir and the dogs began to howl continuously, echoing each other from distant parts of the town, and the thermometer reached 85, the day when the dreadful smell which was to become the chief character in the Agdira tragedy first began to make its presence felt, that I had a bit of luck

I discovered two young Englishmen among the men who were digging in the ruins.

'We were on a sort of tour of Africa, making our way from place to place, getting any sort of work which would keep us going. We only got here last night. At least we can eat while this digging lasts.'

'You don't look very good at it,' I said.

'Well, we're not used to it.'

'I'll give you a job,' I said. 'It'll be a flat-out job day and night, sleep when you can. It'll last you for a week and I'll give you £4 a day and your expenses.'

From then on they ferried my tapes to Casablanca radio station. They hung about Agadir airport cadging lifts, and they became expert in this craft. As soon as one of them had a seat on the plane, he would take all the tapes with him, taxi for six miles from Casablanca Airport to the radio station, taxi back to the airport, thumb a lift back to Agadir, eat an enormous meal and off to Casablanca again.

By now the driver had managed to drive his car up to the airport and return the one we borrowed.

What I had not yet discovered was any living soul who could give me an outside picture of what happened when the earthquake struck. I tried the American Marines but they'd been too far out to sea to get any of the detail. They all agreed that for them, or those of them who'd seen anything, the earthquake had manifested itself as a tremendous flash of light followed by a long very loud rumbling noise and then a crash. Many of the Arab refugees had this impression too, and it was the basis of a rumour that Agadir had perished by atom bomb. The Moroccan refugees still believed this and couldn't be persuaded that it wasn't so. 'It was the French atom bomb,' they said. 'We saw the flash, we heard the rumbling noise—it was exactly like the film—and there was dense smoke. We couldn't see a mushroom cloud because it was too dark.' In the end, the Moroccan government had to squash this rumour publicly.

By day five, Operation Agadir was in full swing, and it was a splendid operation. Every few minutes, aeroplanes from all the nations of the world, it seemed, landed, unloaded, and were off again. The Americans flew in six whole hospitals with all their staff. About three thousand men were now digging in the ruins. Squads of armed Moroccan police patrolled the city in surgical gauze masks, for the smell of Agadir was now so horrible that only short shifts of work were possible in there. It was on day five that the police shot the dogs which had begun to run mad. It wasn't until day six that they began to shoot the looters. Alongside the airport, the bodies lay in rows two miles long by the sides of the road, while bulldozers dug great trenches for their graves, and still the living were being prized out of their tombs below the mounds of wreckage. On day six huge spraying machines on caterpillar tractors were to be seen moving slowly about the streets in clouds of disinfectant fog and now the police closed the city and built a stone wall across each exit road.

On day seven the Morrocan government announced that Agadir was irreclaimable. The risk of plague was now so great that bulldozers would plough it flat and then cement the whole town over. But that day another living being was rescued from his tomb, and such a cry of outrage went up from the press at the thought that any human creature might be walled up alive beneath the concrete that the operation was postponed for three days. By now the Red Cross and the Red Crescent and the Moroccan government between them had scoured the countryside for the refugees and organized them all in camps. Some of them came in from villages twenty miles away which they'd reached on the first night of the panic. So it was on the tenth day that the bulldozers and the concrete mixers moved in, and Agadir was officially dead and buried.

Ten days later, two Arabs, speechless skeletons, were found making their way up the Inezgane road at night on their hands and knees. When their house collapsed in the old city and they were buried yards deep in the earth, they had found themselves alive in a little pitch-black tent of space under the roof beams and with them, miraculously, a great jar of water, untouched by the earthquake. They had tunnelled their way through to the outside world, using pieces of broken pot for spades, after twenty-one days underground. They both survived.

Long before that, on day eleven, I left for Casablanca and telephoned the B.B.C.

'We did get some of your dispatches,' they said, 'but not as many as we would have liked.'

I spoke at some length about the circumstances.

'Yes, it must have been a bit rough,' they said. 'One thing you'll be pleased to hear. The French authorities won't renew your visa in Algeria for at least a couple of months. So you'd better come back to London.'

It was like a reprieve.

But not for long. There is no permanent reprieve for those like me who rejected the original site offered them to build a life on because their times had rendered it unfit for human habitation. We are an odd lot. We can settle, as the beatniks do, for a life made of the lyrical content of a time and a place, constantly changing, or we develop a compulsive itch to experience the quality of life wherever our times have made an impact on it, in which case we are reporters. It is a fretful occupation like a wine-taster's, and like them, it is late in the day when we settle down with our own bottle.